PARIS À TABLE

PARIS À TABLE

1846

EUGÈNE BRIFFAULT

TRANSLATED AND EDITED BY J. WEINTRAUB

WITH A FOREWORD BY DAVID DOWNIE

Illustrated by Bertall

OXFORD
UNIVERSITY PRESS

OXFORD
UNIVERSITY PRESS

Oxford University Press is a department of the University of Oxford.
It furthers the University's objective of excellence in research, scholarship,
and education by publishing worldwide. Oxford is a registered trade mark of
Oxford University Press in the UK and certain other countries.

Published in the United States of America by Oxford University Press
198 Madison Avenue, New York, NY 10016, United States of America.

© Oxford University Press 2018

Library of Congress Cataloging-in-Publication Data

Names: Briffault, Eugène, 1799–1854, author. | Bertall, 1820–1882, illustrator.
Title: Paris à table : 1846 / Eugène Briffault ; translated and edited by J. Weintraub ;
Illustrated by Bertall.
Other titles: Paris à table. English
Description: New York, NY : Oxford University Press, 2018.
Identifiers: LCCN 2017044123 (print) | LCCN 2017050196 (ebook) |
ISBN 9780190842048 (Updf) | ISBN 9780190842055 (Epub) |
ISBN 9780190842031 (hardback)
Subjects: LCSH: Paris (France)—Social life and customs—19th century. |
Dinners and dining—France—Paris—History. | BISAC: COOKING / Regional &
Ethnic / French. | HISTORY / Europe / France.
Classification: LCC DC733 (ebook) | LCC DC733 .B713 2018 (print) |
DDC 944/.361063—dc23
LC record available at https://lccn.loc.gov/2017044123

Earlier versions of Chapter 3 and Chapter 10 appeared in the
journal *Gastronomica*, respectively, as
"Dinner in the Current Age: A Translation from Eugène Briffault's
Paris à table," *Gastronomica: The Journal of Critical Food Studies*, Summer 2015,
and "The Restaurants of Paris: A Translation from Eugène Briffault's *Paris à table*
(an annotated translation)," *Gastronomica: The Journal of Critical Food Studies*,
Spring 2014.

1 3 5 7 9 8 6 4 2

Printed by Edwards Brothers Malloy, United States of America

CONTENTS

ACKNOWLEDGMENTS

First of all, I would like to thank my editor at OUP, Susan Ferber, for rescuing this project from the academic version of the slush pile and, along with the OUP staff, providing excellent guidance throughout the publishing process. I am especially grateful to Isabelle David for her translation review and suggestions, her insights into what my French author of the nineteenth century really meant to say, and an unexpected knowledge of French culinary ways. The anonymous reviewers of the manuscript are also in my debt for their restraint, helpful advice, and for leading me down profitable paths for additional research. Similar gratitude is due to the librarians and staff of the Regenstein Library at the University of Chicago, the Bibliothèque nationale de France, and the Alliance française de Chicago. And, of course, I want to thank my wife, Denise, for allowing me, without complaint, to resurrect the antisocial schedule and demeanor of my graduate-student days—at least for a couple of months.

FOREWORD

David Downie

―――――――――――

•

What lover of victuals and lore, what bona fide history buff or wild-eyed Paris enthusiast, can be anything but thrilled by the first complete English translation—at long last—of Eugène Briffault's perennial, gorgeously illustrated *Paris à table*? This mid-nineteenth-century exploration of the French capital during the reign of the gluttonous King Louis Philippe (1830–1848), the mores and manners of its denizens high-born and low, the culinary foibles and florid gastronomic fantasies of a gimcrack age, bristles with unadulterated irreverence and is a joy to dip into time and again.

Be warned: the gleeful hyperbole and painterly prose readers discover in these pages have contagious effects. You may find yourself, as I do, mimicking the Rabelaisian Briffault and his band of merry gourmands tramping through Paris's strangely familiar cityscape, fork, glass and volume in hand.

Briffault, like his friend and colleague Honoré de Balzac, is one of those preternaturally Parisian gastronome-heroes endowed with insatiable appetites and inexhaustible energies. A worldly, jack-of-all-trades journalist with a sardonic sense of humor, he delights in stitching together historical anecdotes sourced with the intrepidness of a scavenger. Briffault's is a tour de force of panache, showcasing the nativism typical of his times: "When Paris sits down at the table," Briffault announces, "the entire world stirs."

What, only the world and not the galaxy? "Nowhere can the exquisite delicacy of taste and elegance be satisfied as well as in Paris," he continues. The city "blends the delights of the mind with the satisfactions of the sensual."

That may be the best one-line description of this cult book: an immersion blend of intellectual and sensual pleasures.

Equally compelling are the wickedly funny, subversive illustrations by Bertall, an orgy of edible still-life compositions, caricatures of Parisian eaters elephantine or diminutive, and bizarre, toothy creatures or disembodied, yawning mouths devouring not just delicacies but the very monuments of Paris—the Pantheon, Invalides, and Arc de Triomphe among them.

May I make a confession? When, as an unpublished starveling, I resettled in Paris in the mid-1980s, exactly 140 years after the original *Paris à table* appeared, I came across a lavishly well-thumbed copy of the sainted volume at the stall of a grizzled *bouquiniste* on the Seine. Rushing back to my seventh-floor cold-water walk-up garret I pored over the book's tattered mustiness, instantly falling under Briffault and Bertall's spell. Decades later, as I set out to write *A Taste of Paris: A History of the Parisian Love Affair with Food*, I lifted and transposed more than one of Bertall's illustrations—they are in the public domain. My secret hope was to reach back to Ancient Roman Paris and then craft a twenty-first-century version of Briffault's book following the city's surprising gastronomic topography.

Unsurprisingly, then, I was doubly honored to be asked to contribute this foreword to J. Weintraub's sprightly translation, illuminating introduction, and indispensable footnotes. I will therefore shamelessly use the occasion to comment on one particularly startling fact.

It is that Briffault's Paris, including several of the haunts he describes and many of the dishes he favors, lives on today, nearly 180 years later, not so much defying as merrily tweaking its nose at our digitized, standardized, globalized age of exhilarating fusion and culinary confusion.

Where, then, can we eat in the company of Briffault's ghost? For a start, go to the jewel-box Véfour (now Le Grand Véfour), or Procope, Le Rocher de Cancale, La Petite Chaise, Au Vieux Paris d'Arcole, and others still. They exude an attainable past, if I may quote myself, and do a lively business. So too do a host of similar establishments from the latter half of Briffault's century.

There is more: many a favorite recipe from Briffault's age—or earlier—endures, along with that sometimes endearing and always breathtaking self-adoring panache of certain Parisians. While considering themselves cosmopolitan sophisticates, they go on believing everything French is superior, more succulent and delicious, lovelier and more luscious, more artful, ingenious and remarkable than anything from anywhere else on the planet and perhaps the universe of universes.

Today Paris—and New York, London, and Tokyo—have their temples of gastronomy presided over by Alain Ducasse, Guy Savoy, and Joel Robuchon, a holy trinity of twinkling French stellar practitioners. Briffault's was the age of these men's spiritual forefather, the prototypical superstar-chef Antonin Carême. "In our belle France," sang Carême, "we are served to our heart's desire by Providence: everything that constitutes fine eating is here at hand."

Hallelujah! While propounding the Paris-centric gospel of earlier gastronomic authors, Briffault takes Carême's missionary message and gives it a twist: "The magnificence of our tables intrudes," he snipes, "gaiety is afraid of it; luxury, when it is pushed to excess, begets uniformity: from its desire to be all things from all countries, it ends up no longer being from its own."

To my ears, after thirty-odd years living and eating among Parisians high and low, this rings like a premonitory panoramic of Michelin's multiple-starred cosmos about to be swallowed by a voracious black hole.

What, pray tell, do we eat today that the people populating Briffault's Paris ate? Carême's own famed Tournedos Rossini, for one mouthwatering classic, or unctuous, creamy blanquette de veau, meltingly tender boeuf aux carottes, and sweet, tangy crème-brûlée with lemon zest, proudly featured on Parisian menus then and now. Swap out the clothing, and even the caricatures seem eerily contemporary.

One can't help wondering why it has taken so long for Briffault, Bertall, and this, their most acclaimed collaboration, to be discovered and presented to the English-speaking world. It's worth noting that the author and illustrator were never forgotten by Parisians, especially those who love to eat and drink. This book has been reissued in French more than once in recent decades and, in my experience, has always been findable in Paris bookstores or chez *les bouquinistes*. It is an enviable long-seller.

However, it is true, Briffault's followers never crossed the Channel and navigated beyond, to the shores of the New

World. Briffault lived and died in the long shadows of the twin giants of early French gastronomy, Alexandre Balthazar Laurent Grimod de la Reynière and Jean Anthelme Brillat-Savarin. It is also safe to say that without them there would be no *Paris à table*. In the spirit of the times, Briffault borrowed freely from Grimod de la Reynière's many guidebooks and entertainment manuals and pilfered Brillat-Savarin's phenomenally successful *The Physiology of Taste*, which has never been out of print since it first appeared on bookshelves in the 1820s.

Briffault also drew lavishly on another of my favorite, little-known works, *Comme on dîne à Paris*, by the writer-explorer Jacques Arago, published in 1842, a mere four years before *Paris à table*. Originality was not a priority of the age. Au contraire. Without Grimod de la Reynière, I would argue, there would be no Brillat-Savarin, and so forth, ad infinitum.

Yet to a commentator of our own times reading these and myriad other works on French gastronomy from the first half of the nineteenth century, Briffault's playful bric-à-brac certainly stands out and also stands the test of time. The stylish delivery of pithy home-truths is irresistible. I have often come across the "dictums" and "aphorisms" of Grimod de la Reynière or Brillat-Savarin, and, indeed, I translated and collected several score of them in my own book. In retrospect I should have created a third column to include a selection of Briffault's bon mots.

"A banquet is not a pleasure," he writes, "but a duty to be endured." Or "Candles are the table's sunlight." And "The abuse of sauces…and the chemistry of spices…long made French cuisine a threat to health." There are countless others ripe for citation.

So, let us give credit where credit is due. Bertall rightly occupies a place of honor in the pantheon of French illustrators.

It is my humble, mirthful opinion that Eugène Briffault deserves to stand on the podium with his Olympian forebears, a medal perhaps not of gold or silver but of good, solid bronze around his rather rough neck.

The time has come for you to dig into the next course of this bibliophilic feast. Bon appétit and above all bonne promenade *gastronomique*!

INTRODUCTION

Eugène Briffault and Paris à table
A Panorama of Dining

J: WEINTRAUB

"With the magic title of Paris, a play, a review, a book is always
sure of success. Paris draws an unquenchable curiosity that
nothing has yet been able to satisfy.... Put the word on a poster
and there, for six months, you'll have lines and crowds."

—THÉOPHILE GAUTIER, *PARIS ET LES PARISIENS AU XIXe*
SIÈCLE: MOEURS, ARTS ET MONUMENTS (1856)

"M. Briffault is the complete newspaper man.... His pen is a
locomotive driving across the paper; his politics and literature
are powered by steam."

— *PHYSIOLOGIE DE LA PRESSE* (1841)

Eugène Briffault was an editor, journalist, theater critic, and
man of letters who, as a chronicler of nineteenth-century
Paris, was a prolific contributor to its newspapers, reviews, and
anthologies. He was also a celebrated bon vivant, "the most
joyful adventurer of literary Bohemia," according to one contemporary,[1] well qualified to write about a culinary scene he

knew intimately. In 1846 he published *Paris à table*, perhaps the most important book on the subject in the half-century between the appearance of Jean-Anthelme Brillat-Savarin's *Physiologie du goût* (1825) and the elder Alexandre Dumas' *Grand dictionnaire de cuisine* (1873).[2] Referenced by observers of the Parisian dining scene almost from the time of its publication,[3] *Paris à table* is still frequently cited by culinary scholars and critics today, as well as by those who feel that it transcends its immediate subject. The historian Pascal Ory, for instance, characterized its author as "an authoritative voice, speaking on behalf of French culture," and in a *Le monde* review of the 2003 edition of the book, P.-J. Catinchi, declared *Paris à table* to be "the richest view of Balzac's time, seen from the table."[4]

●— —● ●—

Eugène-Vincent Briffault was born on December 31, 1799, in Périgueux, the main city in the Dordogne region in the southwest of France. Beginning his schooling in Paris, he finished in Strasbourg, where he then took up the study of law. After a few years of travel in Italy, he returned to Paris where he obtained his law degree and was admitted to the bar. But in 1828 he set aside the law for political journalism, and, joining with a group of young writers, he helped the liberal editor Jean-Denis Magalon revive his journal *L'album*.[5] In 1823 the Restoration authorities then in power had suppressed the journal, and Magalon had been sentenced to thirteen months in prison. Five years later when Briffault began to write for it, *L'album* was apparently no less controversial, since one of his first articles, on the murder of August von Kotzebue in Germany, was construed by the government of Charles X to be a defense of political assassination. It resulted in a two-month jail term for its author.

Rather than being discouraged by the ordeal, Briffault continued his political journalism, taking a position with the satirical newspaper *Le corsaire* and eventually becoming one of its principal editors. After a disturbance in June 1830, just prior to the July Revolution and the overthrow of Charles X, Briffault spent three days in jail for reputedly exhorting a crowd to rebellion and obstructing the arrest of several of the participants. During the Revolution itself, and especially during the "three glorious days" (July 27 through July 29), *Le corsaire* was often publishing two numbers daily.

In 1832 his political writings cost Briffault, at least temporarily, the use of his right arm. *Le corsaire* was the first to announce that the presumed illness of the Duchesse de Berry—then incarcerated for her role in a failed insurrection to place her son, the "legitimate" heir, on the throne—was the result of a pregnancy. Her "legitimist" supporters considered this correct appraisal to be a dangerous insult, and Briffault, who admitted to having written the article in question, was challenged to a duel by a M. Barbot de la Trésorière. The encounter, with pistols, took place the next morning in the Bois de Boulogne. Apparently the royalist was a better shot than the journalist, since Briffault suffered a bullet wound in his right arm. Afterward, his antagonist was reported to have said, "I only wanted to break his arm. He won't be writing anything more for a while."[6]

If silencing the journalist were his object, the royalist did not succeed. Briffault continued to write charged articles, presumably with his left hand, that provoked additional challenges. One of these was taken up by his colleague Armand Carrel, who had earlier criticized Briffault for having so rashly accepted the initial duel.[7]

From *Le corsaire*, Briffault wrote, in succession, for a diverse group of periodicals—*Le constitutionnel, Le courrier
français, Le charivari, Le siècle, Le Figaro, La presse*—assuming
a variety of editorial positions for several of them. By the end
of the decade he was employed by *Le temps* as its theater
critic and also writing general articles for *L'artiste*. In fact,
by 1839 Briffault was probably better known for his prolific
and eclectic journalism than for his political writing; one of his

Portrait of Eugène Briffault by Marie-Alexandre Alophe from
*Galerie de la presse, de la littérature et des beaux-arts: première
série*, Louis Huart, ed. (Paris: Aubert, 1839), n.p.

colleagues, Louis-Adrien Huart (also a writer and editor for
the humorous periodical *Le charivari*), doubted that there was
any other journalist in the profession who could claim to be
more active, varied, steady, or witty in his production than
Briffault.[8]
A similar portrait was painted by another commentator in
1841: "M. Briffault enters the newspaper office, discards his
coat, rolls up his sleeves.... Is a lead article needed, a short
item, a column, some opinions? *Voilà*, you only have to speak
up to be served. In fact, M. Briffault is the complete newspaper man: he does the long political diatribes, the theater columns, the petty and witty gossip, and I believe he is not a total
stranger to the editing of fashion bulletins.... His pen is a locomotive driving across the paper; his politics and literature are
powered by steam."[9]
In the 1840s, Briffault became more active as an independent writer and editor. He inaugurated his own fashion annual,
La toilette: almanach des femmes, pour 1843, but only one
number was published. Equally unsuccessful was his venture
of the previous year, the monthly *Historiettes contemporaines:
courrier de la ville*, a mixture of cultural observation, anecdotes, and humor ("while others strive to instruct, we will seek
to amuse, but without renouncing enlightenment").[10] Begun
in January 1842, and written almost entirely by Briffault,
Historiettes contemporaines was published only through the
September issue.
With the collapse of these two periodicals, Briffault may
have required additional funds, and he quickly became the
author of several books and pamphlets. Along with *Paris à
table*, Briffault published two other full-length volumes in the
1840s. The first, *Paris dans l'eau* (1844), a social and cultural

study in the manner of *Paris à table*, examined the importance of the river Seine to the city, along with the work, the water sports, the bathing, and the other activities that occurred on its banks. The second of these books, *Le Secret de Rome au XIXe siècle* (1846), was a detailed exposé of the corruption inside the Catholic Church, but despite its polemics, one complimentary reviewer described its author as someone who "states himself to be a Catholic, and appears to us an enlightened and sincerely devout one."[11] Briffault also published several pamphlet-sized titles including one on the game of dominoes (*Manuel complet du jeu de dominos*, 1843) and two on the Duc d'Orléans, the heir to the throne of Louis-Philippe, shortly following his tragic death from a carriage accident.[12] The first of this pair was a standard laudatory biography (*Le Duc d'Orléans, Prince Royal*, 1842) and the second an account of his funeral (*Le Duc d'Orléans, les funérailles*, 1842), an intricately detailed report and description created as if to memorialize the event for posterity. These last two titles revealed a sympathetic relationship with the royal family, one that encouraged a colleague to suggest that Briffault had lost his "bold spirit" (*verdeur*) of political protest and could no longer be counted among journalists supporting freedom of the press and opposition to the ruling power.[13]

Briffault was also a frequent contributor to the omnibus collections categorized by the twentieth-century critic Walter Benjamin as "panoramic literature." These were multivolume sets, often published over several years, in large formats and usually copiously illustrated, containing essays or sketches of characters—"The Bourgeois of Paris," "The Adulterous Woman," "The Chess Player"—or activities and professions—"Summer Balls," "A Doctor's Day," "Students on Vacation"—or sites—

"The Morgue," "Les Tuileries," "The Street Where No One Dies"—and the like. With the use of the term "panoramic," Benjamin was making a particular reference to the spectacles, first produced by Louis-Jacques-Mandé Daguerre in the early 1820s, in one of the shopping arcades that, as a result of these representations, soon became known as the Passage des Panoramas. "Panoramas" and the related "dioramas" became popular in the other Paris arcades, too, and were often elaborate productions employing theatrical devices—light, music, sound, mobile backdrops, and three-dimensional figures—to portray natural occurrences (volcanic eruptions, earthquakes) or historical and topical events. For Benjamin such spectacles were an art form that paved the way for photography and cinema. The "panoramic literature," on the other hand, consisted of "sketches, whose anecdotal form corresponds to the panoramas' plastically arranged foreground [i.e., in three dimensions] and whose informational base corresponds to their painted background. This literature is also socially panoramic."[14] In other words, these writings portrayed social types and activities integrally attached to their social environments. As examples of this genre, Benjamin cited *Paris ou le livre des cent-et-un* (*Paris, or the Book of the Hundred and One*), *Les Français peints par eux-mêmes* (*The French Portrayed by Themselves*), *Le Diable à Paris* (*The Devil in Paris*), and *La grande ville* (*The Great City*).

Eugène Briffault contributed to all four of these. The first, *Paris ou le livre des cent-et-un*, was published in fifteen volumes from 1831 to 1834; Briffault wrote two articles, one on "The Paris Night" and an essay on "The Opera" (which was also published separately in 1834 as a sixty-page pamphlet).

For *Les Français peints par eux-mêmes* (9 vols., 1840–1842), subtitled *Encyclopédie morale du dix-neuvième siècle*, Briffault contributed a pair of character sketches, "The Deputy" and "The *Viveur*." *La grande ville*—published in two volumes in 1842 and 1843, and which advertised itself as a *"nouveau tableau"* of Paris—featured from Briffault a narrative about "A Society Actress" and a report on "Le Marché des Innocents" (the central market until it was replaced by the new pavilions of Les Halles in the late 1850s). For *Le Diable à Paris*, subtitled *Paris et les parisiens, mœurs et coutumes, caractères et portraits* and published in two volumes in 1845 and 1846, he borrowed material from his book *Paris dans l'eau*, offering a chapter on "A Day in the Swimming School."

Briffault also made contributions to more specific anthologies such as *Paris revolutionnaire* (1833–1834; a collection in support of the July Monarchy), *Nouvelles parisiennes* (1843; primarily reprints of newspaper columns), *Les rues de Paris* (1844; histories and descriptions of various Parisian streets and districts), *Nouvelle galerie des artistes dramatiques vivants* (1855; capsule biographies of theater artists to accompany their engraved portraits), and *Dictionnaire de la conversation at de la lecture* (1832 to 1839 in fifty-two volumes with a sixteen-volume supplement published from 1844 to 1851).

Whatever foundational impact the volumes of "panoramic literature" may have had on the development of the realistic novel or the study of society and its culture, they certainly attracted the most esteemed writers of the time. Briffault shared bylines with novelists Honoré de Balzac, Alexandre Dumas *père*, Eugène Sue, George Sand, and Paul de Kock, as well as with Théophile Gautier, Albert de Musset, Arsène Houssaye, Gérard de Nerval, Charles Nodier, and a host of others. Many of their pages were also illustrated by the most notable artists and engravers, including Paul Gavarni, Honoré Daumier, J. J. Grandville, and Bertall.

"The *Viveur*," published in *Les Français peints par eux-mêmes* and a piece occasionally cited separately by his contemporaries, was perhaps the most revealing of Briffault's contributions, since the author himself was a prime example of "le sublime viveur, la gaieté incarnée," as he was characterized by James Rousseau in *Physiologie du viveur*.[15] The *viveur*, as both Briffault and Rousseau described him, was a kind of bon vivant who especially prized food and drink and the conviviality that usually accompanied their consumption.[16] The product of enlightened times, he applied reason to the sensations "to find the liveliest and least affected of pleasures." The *viveur* seems to have had little interest in fashion, possessions, luxurious surroundings, or sexual adventures, and although there was a bit of the Don Juan in him, as Briffault contends, there was little of the Don's villainy ("scéléretasse") or love of women ("feminine amour"). The *viveur* lived in the moment, having no regard for the future, fearing only the onset of gout, which was likely to afflict his old age as does "remorse the life of the guilty." As if to clarify his own identification with the type (as well as his altered priorities), Briffault told the tale of one *viveur* who, having just had his right arm shattered by a bullet during a duel, calmly announced, "I will now drink with my left hand."[17]

Briffault was a formidable eater and drinker. Early in his career Louis Huarte had warned him, to no avail, about his "immoderate portliness," a "maladie" that had attacked other writers of his generation, such as Jules Janin and Honoré de Balzac.[18] Roger de Beauvoir (the *nom de plume* of

Eugène-Auguste-Roger de Bully), in his recollections of several "soupeurs" ("viveurs") of which he, too, was an exemplar, described Briffault as "the godfather of all the boulevard kitchens."[19] As with other writers who were "barons of the fork," his most agreeable writings were composed "in shirt sleeves, with both elbows on a restaurant table...among ravaged dishes and empty bottles."[20] Beauvoir accused him of having killed off more than thirty restaurants (presumably by not paying his exorbitant bills),[21] and another commentator warned newly published authors and playwrights about inviting Briffault to dinner in the hope of buying positive publicity, since his "gastronomic indiscretion" could be "frightening."[22] One of the witticisms for which he was known was his response to the observation that two were required to eat a chicken: "Right. Me and the chicken."[23]

He was also a legendary drinker, and he was particularly renowned for his ability to "do the *cloche*." This involved filling a large *cloche à fromage* (a sort of bell jar used to cover plates of cheeses) with champagne and draining it in a single draft, culminating with a resonant *bing* as the empty *cloche* was dropped to the table.[24] Even the seasoned *viveur* François-Auguste Romieu, a man reputed to be the "plus gai de France," declined to attempt "la cloche de Briffault."[25]

In 1842 the artist Benjamin Roubaud created a long scroll-like caricature, the "Grand chemin de la posterité," depicting a procession of novelists, poets, playwrights, and journalists following Victor Hugo into a future heralded by Romanticism. Near the end of the cortege of journalists, facing the viewer, stood a smiling and portly Briffault. His name was inscribed beneath him and above that the title, "Le mélancolique," which

would appear to be an odd label for someone renowned for his wit and conviviality ("la gaieté incarnée"). But perhaps the illustrator suspected something, for, as Roger Beauvoir later expressed it in his capsule biography of Briffault, "One fine day he went mad and had to be shut up inside [the asylum] Charenton."[26]

Beauvoir, who was repelled by Briffault's politics, described his later life as being one of considerable decline. He seemed to be working harder and harder for less and less, and he gave some indication of being in extreme debt. Eventually he switched from champagne to strong liquors and absinthe. In conformance with Roubaud's "melancholy" characterization of him, Beauvoir described him as having become "serious, morose, taciturn," with a livid brow, sunken cheeks, and a "cadaverous" appearance: "Nocturnal

Paris . . . no longer found in him anything but a ragged phantom, the ghost of his gaiety."[27]

His temperament and his financial affairs were not helped apparently by a late and unexpected marriage to a woman who was said to be pretty, half his age, and, according to Beauvoir, "a princess of the sidewalk," registered with the police as a prostitute.[28] The critic Edouard Thierry, who considered the marriage to be "an astonishing surprise," was troubled by the fact that shortly thereafter, thieves "were admitted" into Briffault's dining room and stole all of his silver.[29] In fact, Beauvoir attributed his mental collapse to the use of a toxic aphrodisiac, whose danger Briffault never suspected and which finished the job brandy and absinthe had apparently begun.[30]

Of course, his illness may have instead been the result of a physical ailment, and considering the company he was keeping, he may have succumbed to the same sexually transmitted disease that drove other writers and artists—Charles Baudelaire, Gérard de Nerval, Guy de Maupassant, Alphonse Daudet, Henri de Toulouse-Lautrec—into sanatoriums and eventually to their premature deaths. Charles Maurice, a theatrical critic and colleague of Briffault, reported that a doctor at the asylum had attributed his illness to a "paralysis" that had invaded one side of his brain and would "irresistibly strike the other." This same friend mentioned that whenever he and his wife visited him in the sanatorium, Briffault was calm and quiet, and, although melancholy, he could always recognize the two of them. He enjoyed discussing the pleasurable former times they had spent together, but although his memory was clear, it tended to weaken by the end of the visit.[31] Another acquaintance described similar moments of clarity in Charenton, although

Briffault once mistook him for a restaurateur to whom he owed six hundred francs. To this same visitor he also seemed to recall the pain of his marriage, one time pleading with him not to tell "her" he was there. When asked whom he meant, Briffault pointed to a woman in a nearby alley with a fan in one hand and the straps of her bonnet dangling, giving her arms to two young men as she joined them in a burst of laughter.[32]

When Charles Maurice on one visit asked after Briffault's wife, he replied, "She came at the beginning, but she doesn't come anymore."[33]

Briffault died in Charenton on October 11, 1854.

•—• •—• •—•

According to Jean-Paul Aron, during Louis-Philippe's "July Monarchy" (1830–1848)—when Briffault was active as both a writer and *viveur*—dining in France, and particularly restaurant dining, had entered a period of relative decline. Paris was still, by far, the center of the gastronomic world but "the golden age that culminated between 1812 and 1825 [had] slowly deteriorated into the *petit-bourgeois* grey dullness of the constitutional monarchy."[34] Many of the historic restaurants that had created and secured that "golden-age" reputation—Café Anglais, Véry, Les Trois Frères Provençaux, Le Cadran Bleu, Le Rocher de Cancale—were still in operation, but some had changed owners or locations and clientele while others had become complacent and were overly dependent on their celebrity and luxurious surroundings or had simply become overwhelmed with tourists and provincial diners. For instance, a character in one of Edward Bulwer-Lytton's novels declared, "Véry is, indeed, no longer the prince of restaurateurs. The low English who have flocked thither, have entirely ruined the place!"[35] In addition, one writer in 1841 complained that most quality ingredients were then being sent first to private residences rather than to restaurants and that "the decadence" was complete: "The time where Legac, Grignon, the old Frères Provençaux, the first Véry made their delicacies are now far away from us."[36] Briffault shares these opinions, and in Chapter 10 of *Paris à table*, after praising the restaurants of Napoleon's Empire and the Restoration, he finds that, despite some exceptions, "the general condition has been altered and is deteriorating more and more." He considers the best dining to be occurring instead in private residences: at an occasional banquet, at a few noble tables, and in the homes of the affluent bourgeoisie. In fact, claims Aron, it was not until the "bourgeois of the Second Empire" resumed dining out publicly in town, "breaking with their *Louis-Philippard* fathers who aspired only to get back home,"[37] that a new "golden age" was established during the economic resurgence of the Second Empire (1852–1870). Of course, this revival of eminent restaurants was also supported by the emergence of another generation of master chefs, such as Adolphe Dugléré, who restored the Café Anglais to its former grandeur; Jules Gouffé, who made a reputation for the Jockey Club; and Paul Brébant, who founded the eponymous Brébant.

Along with the initial establishment and rise of great restaurants, the early decades of the 1800s can also be characterized by the beginning of a unique gastronomic literature. As if to inaugurate the phenomenon, the word *gastronomie* in its current usage entered the language through a popular poem written by Joseph Berchoux in 1801, "La Gastronomie ou l'homme des champs à table," establishing at its origin a rapport between gastronomy and literary culture.[38] In fact, Pascal Ory has declared that "gastronomy" has more to do with the "rules" of eating and drinking, the "art of the table," than with cooking, and that the "gastronome in his most evolved form" is not a professional cook, but "a man of letters."[39] In any case, an intricate connection was forged between eating and writing at the very beginning of the nineteenth century, one that would leave, according to Aron, a deep impression on French civilization: "Cuisine became an object of discourse. The press and literature, both large and small, seized on it like a serious matter."[40]

As early as 1841 one critic isolated the trio of writers who represented the best in gastronomic literature, declaring that "several books alone contained the secret of the finest of traditions: they are the writings of Monsieurs Grimod de la Reynière, Brillat-Savarin, and the illustrious practitioner Carême."[41] Since then, these three very different personalities have frequently been cited as the pillars of culinary discourse in the first part of the nineteenth century, a sort of literary complement to the iconic restaurants of that golden age.[42] Alexandre-Balthazar-Laurent Grimod de la Reynière is often credited with being the first culinary critic and journalist. Before him many books had appeared on food and drink, but these were primarily cookbooks, technical guides, and medical treatises. Grimod de la Reynière's *Almanach des gourmands*, an annual volume appearing eight times from 1803 to 1812, was a regular compilation of reportage and commentary, containing restaurant and supplier recommendations and reviews, advice and guides for the consumer and connoisseur, nostalgic culinary recollections and anecdotes. Along with other publications on the topic, he also founded the first epicurean newsletter, the *Journal des gourmands et des belles* (published from 1806 to 1807 and, from 1808 to 1815, under the title *L'épicurien français*).

At about the time Grimod de la Reynière ceased publishing, Marie-Antoine Carême wrote his first book, *Le pâtissier royal parisien* (1815). Carême, perhaps the first celebrity chef, converted a deep and practical knowledge of cooking and taste into a series of works that were compilations of recipes and best practices, designs and plans for menus and ornamentation, historical discourse and personal recollection. These culminated in the five volumes of *L'art de la cuisine française au dix-neuvième siècle*, which began to appear shortly after his death in 1833.

The pinnacle of this new gastronomic literature, a classic whose influence has arguably yet to be surpassed, was Jean-Anthelme Brillat-Savarin's *Physiologie du goût*. Published late in1825, a few months before the author's death, the book's initial sales were slow, but, at least in France, it has never been out-of-print. Along with considerable anecdotal material and personal reminiscence, the book is a scientific study in the broadest sense (at least in nineteenth-century terms), containing chemical and anatomical analyses of nutrition and taste, a "Philosophical History of Cooking," and a host of meditations and aphorisms on food and eating. Initially published anonymously by "a professor and member of several learned societies," it is the first treatise to attempt a comprehensive treatment of food from its composition, its production, and its preparation, to its consumption, as well as being an exploration of the social world of which it is a part, something of a "sociology of taste ahead of its time."[43]

During subsequent years, the work of these three writers exerted considerable influence—"Journalists pillaged their writings, editors reproduced their recipes, 'anecdotiers' appropriated their stories and sayings"[44]—as commentary on culinary matters continued to be written and published for an expanding press, although without the durability or substance of these pioneers. Among the more serious efforts during the period of the July Monarchy, were two new, though ultimately short-lived, periodicals, Paul Lacroix's *Le gastronome: journal universel du goût* (1830–1831) and *La table: journal culinaire* (1844–1845), edited and published by Victor and César Bouton. In addition, popular journalists and writers were reviewing, commenting, and critiquing in the daily press as well as publishing books and pamphlets on the contemporary dining scene. These latter would include Auguste Romieu and Horace-Napoléon Raisson's *Code gourmand: manuel complet de gastronomie comprenant les lois, règles, applications et exemples de l'art de bien vivre* (1827), Jacques Arago's *Comme on dine à Paris* (1842), and Victor Bouton's *La table à Paris, mystères des restaurants, cafés et comestibles* (1845). There was also considerable development in another literary genre as novelists like Honoré de Balzac and Paul de Kock began to introduce restaurants and other dining sites into their fictions, constructing scenes around the consumption of food and making culinary events an integral part of their fictional worlds.

One other influential publication, whose significance is often overlooked, was more of a summation than a development or a new direction. It too had a wide readership and seemed to have reinvigorated serious interest in gastronomy. First published in 1843 in a single volume of 550 pages, *Les classiques de la table* accumulated content as subsequent editions appeared in 1844 and 1845, until by its fourth and final 1848 edition, it had doubled in size, consisting of two volumes of more than 500 pages each. Edited by Frédéric Fayot, who had been Carême's personal secretary and editor of several of his books, *Les classiques de la table* collected under a single title material from the three essential writers named above, including the complete *Physiologie du goût*, as well as extensive extracts from the work of both Grimod de la Reynière and Carême (with some of Carême's reminiscences appearing for the first time in its pages). It also reprinted Berchoux's poem "La Gastronomie" and texts from the pens of such authoritative voices as the Marquis de Cussy and Lady Morgan (née Sydney Owenson), among several others. By its last two editions, it was labeling itself, with some accuracy, as "a small library of the most distinguished writings published in Paris on gastronomy and the elegant life."[45]

With four editions in five years, *Les classiques de la table* would seem to have been a success. Even though it was not translated, it still received some attention in England. One reviewer, Andrew Valentine Kirwan—an Irish lawyer with a wide knowledge of France and its cuisine—considered the first edition to be a sign of the resurgence of both gastronomic literature and French dining.[46] For the previous fourteen years, he stated in 1844, "the cooks and epicures of Paris...have been altogether silent on the progress, or, perhaps, we should rather say on the 'decline and fall' of their own art." But with the "disinterring" of these "classics of the table," he sensed a change, contending that the "closing and bankruptcy of restaurateurs...is no longer an everyday occurrence," and that "the courtesies and elegances of life are again reviving; the birds of the air, the water, and the earth are again salmied, fricasseed, roasted, crapaudineed, filleted, and supremed."[47] Another English reviewer found the selection of texts to be "admirable" and would think of giving no other book as a gift for the holiday season.[48]

Briffault may not have owned a copy of *Les classiques de la table*, but he certainly had access to one of the editions and it is surely the "book authoritative in gastronomic matters" he mentions in Chapter 10 of *Paris à table*.[49] He draws material and information from it frequently, sometimes citing the author or the extract directly, sometimes simply alluding (occasionally only through quotation marks) to its previous publication there, sometimes providing no attribution at all. These, incidentally, are his usual tactics with his other reference material, practices that range from direct citation of an author or text, to vague mention of a previous source or a quote from an "expert" or a "traveler," to what modern authors would regard as outright plagiarism. One particularly blatant example of Briffault's lax process would be the four anecdotes that conclude his third chapter, which were "quoted" ("On cite plusieurs exemples") almost verbatim, without further attribution, from an 1840 newspaper column written by the poet and pioneering journalist Delphine de Girardin.

This cavalier attitude toward the intellectual property of others was not uncommon in nineteenth-century France, where writing was becoming as much a matter of commerce as of literature, where writers were competing for publishers' attention and often getting paid by the line. To cite some more celebrated examples, Stendhal was not immune to masquerading translated work as his own, and the elder Dumas' hugely prolific output was often the product of unacknowledged collaboration as well as borrowings from both others and his own previous work.[50] Balzac, who knew something of these matters, primarily from being plundered rather than plundering

himself, has a journalist in *Illusions perdues* (1839) declare
that "the secret of fame and fortune in the literary world is not
hard work but the exploitation of other people's hard work."[51]
Briffault, too, was a victim of theft, a crude translation of large
sections of *Paris à table*—the only substantial translation of
the work to be published in English—having appeared as the
chapter "The Science of Good Living in Paris by a Gastronome"
in *Tea-Table Talk, Ennobled Actresses, and Other Miscellanies*
(1857), by a "Mrs. Matthews."[52]

•—•—•—•

Paris à table was initially published by J. Hetzel in twenty parts
at 15 centimes each or three francs for the entire volume.[53] It
was advertised with other Hetzel titles, including Balzac's
Paris marié: philosophie de la vie conjugale (1846), under the
heading *Petits tableaux de Paris* (Small Pictures of Paris). A
poster was also produced to publicize it.[54] A cheaper, popular
edition (2 fr.) from Havard appeared in 1851 in a two-column
format as part of an eclectic series of titles, *Romans du jour
illustrés (Illustrated Narratives of the Day)*. The book's publication history was identical to that of Briffault's previous title
with Hetzel, *Paris dans l'eau* (1844), and like its predecessor,
it was also profusely illustrated with woodcuts by Bertall.

Bertall, an anagram of his middle name (the second "l" was
Balzac's suggestion), was born Charles-Albert d'Arnoux in
1820. Against the wishes of his family, he trained as an artist
and illustrator. Perhaps it was his early acquaintance with
Balzac that led to a recommendation to either Briffault or the
publisher Pierre-Jules Hetzel, since the 120 vignettes he produced for *Paris dans l'eau* represented some of his earliest

published work. Apparently both author and publisher were satisfied with the results, since he was also assigned to illustrate *Paris à table* two years later, earning equal billing with Briffault in advertising and on the cover. By then Bertall had also established a professional relationship with Balzac, having produced drawings and a poster for *Petites misères de la vie conjugale* (1845–1846), and he was responsible for almost half of the illustrations for the first edition of the novelist's complete works, *La comédie humaine* (1842–1855). He would go on to become one of the most prolific graphic artists of the century, contributing to anthologies, popular fiction, the periodical press, and children's literature, as well as illustrating two subsequent editions of *Physiologie du goût*.[55] In addition, he played a role in the development of photography, opening his own portrait studio in 1866.[56]

On their first meeting, Balzac asked the young Bertall how he had managed to draw such an accurate portrait of *Père Goriot*'s Madame Vauquer, which the artist had submitted to introduce his work to the novelist. Bertall answered, "I copied word for word, feature for feature the description you made of her, and I tried never to forget neither a single feature nor a single word." Balzac replied, "Very good, my boy, nothing could resemble her more. The type is the one I depicted."[57] This close, integral relationship of the drawing with the text, as well as Bertall's concern for the intent of the author, is characteristic of his work for Briffault.

Other than the occasional spot art, Bertall's drawings in *Paris à table* go well beyond simple adornment. The image that serves as cover and frontispiece—featuring a portrait of the author as a colossal chef straddling the river Seine, with a huge fork piercing the Left Bank and a bottle of wine replacing the

Vendôme column on the Right—blends realism and imaginative fancy to present a panoramic introduction to the book's content. Continuing the gigantic metaphor into the first chapter, Bertall offers several outsized and grotesque images to represent the immensity and power of the culinary scene described by the author, "the Cyclopean and gargantuan mass of Paris consumption." In subsequent chapters he usually sketches more realistic figures to depict the types and circumstances described by the author, adhering closely to specific language of the text, sometimes simply representing it, sometimes clarifying or commenting on it. Occasionally he draws attention to a humorous punch line or even a pun, and he sometimes underscores the ironic tone often deployed by the author. When Briffault in Chapter 4 describes a variety of banquets, including "the philanthropic banquet, where you eat for the poor who are dying of hunger," Bertall depicts not a festive banquet scene, but a destitute man dying in the street.[58]

Certainly, Briffault must have approved of the color, depth, and humor Bertall contributed to his book for, clearly, along with enlightenment, entertainment was one of his primary objectives. As a *viveur* of the first rank, Briffault prized conviviality, and throughout *Paris à table* he proves himself to be an accomplished storyteller. Collected from literary sources and the popular press, both attributed and unattributed, and probably on occasion from his own experience, the various tales and anecdotes scattered throughout the book are used to illuminate historical moments, exemplify unusual or exotic fashions or customs, or, as was the case with Brillat-Savarin, to draw attention to a social setting or mannerism.[59] But on other occasions they seem to be inserted simply to amuse, sometimes stacked at the end of a chapter without any logical relationship

to what went before or any real coherence among them other
than the author's love of a good story, as if Briffault were offering the reader the kind of spirited conversation he found so
often lacking at the contemporary table. Like Balzac, he apparently found the technique of "anecdoter" to be useful not
only as a "passport to all that is moral" but also necessary as an
"anti-narcotic."[60]

Other than the anecdotal material, which is prevalent in
the literature, *Paris à table* has less in common with the gastronomic writing of his predecessors or contemporaries than
might be expected. With the exception of the statistical information in the first chapter, his text has little of the scientific,
medical, or philosophical content found in Brillat-Savarin.
Briffault specifically avoids a scholarly approach. "Having little
curiosity about gastronomic archaeology, we will not be searching, in the archives of the past…erudition at the table would
be no more than inappropriate, annoying, and in bad taste," he
writes in Chapter 2. Although there are observations about
restaurants both past and present, there are no recommendations for dining or judgments about individual meals as would
be found in, say, Grimod de la Reynière. *Paris à table* is not a
practical guidebook for tourists, nor is it intended for cooks,
since there are no recipes, *à la* Carême, or techniques for
preparation. In fact, Briffault almost never enters a kitchen,
and many of the details about food itself or descriptions of individual meals are embedded in the anecdotes and the referenced material.

In retrospect, some critics found *Paris à table* to resemble
a literature of another sort. An anonymous biographer, encap-
sulating Briffault's life for an encyclopedic project, characterized the book as a "petite physiologie,"[61] and Pierre Larousse,

for his dictionary, identified both *Paris à table* and *Paris dans l'eau* as "spirituelles physiologies."[62] Although the term *physiologie* had often been used to give a scientific or pseudo-scientific aura to an occasional title (Brillat-Savarin and Balzac's *Physiologie du marriage* [1829] are obvious examples), for a short period in the 1840s the term also had a specific, generic application. Written and illustrated by many of the authors and artists who contributed to the panoramic literature, these particular *physiologies* were a series of pamphlet-sized caricatures and portraits—often depicted in a light, satirical manner—that presented a variety of social types and typical situations familiar to the contemporary Parisian.[63] One of the first, written by *Le charivari* editor Louis Huart in May 1841, which may have helped to launch the trend, was *Physiologie du flâneur*, a distinctive choice since it featured a quintessentially urban and Parisian specimen. Courtesans and cuckolds, creditors and debtors, grocers and ragpickers—about 120 of them, in all—quickly followed in the path of the *flâneur*. Intended for a mass audience, *physiologies* were published in inexpensive formats, in several uniform series, at about one franc each. For a short time they became immensely popular, with approximately a half-million copies printed between 1840 and 1842. The anonymous author of *Physiologie des physiologies*, a *jeu d'esprit* satirizing the genre itself, lamented the fact that authors like Molière and Hugo had been consigned to the shadows by "these small books—yellow, blue, red—that run riot among the shelves.... *Physiologies, Physiologies*—everything is *Physiologies!*"[64]

Walter Benjamin considered the *physiologie* to be a subgenre of panoramic literature. They were "inconspicuous" paperbacks with limited horizons, designed for sale in the streets, whereas the more expansive and expensive anthologies were "salon attire," clearly intended for the leisured reading of the leisured classes. He had little respect for these lesser publications, and once their coverage of all human types had been exhausted, according to Benjamin, they disappeared, their place subsequently taken by the "physiology of the city." The "city," of course, was Paris. Into this latter category, along with several other books with "Paris" in their titles (including Balzac's *Paris marié*), Benjamin situated *Paris dans l'eau* and *Paris à table*.[65]

Despite his dismissal of the genre, Benjamin's categorization of *Paris à table* with other panoramic literature, particularly writings associated with the city, links Briffault to other authors—journalists, essayists, novelists—who observed and analyzed the contemporary urban scene. This was a self-reflective literature intended for readers who wanted to read about themselves, but the detailed investigation of Parisian life became not only a commentary on their own reality but also an attempt to explain it, to preserve it for posterity, and, on occasion, to reflect on the human condition. Early in his career, Briffault positioned himself as a social critic, equipped with a cold analytical eye. In his 1832 essay "The Paris Night," he compared the major object of journalistic attention—the birth of a new European civilization with its daily and often troubling fluctuations in public, private, and artistic life—to a "cadaver": "We are seeking to discover the mechanism of social existence; the bodies of politics and of civilization lie beneath our scalpels."[66] In this essay, he achieved his purpose by strolling through the nocturnal streets like a *flâneur*, "observing and seeking out everything that Paris, dead or asleep, can still contain within its vibrant and active parts."[67]

He continued to see himself as a chronicler of urban life a decade later when he founded the monthly *Historiettes contemporaines*. Borrowing a phrase from Jean de la Bruyère—the author of a classic collection of portraits, *Caractères, ou les moeurs de ce siècle* (1688)—he interpreted *historiette* as "the common noise of the city." Like many commentators of his time, Briffault viewed the passing scene as transitory but worthy of being recorded: "The world is vast and changing; scenes, men, events, things speedily appear and disappear. You have to look quick!" The *historiettes* would be both amusing and enlightening, offering "notes from the history of these times, the comedy next to the drama, the *moeurs* ("manners") depicted by the deeds."[68]

The word *moeurs* appears almost two dozen times in *Paris à table*, where, depending on its context, it can be translated as "manners," "customary manners," "customs," "ways of life," and so forth.[69] But in one pivotal instance, in his introductory chapter, Briffault uses it to describe his intent: "What a people eats...is known; but nothing is known of those private customs and manners ("moeurs intimes") that show their true character under a picturesque and lively appearance, constantly in motion. That is what we are trying to do for Paris."

The depiction and disclosure of contemporary manners, or *moeurs*, was also uppermost in the minds of many of the writers and editors producing the panoramic literature of the time. For instance, the original subtitle of *Paris ou le livre des cent-et-un*, when the project was first conceived in 1831, was *Paris et les moeurs comme elles sont* (*Paris and Its Manners as They Are*),[70] and its publisher Pierre-François Ladvocat, in his opening notice to the public, declared that he wanted to do for *Paris moderne* what Louis-Sébastien Mercier, in his *Tableau de Paris* (1781–1788), had done for the pre-Revolutionary city: reveal the character of Paris through multiple "pictures of manners" (*tableaux de moeurs*).[71]

When the various chapters of a later omnibus collection, *Les Français peints par eux-mêmes* (1840–1842), were initially sold as separate parts, they were advertised as *moeurs contemporaines*,[72] and the journalist and critic Jules Janin made it clear in his "Introduction" to the first volume that the object of the project was "the study of contemporary manners" (*l'étude des mœurs contemporaines*).[73] He, too, found models in those few previous writers—Molière, La Bruyère, Mercier—who had attempted similar moral portraits, although, as Janin phrased it, they tended to wield satirical daggers rather than the analytical scalpel. The goal of the contributors to the present and subsequent volumes of *Les Français peints par eux-mêmes* would be to preserve, down to the slightest detail, the variety and divisions of a rapidly passing Parisian scene for a future that would want "to know everything about us, how did we mount our horses? How were our tables set? What wines did we prefer to drink?"[74] Two years later, in his conclusion to the completed project, its publisher, Léon Curmer, applauded his authors for not only preserving a variety of "fleeting pictures" from "the immense daily whirlwind that swallows all things," but also, "with the patience and resignation of the surgeon, who holds the scalpel with a sure hand," sounding the depths of "all the social classes, the most elegant salons, the most shameful dives, the noblest of national sentiments, the basest instincts toward vice, the most touching of the heart's emotions." The result was that the volumes, like a "moral mirror," reflected society in its entirety, presenting the reader with "all that the human heart could experience of sensations, all that personal interest, devotion, egoism, love, hatred, modesty, depravity, atheism, charity, ignorance, the love of study, good and bad instincts can engender."[75]

In his "Avant-propos" to *La comédie humaine*, written in 1842 as an introduction to the future compilation of his complete works, Balzac reveals similar attitudes. Declaring that a large portion of his fiction would be organized into six books, *Scènes de la vie privée, de province, parisienne, politique, militaire et de campagne*, he places them all under the heading *Études de mœurs*, and like the physiologists, he, too, was intent on exploring types, both persons and situations: "Not only men, but also the principal events of life are categorized by types.... My work has its geography as it has its genealogy and its families, its places and its things, its persons and its deeds...its nobles and its bourgeois, its artisans and its peasants, its politicians and its dandies."[76] He regretted that historians of earlier civilizations had favored "public life" to the exclusion of the perennial and everyday actions of the individual, but he would rectify that neglect: "French society was going to be the historian, I should be no more than the secretary. In drawing up an inventory of vices and virtues, in gathering together the principal facts of the passions, in depicting the characters...perhaps I could come near to writing the history forgotten by so many historians, that of manners (*moeurs*)."[77] A rigorous and faithful reproduction was the foundation of his work, although as an artist he would need to go beyond being the mere reporter of "the drama of private life" (*la vie intime*), an "archaeologist of social furnishings." To achieve his higher artistic aims, he would need to seek out "that social force" (*ce moteur social*), the "sense" behind this "immense assembly of figures, passions, and events," and to measure its proximity to "the eternal law, to the true and the beautiful."[78]

Eugène Briffault was neither a novelist nor a social scientist, but a journalist, and as with other journalists of his day, his style could be breezy, fashionable, allusive, and sometimes he could be discovered with his tongue firmly implanted in his cheek, as, for instance, in the concluding paragraph of *Paris à table*. But as a journalist, he could also be a documentarian, "observing and seeking out everything," as he wrote earlier in his career, and he adopts this practice for *Paris à table*. In his introduction he presents an overview of the extent of the city's culinary culture—a wide tracking shot, as it were—but he concludes the chapter by promising to focus in on his fellow citizens, investigating them close up and at every level, as if he were a naturalist observing animal behavior, species by species, each in its particular habitat: "There will be no sanctuary impervious to our efforts, we will go sit down at every table, by the side of the most powerful and the most humbled, with the voluptuous, with the artisan and the laborer. We will be at every celebration: the palace, the mansion, the clubs... the cabaret and the backroom, the attic, the workshop, the sleazy dive... diligent to capture nature in the act, we will discover each in its turn, like those who, to study animals, choose the moment they devour their prey." In subsequent chapters, he observes and presents for the reader the manners and habits associated with various types of Parisian meals, linking them to the current times and the recent past, to economic good fortune and adversity, but he also extends his investigation to all levels of society, usually beginning with the affluent and their fondness for the luxurious and the sumptuous, but reporting as well on lesser classes of diners—from the professions, through the artistic community, down to the worker eating hastily in the streets. In his chapter on restaurants, he has a similar trajectory, focusing primarily on the celebrated and first-class establishments, but eventually descending through the mid-range dining rooms down to the *gargotes*, the *tapis-francs*, and the prix-fixe eateries catering to clerks and students. He seems to have a particular fondness for the bourgeois household, but he also visits the *tables d'hôte* and the *pensions bourgeoises*, and the many other options open to the Parisian diner, including even a failed experiment in home delivery and the scavenging in the dumps. As if in response to Jules Janin's aspirations for *Les Français peints par eux-mêmes*, he would enlighten posterity on how "our tables [were] set," and in the process he would construct an unprecedented culinary portrait of Paris at a time when it was not only the gastronomic center of the world, but, to borrow Walter Benjamin's phrase, "the capital of the nineteenth century."

NOTES TO INTRODUCTION

[1] Jean-Bernard Mary-Lafon, "Histoire d'un livre," *Musée des familles,* second series, 7 (1850): 172.

[2] See, for instance, Allen S. Weiss's introduction to the abridged Mercure de France edition of *Paris à table* (Paris: Mercure de France, 2003), 7.

[3] In his book *Drafts on My Memory*, William Pitt Lennox cites a dinner at the Rocher de Cancale mentioned in "a very amusing book entitled *Paris à table*, most graphically written by Eugène Briffault" (London: Chapman and Hall, 1866), 26.

[4] Pascal Ory, "Gastronomy," *Realms of Memory: Vol. II, Traditions*, ed. Pierre Nora, trans. Arthur Goldhammer (New York: Columbia University Press, 1997), 443; P.-J. Catinchi, "La restauration par le menu," July 25, 2003, 11.

[5] Eugène Briffault, "Fontan," *Nouvelles Parisiennes* (Paris: Ledoux, 1843), 377.

[6] Roger de Beauvoir, *Les soupeurs de mon temps* (Paris: Faure, 1868), 180–181. For more on the background of his duel with Barbot de la Trésorière and the duel itself, see also Alexandre Dumas *père*, *Mes mémoires* (Chapter 264).

[7] Carrel, who was one of the most prominent liberal journalists of his time, fought several duels during his career, the last of which, in 1836, led to his death.

[8] Most of the biographical information here about Briffault prior to 1840 has been drawn from the capsule biography written by Louis Huart in his edition of *Galerie de la presse, de la littérature et des beaux-artes* (Paris: Auber, 1839), unpaginated.

[9] [Edmond Texier?], *Physiologie de la presse: biographie des journalists et des journaux de Paris et de la province* (Paris: Laisné, 1841), 44–45.

[10] *Historiettes contemporaines: courrier de la ville*, no. 1 (Jan. 31, 1842): 9.

[11] "Literary Notices," *The Roman Advertiser*, no. 103 (March 31, 1849): 394.

[12] For more on Ferdinand Philippe, Duc d'Orléans, see chap. 2, n. 43.

[13] [Napoléon Gallois], *Petit dictionnaire de nos grandes girouettes* (Paris: Binet, 1842), 52.

[14] *The Arcades Project*, trans. Howard Eiland and Kevin McLaughlin (Cambridge, MA: Harvard University Press, 1999), 5–6. In his essay "The Paris of the Second Empire in Baudelaire," he defines this literature in similar language, as works consisting of "individual sketches which . . . reproduce the dynamic foreground of those panoramas with their anecdotal form and the sweeping background of the panoramas with their store of information" (Walter Benjamin, *Selected Writings: Volume 4, 1938–1940*, ed. Howard Eiland and Michael W. Jennings, trans. Edmund Jephcott et al. [Cambridge, MA: Harvard University Press, 2003], 18).

[15] (Paris: Laisné, 1842), 79.

[16] "The *viveur* thinks only of eating and drinking" (Rousseau, 4). "Wit, gaiety, *insouciance.* That's what constitutes the *viveur,*" writes Rousseau elsewhere in his *Physiologie* (11).

[17] *Les Français peints par eux-mêmes* (Paris: Curmer, 1841), 365–372. The collection went through several editions, including an English one, *Pictures of the French: A Series of Literary and Graphic Delineations of French Character* (London: Orr, 1840). This edition included both "The Deputy" (255–233) and "The Viveur" (329–337), and these represent the only English translations of a complete work by Briffault.

[18] Huart, n.p.

[19] Beauvoir, *Les Soupeurs de mon temps*, 153. According to Anne Marie-Fugier (*La vie élégante ou la formation du Tout-Paris: 1815–1848* [Paris: Fayard, 1990], 372), Beauvoir was an occasional dinner companion of Briffault.

[20] Ibid., 184.

[21] Ibid., 153.

[22] Mary-Lafon, 172. Armand de Pontmartin recounts the tale of a friend who, wanting to treat Briffault to a 40-sous dinner in gratitude for a complimentary article, was unaware he was dealing with "la gloutonnerie de Gargantua" and wound up underwriting a "prodigieux" feast at Les Trois Frères Provençaux (*Souvenirs d'un vieux critique* [Paris: Calmann Levy, 1884], 3:21).

[23] Beauvoir, 155.

[24] Ibid., 154.

[25] Alfred Marquiset, *Romieu et Courchamps* (Paris: Emile Paul Frères, 1913), 36–37.

[26] Beauvoir, 185. Founded in 1645, Charenton was the major Parisian insane asylum, located just southeast of the city.

[27] Beauvoir, 183–184.

[28] Ibid., 184.

[29] Cited in M. W. Duckett, ed., *Dictionnaire de la conversation et de la lecture: supplément* (Paris: Firmin-Didot, 1864), 1:692.

[30] Beauvoir, 187.

[31] Charles Maurice, *Histoire anecdotique du théâtre* (Paris: Plon, 1856), 2:346.

[32] Beauvoir, 188–189.

[33] Maurice, 347.

[34] Jean-Paul Aron, *Le mangeur du XIXe siècle* (Paris: Laffont, 1973), 90.

35 Edward Bulwer-Lytton, "Chapter 12," *Pelham, or the Adventures of a Gentleman* [1828] (Philadelphia: Lippincott, 1883), 78.

36 [Anon.], "Revue gastronomique: Paris et aujourd'hui, les restaurants de Paris," *Journal des femmes*, no. 13 (Oct. 1841): 308–311.

37 Aron, 89.

38 For the early use of the word and its related nomenclature, see Alberto Capatti, "Gastronomie et gastronomes au XIXe siècle," *À table aux XIXe siècle* (Paris: Flammarion, 2001), 102–113; also Christian Guy, *La vie quotidienne de la société gourmande en France au XIXe siècle* (Paris: Hachette, 1971), 92–94.

39 Pascal Ory, "Gastronomy," in *Realms of Memory: The Construction of the French Past, Vol. II: Traditions*, ed. Pierre Nora, trans. Arthur Goldhammer (New York: Columbia University Press, 1997), 448.

40 Aron, 14–15. See also Priscilla Parkhurst Ferguson, *Accounting for Taste: The Triumph of French Cuisine* (Chicago: University of Chicago Press, 2004), 33–34 ("The crucial period of culinary textualization began in the early nineteenth century, when the growing market for all kinds of writing initiated a notable… growth that lasted until the end of the century" [34]).

41 [Anon.], "Revue gastronomique: Paris et aujourd'hui, les restaurants de Paris," *Journal des femmes*, no. 13 (Oct. 1841): 310.

42 See, for instance, Ferguson, *passim*; and Ory, *passim*.

43 Ferguson, 31.

44 Capatti, 109.

45 For the publication history of *Les Classiques de la table*, see Georges Vicaire, *Bibliographie gastronomique* (Paris: Roquette, 1890), 176–181. For more on the Marquis de Cussy and Lady Morgan, see chap. 2 (nn. 19 and 59, respectively).

46 "Gastronomy: The Classics of the Table," *Fraser's Magazine* 29 (May 1844): 604–615. Originally published anonymously, the article was reprinted in *The New World* 8 (June 1, 1844): 677–682 and *Campbell's Foreign Semi-Monthly Magazine* 6 (June 16, 1844): 241–252. The piece was also extended into a series of articles for *Fraser's*, but only the second ("Dinner, Dessert, Wines, Coffee," 30 [July 1844]: 48–61) continued to review *Classiques*. The third article ("Dessert, Fruits, Sweetmeats, and Liqueurs," 30 [Sept. 1844]: 269–79) and the fourth ("Sweetmeats, Beer, Cider, Perry, Liqueurs, and Wine," 30 [Oct. 1844]: 427–436) covered general culinary issues, much of which was repeated in *Host and Guest: A Book about Dinners, Wines, and Desserts* (London: Bell & Daldy, 1864), a book for which Kirwan acknowledged authorship.

47 "Gastronomy: The Classics of the Table," *Fraser's Magazine* 29, 604–605.

48 A.D., "*Les classiques de la table*, un beau volume illustré," *Revue britannique* 18 (Nov. 1843): 252–253.

49 He also mentions the collection by name in his *Paris dans l'eau* (Paris: Hetzel, 1844), 11, describing it as a book where "the taste, the intellect, and the succulent intelligence are authoritative," a book that has "gathered together in one doctrinal body all the pleasant and useful, salutary and delectable truths of real eating and drinking."

50 See, for instance, Hélène Maurel-Indart, *Du plagiat* (Paris: Presses Universaires de France, 1999), 24–27.

[51] Cited in Graham Robb, "The Pens of the Musketeer," *New York Review of Books*, March 20, 2008, 35.

[52] This chapter was a lengthier version of articles published in *Bentley's Miscellany* ([London: Richard Bentley, 1850], 27:487–492 and 574–581). Its author, also identified here as "Mrs. Matthews," was probably Lucia Elizabeth Vestris, a well-known actress and theater manager who in 1838 married Charles James Matthews, also an actor and the first editor of *Bentley's Miscellany*.

[53] It is difficult to determine equivalence of value between modern and earlier currencies, but in 1843 Frédéric Soulié calculated that the average clerk earning 1,800 francs annually would have basic expenses of 119 francs per month ("Restaurants et gargotes," *La grande ville*, ed. Paul de Kock [Brussels: Muquardt, 1843], 3: 90–91.

[54] The poster was on display at the exhibit *À table au XIXe siècle* at the Musée d'Orsay (from Dec. 4, 2001, to March 5, 2002), and it appears in the catalog of the same name (Paris: Flammarion, 2001), 179.

[55] The two editions were published respectively by Gonet (1848) and Barba (1858).

[56] For more on Bertall, see Henri Béraldi, *Les graveurs du XIXe siècle* (Paris: Conquet, 1885), 2:45–49. For his relationship with Balzac, see also the website of the Balzac Museum in Paris, maisondebalzac.paris.fr.

[57] Bertall, "Souvenirs intimes," *Supplément littéraire du dimanche, Le Figaro*, no. 34 (Aug. 20, 1881): 135.

[58] The journalist Jules Janin in his "Introduction" to *Les Français peints par eux-mêmes* described a similar partnership between writer and graphic artist where both have united to "share their observation, their irony, their *sangfroid*, and their mischief," reaching mutual agreement on "that great task, the study of contemporary manners ('*moeurs contemporaines*')" (Paris: Curmer, 1840), 1:xv.

[59] For the importance of stories and anecdotes in the maintenance of "consciousness" of "the culinary self" among the French, as well as their use by Brillat-Savarin, see Ferguson, *Accounting for Taste*, 30–31.

[60] *Physiologie du marriage* [1829] (Paris: Charpentier, 1838), xxi.

[61] M.W. Duckett, ed., "Briffault (Eugène)," *Dictionnaire de la conversation et de la lecture: supplement* (Paris: Firmin-Didot, 1864), 1:692.

[62] Pierre Larousse, Briffault, *Grand dictionnaire universel du XIXe siècle* (Paris: Grand Dictionnaire Universelle, 1867), 2:1267. In the article on "Physiologie," Larousse categorized *Paris à table* and *Paris dans l'eau*, along with other "*études de moeurs*," under the general title of "physiologies parisiennes" (1874), 12:918.

[63] In many instances, these pamphlets could also have been easily converted into chapters for the larger anthologies. The editor of *Les Français peints par eux-mêmes*, in fact, termed his own opus a "galerie physiologique" (L. Curmer, "Conclusion" [Paris: Curmer, 1842], 8:460).

[64] (Desloges, 1841), 30. Most of the details in this paragraph are drawn from Richard Sieburth, "The French *Physiologies*, 1840–1842," *Notebooks in Cultural Analysis: An Annual Review*, Norman F. Cantor, ed. (Durham, NC: Duke University Press, 1984), 163–200. See also Margaret A. Rose, "Flâneurs and Idlers: A 'Panoramic' Overview," *Flâneurs & Idlers* (Bielefeld: Aisthesis, 2007), 1–74. The phenomenon was noted across the Channel: "Our lively neighbors … have lately shot off a flight of small, literary rockets about Paris, which have

exploded joyously in every direction…termed *Les Physiologies*—a series of graphic sketches, embodying various every-day types of characters" (Albert Smith in the October 2, 1841, edition of *Punch*, cited in Rose, 27).

[65] Walter Benjamin, *Selected Writings*, 18.

[66] "La Nuit de Paris," *Paris ou le livre des cent-et-un* (Brussels: Meline, 1832), 12:119.

[67] Ibid., 128.

[68] *Historiettes contemporaines: courrier de la ville*, no. 1 (Jan. 31, 1842), 8–9.

[69] I have not translated *moeurs* as the more literal "mores" in the text, because the latter, I think, has a more restrictive connotation in English, referring not only to conventional but usually to acceptable behavior. Although this usage is also common in French, *moeurs* usually has a general, more neutral definition, as defined by the 1835 *Dictionnaire de l'Académie française: sixième edition* (Paris: Firmin Didot), 2:217): "The manner of living, the inclinations, the habits, the particular customs of each nation." Briffault also uses the term "habitude" almost twenty times, but with more limited significance; I have translated it on most occasions, as "habits" or "customs." For more on the use of the term *moeurs* in the literature of the time (as well as the place and impact of the *physiologie*), see Martina Lauster, *Sketches of the Nineteenth Century: European Journalism and Its Physiologies, 1830–50* (New York: Palgrave Macmillan, 2007), 18 and *passim*."

[70] Marie Parmentier, ed., *Paris, ou le livre des cent-et-un: Anthologie* (Paris: Champion, 2015), 26.

[71] Cited in Parmentier, 29.

[72] Ségolène Le Men, *Les Français peints par eux-mêmes: panorama social du XIXe siècle* (Paris: Réunion des Musées Nationaux, 1993), 6.

[73] *Les Français peints par eux-mêmes* (Paris: Curmer, 1841), 1:xvi.

[74] Ibid., v.

[75] *Les Français peints par eux-mêmes* (Paris: Curmer, 1842), 8:457.

[76] *La comédie humaine* (Paris: Furne/Durochet/Hetzel et Paulin, 1842), 1:27–29.

[77] Ibid., 14–15.

[78] Ibid., 15–16. For more on the relation between Balzac and panoramic literature (primarily editorially, but also conceptually), see Ségolène Le Men, "La 'littérature panoramique' dans la genèse de *La comédie humaine*: Balzac et *Les Français peints par eux-mêmes*," *L'année balzacienne* 1, no. 3 (2002), 73–100.

NOTES ON THE TRANSLATION

I have for the most part retained Briffault's punctuation and paragraphing. Like many of his colleagues in the nineteenth century, he was inordinately fond of the semicolon, but he does use it in a variety of ways to subordinate and qualify his observations; on a few occasions, though, I have converted phrases into sentences or into relative clauses to clarify meaning.

I have treated "technical" and "untranslatable" terms in several ways. Where there is a close equivalent term in English (such as "reduction" from "glace"), I have translated it without comment. Where a French term is similar to an English term but with variation (such as "surtout," which is an elaborate form of a "centerpiece"), I have converted the term in the text to the English equivalent, but provided an explanatory footnote. In a third case, where there is no true English equivalent, or translation might lead to confusion (such as "table d'hôte" or "cercle"), I have retained the French in the text, in italics, and provided an explanatory footnote.

Occasionally, Briffault's spelling—usually of proper names—differs from modern usage, and in those cases I have used the modern version without comment.

All translations from the French in both the text and the citations are mine, unless otherwise indicated.

A BRIEF CHRONOLOGY OF RELEVANT DATES

For Paris à table: 1846

1643–1715	Reign of Louis XIV, the Sun King
1715–1723	The Regency; governance by the Regent, Philippe d'Orléans, while Louis XV is a minor
1715–1774	Reign of Louis XV
1774–1792	Reign of Louis XVI; from Sept. 1791 to Sept. 1792, Louis XVI becomes officially a "constitutional monarch" until the monarchy is abolished
1789	Storming of the Bastille and the beginning of the French Revolution
1792	Establishment of the First French Republic
1793	Louis XVI is guillotined on Jan. 21
1795–1799	Directory; a five-member committee replaces the Revolutionary Committee of Public Safety, and governs France until it is replaced itself by a coup d'état
1799	Birth of Eugène Briffault

1799–1804   Consulate; established after the 1799 coup
d'état and run essentially by three executives
("consuls"), with the true power remaining in
the hands of the First Consul (Napoleon
Bonaparte)

1804–1814   (First) Empire; Napoleon is granted the title
Emperor of the French by the French Senate
in 1804, and France becomes the dominant
power in Europe until its defeat by the Allied
powers in 1814 and Napoleon's abdication

1814–1815   (First) Bourbon Restoration; Louis XVIII, a
brother of Louis XVI, is restored to the throne
of France by the Allied Powers

1815   "The Hundred Days"; Napoleon escapes from
exile in Elba, regains power over the French
military, and is defeated at Waterloo by the
Allied Powers on June 18, 1815; Napoleon
abdicates on June 22 and is exiled to St. Helena

1815–1830   Bourbon Restoration; Louis XVIII returns to
Paris on July 8, 1815, and remains on the
throne until his death in 1824, when he is
replaced by his brother, Charles X

1825   Publication of *Physiologie du goût*

1830   July Revolution; the "three glorious days" of
uprising in Paris, July 27 to 29, results in the
abdication of Charles X and the election of
Louis Philippe, Duc d'Orléans, as a constitutional monarch, the "King of the French"

1830–1848	July Monarchy; the reign of Louis-Philippe, generally dominated by the wealthy bourgeoisie, becomes increasingly conservative as France enters a period of relative peace and colonial expansion
1846	Publication of *Paris à table*
1848	February Revolution; Louis-Philippe is overthrown and the Second Republic is established
1848–1851	Second Republic; it begins with highly revolutionary aims that are soon suppressed by a conservative electorate and the election of Louis-Napoleon Bonaparte as President of the Republic
1852–1870	Second Empire; having organized a coup-d'état in 1851, Louis-Napoleon Bonaparte arranges to restore the Empire and become head of the Second Empire as Napoleon III, until his government collapses after its defeat in the Franco-Prussian War of 1870
1854	Death of Eugène Briffault

A LIST OF SELECT BERTALL ILLUSTRATIONS

• I •

INTRODUCTION

The Parisian Dinner

A diplomat, not M. de Talleyrand,[1] said that he liked to deal
with people only after having seen them at the table. Indeed,
it seems that for humanity, as for the other animals, inherent
instincts reveal themselves with greater energy and candor
when accomplishing those functions so necessary for life.

There is, in our opinion, an infinite charm in looking at the
way a town lives, acts, and moves about, as if the examination
were linked to the deeds and actions of a single person. If it so
happens that this town is a city, significant not only for its

---

[1] Charles-Maurice de Talleyrand-Périgord is still regarded as one of the most skilled,
influential, and, certainly, most resilient statesmen in European history (see also
chap. 2, n. 10).

splendor and scale, but for its power and the stimulus and animation it imparts to civilization; if this city is named Paris, everything is magnified and raised up with her. The stature of the scholars who measured Micromégas[2] did not surpass the height of the giant's toe, the peak of which, carefully appraised, revealed to them his size.

Let no one be surprised, then, by this fervor to explore, linked to the slightest details of the life Paris leads. This is not a cult of fashion or infatuation; this is not a craze or fad; it is the rigorous consequence of that law of moral and physical nature by virtue of which everything radiates from the center to the circumference.

We are not writing a work of gastronomy here, sincerely convinced by our own experience that appetite can no more be given to a sour stomach than wit to a fool.

Within the Cyclopean and gargantuan mass of Parisian consumption, we have discovered such a number of lively and useful facts and insights that we wanted to show how sharp and savory is the variety of this colossal menu that every day sets the Parisian table.

The petty prince of a small African tribe, it is said, has a herald proclaim after his royal meal that all the world's kings can dine now that he is full. This tale, told by travelers come from afar, has circled the globe.

Our reality is much more marvelous than this arrogant fiction.

When Paris sits down at the table, the entire world stirs: from every part of the known universe, all things created, the products of every kingdom, those the earth sees growing on its

---

[2] Micromégas, who was 120,000 feet tall, is the extraterrestrial visitor in Voltaire's story of the same name (1752).

surface, those it clasps within its womb, those the sea contains and feeds, those populating the air: all run, hurry, and hasten to gain the favor of a look, a caress, or a quick bite. For France, the Parisian dinner is the country's main event. The plains, the hills, the mountain and the valley, the wood, the forest, the vineyard and the field, the garden and the orchard, the land and the water are its tributaries. All wish to be fruitful and breed marvels if only to please this sovereign city whose voracity delights them and bestows happiness and wealth upon them.

Every year sees an increase in the quantity of the victuals swallowed by this abyss, which, rather than filling up, expands, and the more it absorbs, the vaster and deeper it becomes. A tremendous and terrifying progression!

It is generally believed that there is nothing more uniform than the dietary habits of a people. That is the case, perhaps, for those whose views stop at the surface. Their hasty observation readily assigns the same time and an invariable form to the meals of an entire nation, hardly deigning to indicate—within the different classes of the society visited—the nuances inseparable from the diversity of position and fortune.

For such a careless attitude, each human collective has its own manner of "black broth":[3] these local dishes are called "potage" in Paris;[4] "roast beef" in London; "olla podrida" in Madrid; "sauerkraut" in Vienna, Berlin, and all of Germany; "macaroni" beyond the Alps; "stockfish" along the Baltic; "herring" in Holland; "caviar" in the North; and "pilau" in all of the East.[5]

What a people eats, then, is known; but nothing is known of those private customs and manners that show their true character under a picturesque and lively appearance, constantly

---

[3] This is a reference to the "black broth," mentioned in Plutarch's *Lives* ("The Life of Lycurgus"), a staple of the Spartan diet, and although no recipe has come down from ancient times, it reputedly consisted of pork boiled in its own blood, seasoned with vinegar and salt.

[4] "Traditional and root vegetables are added to bouillon to pick up its flavor...that is what we call *potage*....*Potage* is the base of the French national diet, and it needed the experience of centuries to bring it to its perfection" (Jean-Anthelme Brillat-Savarin, Méditation 6, *Physiologie du goût*).

[5] An "olla podrida" (literally: "rotten pot") is a Spanish stew composed of a variety of meats and vegetables, depending on the recipe and the region; "macaroni" was often used in the nineteenth century (and it still is in some languages) as a generic term for "pasta"; "stockfish" is cured cod or haddock, usually dried in the air without salt; "pilau," or "pilaf" in both French and English, is a dish of seasoned rice to which fish, meat, or other ingredients have been added.

in motion. That is what we are trying to do for Paris.

Homer's heroes and the children of Master François' imagination[6] are dwarfs whose pygmy
proportions cannot compare with
the grandeur of our city. To feed it
every day, thousands of individuals
devoted to the service of its gullet

voluntarily condemn themselves to continual labor. For Paris,
in the year 1844, five slaughterhouses killed and carved up:
76,481 steers, 16,374 cows, 77,881 calves, 437,385 sheep,
90,000 hogs.[7] Such is its appetite!

The small bites, pâtés, terrines, preserved meats, crawfish
and lobster, delicacies that Paris eats for its pleasure as hors-
d'oeuvres, to add charm to its leisure and sharpen its appetite,
constitute a weight of 112,000 kilograms. The local meats,
small gifts that come from the surrounding area, contribute
only 821,000 kilograms to its diet; sausages and cold cuts play
a more important role there, Paris consuming some 3,418,000
kilograms, sufficiently warranting the burning thirst by which

---

[6] François Rabelais was the author of the novels comprising *La vie de Gargantua et de Pantagruel* (1532–1564), both of whose appetites were indeed gargantuan.

[7] Statistics like these, often from government reports, were occasionally cited in the newspapers and periodical literature of the time, from where Briffault may have drawn them. These same numbers, for instance, were cited in the newspaper *Journal des débats politiques et littéraire* (Jan. 7, 1844), 3, as well as in *Journal d'agriculture pratique et de jardinage: July 1845–June 1846* (Paris: Librairie Agricole de Dusacq, 1846), 3:325. The five slaughterhouses were constructed primarily between 1808 and 1818, near the barriers at the outskirts of Paris in, respectively, Montmartre, Ménilmontant, Villejuif, Roule, and Grenelle; three would close in 1848 and others would open throughout the century. (See, e.g., Christian Guy, *La vie quotidienne de la société gourmande en France au XIXe siècle* [Paris: Hachette, 1971], 46–47.)

it is constantly tormented. There are also the extremities and the offal; these are the leftovers from the butchering that reaches just about 1,240,779 kilograms.

Such are the principal elements of the animal part of its nutritional diet.

The other amenities of its table are not any less than those of which we have just spoken.

The poultry and game, the butter, the oysters, the seafood, the eggs, the cheese consumed annually by Paris are worth twenty-five million francs: ten million for the poultry and game alone, eight million for the fish and the oysters, five to six million for the eggs, close to one and a half million for the cheeses.

In 1845 Paris consumed more than a million hectoliters[8] of wine; about 115 liters for each resident. This quantity is for

real wine, introduced legally into Paris; but who will say how much it was extended by fraud and processing. The committee for viniculture estimates water sold for wine at 500,000 hectoliters.[9] This is still only a probable figure.

In addition, Paris drank 119 hectoliters of beer and 14,000 liters of apple and pear cider. Alcoholic

[8] A hectoliter is equivalent to a hundred liters, or 26.4 gallons of liquid measure.

[9] This figure derives from a report on taxation and fraudulent practices in the wine industry delivered to the Chambre des Députés by its *comité vinicole* in 1843 and publicized in the trade press. (See, e.g., *Moniteur de la propriété et de l'agriculture*, July 31, 1843, 8:196.) In the first issue of his journal *Historiette contemporaine* (Paris: Lang-Vevy, 1842), 65, Briffault tells this story: "'Sir,' the military paymaster said to the wine purveyor, 'there's too much water in the wine,'—'No, sir.' replied the supplier, 'there's not enough wine in the water.'"

spirits contributed to its consumption 36,000 hectoliters, which include, admittedly, liqueurs and fruit brandies, perfumed waters, alcoholic varnishes, and pure alcohol in barrels. We think that four-fifths of this quantity should be allocated to consumption down the gullet.

Recalling that grapes alone account for 623,962 kilograms will give some idea of the fruit eaten here. Let us not forget to mention that every year Paris puts into its salads 18,000 hectoliters of vinegar and therefore three times as much oil.

The provinces surrounding it supply its vegetables, coming from more than two hundred kilometers all around: it enlists the entire French countryside. Provence is its greenhouse; Touraine its garden; Normandy raises and fattens its cattle; the flocks of sheep destined for its table graze in the robust meadows salted by the ocean's waters and along the aromatic crests of the Ardennes; it fishes in three seas; like no other, it is rich in rivers, streams, lakes, and ponds; it holds within its waters the fish most in demand; in its torrents,

the ponds of its mountains, it sees trout multiply; at the mouths of its rivers, it finds salmon, sturgeon, and those hybrid species, whose time in fresh water, close to the sea, endows them with such delicate flavors. Its forests and woods do not let it lack for game; those bands of riflemen, those panting hounds, those stallions and hunters surge forth for Paris; the horns sound out for Paris. It counts among its purveyors the most illustrious of names: there have been kings, and there are still princes who kill game for it.[10]

Who will count the number of people who put something in the oven and take it out every day for Paris: cooks, grill men, bakers of pastry and bread, cupbearers, confectioners, cheese

and dairymen, ice-cream makers; those who watch over the saucepans, the kitchens, the spits, the service, the ovens, the cellars and liquor cabinets, and those who preside over the fruits and buffets; who then will undertake the census for all this?

The Paris kitchen requires the use of more than 2,773,000 hectoliters of charcoal, not including 98,000 hectoliters of coal dust, separate from the coal itself used more and more for this purpose. Today more than two million hectoliters of that last fuel are consumed.

---

[10] Charles X, in particular, was associated with hunting, having on one occasion, according to Talleyrand, killed 1,793 pieces of game, a figure attained by no previous French king (Philip Mansel, *Paris between Empires: 1814–1852* [London: John Murray, 2001], 224).

In every corner of the world, Paris has people mindful of its tastes, its fantasies, its desires, its whims; if its appetites languish, they work to revive them, they think about generating new ones in place of those that have gone away; imagination, art, and industry are united in this competitive rivalry to win the good graces of the master. Paris has thus become the only place where the magical power of gold has been applied to its fullest extent: with gold, Paris knows nothing is impossible.

Elsewhere, greater pomp and greater magnificence can be deployed; but nowhere can the exquisite delicacy of taste and elegance be satisfied as well as in Paris; Parisian comfort does not have the refinements of egoism; but it has the understanding of a life that blends the delights of the mind with the satisfactions of the sensual. This charming secret, whose tendencies are on full display and which retains the natural graciousness of its customary manners, is, for all measures of its existence, an inexhaustible source of attractions, and a privilege belonging to Paris alone; it is envied, it is copied; but it cannot be stolen away.

At the table is where Paris loves to assemble those riches that shape its pride and its happiness.

All the arts are invited to adorn and embellish meals where each, according to the means of the household, endeavors to please and charm; from the most splendid setting to the most humble dinner, hosts strive to be fully worthy of those they are welcoming; these celebrations are in all dwellings; even the poorest still find in them moments of gaiety and forgetfulness.

Sculpture and metalworking have shaped, embroidered, and chiseled the dishware; glassworks have cut crystal with surprising skill; its forms, its designs, its incisions, its engravings, its colors, its reflections and transparencies, the play of light, all

have been set to work to enhance the brilliance of the table; ceramics, which has molded and fashioned the vases, has known how to prepare them for every use, to make them pleasing, convenient, easy, and light enough for every service; the refinement of the linen borders on the marvelous. The strangeness, the grace, the quirks, and the freshness of the settings surprise and seduce the eye; an enlightened care, miracles of imagination, work, and patience are found in the slightest details; flowers and paintings have complemented these ornaments that are so attractive and of such a ravishing variety. With so much taste, opulence has been forgiven its wildest extravagances, and the fortunate guests do not know whether they should admire more the profusion of this luxury or the harmony that presides over the balance of all of its parts.

To these joys of our tables, add the delicious delicacies which have raised the reputation of our meals so high, and you will discover all that humanity can wish of the pleasures worthy of it; the spirit cannot fail with so many things honoring, glorifying, and calling to it. France is the most succulent country in Europe; no land is more fertile with prized foods than ours; each department, each town has its preeminent productions and its celebrated morsels; the talent and abilities of our cooks in the art of their preparation are exceptional, and the entire world asks for these masterpieces from our soil and our ovens. Paris gets the first fruits of these offerings; there are few towns that do not have some marvel of this type, some phenomenon or masterpiece to present to it.

The wines of France have a glory that praise can only diminish; Paris is the center, and all the assets with which the

heavens have gilded our vineyards flow toward it. Its cellars need to be seen at Bercy.[11]

Paris collects its tribute and the best part of what Providence thought to have distributed equally. The prime cut of filet is for Paris; the miracles of cultivation are reserved for Paris; Bresse and Maine have driven the perfection of their chickens and capons so far forward only to make a fine showing at the Paris markets.[12] Whatever is destined for consumption at the Paris table cannot be had on its native ground for its weight in gold; these chosen foods become sacred and inviolable, like the beautiful slaves reserved for the sultan's harem. Seaports watch with sorrow as their shores are stripped, for Paris, of what sometimes they would like to keep for themselves; nothing can hold back what has been designated for the jealous master whose table suffers no rivals. If one day, on one single day, Paris were deprived of those things over which it has established its right of supremacy, it would withdraw its generous bounty from the ingrates who had misconstrued their prerogatives. Paris is a profligate

[11] Located just beyond the Paris city limits (where city taxes on wine and other goods, the *octroi*, could be avoided), Bercy, with its massive warehouses, was one of the nineteenth century's largest repositories and markets for the wine trade.

[12] The former provinces of Maine (in the Loire region) and, in particular, Bresse (in eastern France) are still celebrated for the quality of their poultry.

that commerce is far too interested in indulging to cause it the slightest bother.

What a picture are those Parisian dinners! At the top, in the radiant and resplendent zones, customary manners are reflected and contemplated with vanity and pride in the table's luxury; moving down we will find pleasures still brilliant but less dazzling; the more tranquil gaze will be able to regard them with deference; at each step down the ladder, we will see luxury giving way, with intelligence, to comfort until, having reached the middle regions, we will encounter that openness and integrity non-existent higher up and that ease unknown lower down. During this journey, we will attend those solemn and sumptuous meals where ambition, politics, and boredom take their seats: the silliness and vanity of the social climbers, the triviality of assured opulence, the ridiculous bourgeoisie,[13] the parsimony, the destitution concealed beneath the luxury, all will in turn be revealed to us. The uncertain life, active and animated by a young population, the pleasures of a free existence, the gourmandizing, the gallantry and intrigues, the mysteries of the tête-à-tête at the table will also supply us with portraits; to complete this gallery of pictures, we will summon our courage and zeal; there will be no sanctuary impervious to our efforts, we will go sit down at every table, by the side of the most powerful and the most humbled, with the voluptuous, with the artisan and the laborer. We will be at every celebration: the palace, the mansion, the clubs, the tavern, the dining rooms of bankers and the halls of restaurateurs, the cabaret and the

---

[13] I have retained Briffault's usage of "bourgeois" (and "bourgeoisie"), a term which seems to have had a fairly wide application in his time, referring, in general, to any city dweller (or class of such) not a member of the aristocracy or the laboring class.

backroom, the attic, the workshop, the sleazy dive, and sometimes the sustenance taken on the run by the Parisian *lazzarone*[14]—diligent to capture nature in the act, we will discover each in its turn, like those who, to study animals, choose the moment they devour their prey.

[14] Italian for "rascal" or "idler."

THE HISTORY OF DINNER UP TO OUR TIME

In France, the principal meal of the day has, historically, been called "dinner." Having little curiosity about gastronomic archaeology, we will not be searching, in the archives of the past, for the precise times for dinner. What is most important for us to know are its true manners and customs, and we will ask of memory only what is necessary to clarify the present; and that is just as well, since erudition at the table would be no more than inappropriate, annoying, and in bad taste.

In 1667, in Paris, you dined around noon; this time is confirmed by the line in Boileau's third satire:

"I rushed over, at the end of Mass, just as noon sounded."[1]

Not only do we find, in this citation, the precise hour for dinner, but it also tells us that this meal, among civilized nations, has always been placed near the day's most important event. During the iron ages, the centuries of combat, you dined when you could, sometimes after the battle, sometimes before. Charlemagne wanted feats to be performed before any

---

[1] Nicolas Boileau was one of the leading French poets and critics during the reign of Louis XIV, and probably its most celebrated satirist. The "Third Satire," probably composed in 1665, was an imitation of Horace and known as "the ridiculous meal."

nourishment was taken; Henri IV, on the other hand, wanted his soldiers to have a bit of beef in their stomachs before facing the enemy.[2] When leisure became the ultimate object of French society, dinner, taken by warriors during the first hours of daylight, drew closer to the middle of the day, settling in between eleven and twelve. In the seventeenth century, the daily devotions, whose duties and requirements marched in step with the splendors and rigorous etiquette of the court, fixed the time for dinner, placing it at the close of the divine office, "at the end of Mass."

Later, dinner seemed to interfere with the dissipated life publicly avowed by the entire court; the previous century's timing seemed impractical when bedtime was at daybreak; it became far too troublesome to sit down at the table at noon; for a long time, then, dinner was only an inclination; it was endured, not accepted. Under Louis XIV, dinner was after Mass; under Louis XV, supper came after the theater; among the nobility and for the wealthy class, supper was thus created out of a loathing for dinner.[3]

In the following regime, habitual ways calmed down a bit: dinner was around two o'clock; supper, without shedding much of its brilliance, was maintained. At the court of Louis XVI, a leisurely protocol was observed and without any fuss, daily life followed a plan, and hours were fixed for eating. A few of the chosen—appearing at their head the Lauzuns, the Richelieus, the Comte d'Artois, and the Queen's intimates—preserved for

[2] Charlemagne became King of France in 768 and eventually Emperor of the Romans in 800. Henri IV was King of France from 1589 to 1610.

[3] Louis XIV, the Sun King, reigned from 1643 to 1715, Louis XV from 1715 to 1774. For Briffault's full discussion of "supper," see Chapter 8.

themselves the privileges of another time;[4] but despite these brilliant exceptions, court and city took pride in regularity: dinner was generally between noon and three. It would be quite difficult to say at what time the era known as the Revolution dined.[5] During that upheaval, the country's entire being was drawn toward political meetings and public places; the private person's life had disappeared completely, leaving visible only the life of the citizen. Eating was done quite hastily, and, if some excesses persisted through these times agitated by such violent and terrible passions, they left no trace. Most of the men on whom the destiny of the country seemed to depend are remembered only as being sober and showing little concern for the pleasures of the table.[6] Two years ago, in rue du Dauphin at the corner of rue de Rivoli, a humble eating house—designated as the place where the most ardent orators then gathered at the dinner hour—could still be seen; their words are retained in our memory, but what constituted the meals to which they themselves were totally indifferent, is no longer known.

[4] Louis XVI reigned from 1774 until he was deposed by the Revolution in 1792. The Lauzuns are probably the family of Armand-Louis de Gontaut, Duc de Lauzun, who, as well as being noted for his elegance and fashion, commanded armies in both American and French Revolutionary wars. Armand de Vignerot du Plessis, Duc de Richelieu, was a noted bon-vivant and general during the reigns of both Louis XV and Louis XVI. The Comte d'Artois was a brother of Louis XVI and later became Charles X, King of France. The "Queen" is, of course, Marie Antoinette, who found it difficult to follow any kind of "régime" or plan.

[5] It would also be difficult to say exactly when the Revolutionary "era" began (or ended) but the storming of the Bastille on July 14, 1789, would be a reasonable candidate for the onset of the "upheaval."

[6] Georges Danton, who had a considerable reputation as a fine eater, was an exception, and was accused of "bathing in Burgundy and eating game off of silver plates" before being condemned to the guillotine in 1794 (Béatrix de l'Aulnoit and Philippe Alexandre, *Des fourchettes dans les étoiles: brève histoire de la gastronomie française* [Paris: Fayard, 2010], 126).

The Directory[7] restored dinner to favor; it even brought
opulence, luxury, wealth, and finery to a point that recalled the
pomp and the taste of the most brilliant chronicles of the table.
In the wake of passion, vice followed; society was as debili-
tated and corrupt as it appeared to be rough and austere; for
the excess of heroism, the excess of egoism was everywhere
substituted; those growing wealthy with the most scandalous
speed imitated or rather aped, through the pride and the foolishness of their extravagance, those financiers of a former time
whose prodigality had so amused the nobility they had intended to humble. There were also, among the bourgeoisie,
sudden fortunes recalling those of rue Quincampoix;[8] to satisfy
their vanity, they spent wildly money so easily earned. Politics
ruled the nation's affairs only by means of seductions, the

---

[7] Administered by five Directors and two legislative houses, the Directory governed
France from 1795 to 1799 during a period of extreme economic and social distress,
government repression, corruption, and military adventurism. It was eventually
overthrown by Napoleon Bonaparte.

[8] Rue Quincampoix, a narrow street in the Third Arrondissement, had long been a
meeting place for moneylenders, speculators, and entrepreneurs seeking investors,
but it is probably best known as the address of John Law's Mississippi Company,
the home of the "Mississippi bubble" and its subsequent financial crash (1720).

choice of which, on the part of both sides, appeared to be far from scrupulous; pleasure was the means most often put to use. There was, throughout all of this world, a feverish disorder, an insane dissipation, and a passion for sensuality that generated only fierce or bizarre pleasures, whose extravagant

prodigality did nothing for elegance or for taste. Among those who shone the brightest during this time where lunacy and debauchery held such a large place in the business and amusements of the day, only a few knew how to evade these ridiculous impulses. This delirium of the Directory was a necessary crisis between Republican rigidity and the Empire's civilization, the first light of which was illuminated by the Consulate.[9]

There is an unavoidable name, and one that the chronicle of the first thirty years of this century always encounters along the way: it is the name of M. de Talleyrand.[10] There is not a single quality envied by the world that has not been attributed to him: he was deemed the first among political men and the last of the great lords; the spirit of France, in its entirety, was granted to him; his high office

---

[9] The Consulate was the government of France between the coup d'état of 1799, engineered by Napoleon Bonaparte (the First Consul) against the Directory, and the establishment of the Empire in 1804.

[10] Charles-Maurice de Talleyrand-Périgord, one of the most celebrated (and despised) statesmen of his time, held a variety of offices in a variety of regimes, from the reign of Louis XVI to that of Louis-Philippe. Immensely wealthy, he was also celebrated as a gourmet, and his name appears frequently in both of those capacities throughout *Paris à table*.

and his fortune always placed him near a throne he often dominated with his skill; he drew the good will of sovereigns, the favors of women, the adulation of the ambitious, the hatred of honest people, and the sarcasm of the crowd. As if all that were not enough to make a man famous, gastronomy took hold of him and ruthlessly placed him in the pantheon of the culinary arts. We do not intend to protest against this part of his fame; the facts have often taken care to correct whatever was askew and mispraise bestowed guided in the epicurean ways. on Talleyrand's hospitality and For him, refined only a means to fine food were serve his purposes and in no way his inclinations.

The first and most precious of Talleyrand's qualities was his tact; it was for him swift and sound, exquisite and sure, almost infallible; his wit was endowed with all that was lacking in his heart. He came from the Old Regime; he had tiptoed through the Revolution, and the Directory's bad taste horrified him: but he joined in on the Luxembourg voluptuousness without a single complaint, disguising his disgust, taking care to reduce those enormities to reasonable and just proportions.[11]

[11] The Directory chose the Luxembourg Palace, which had been a prison during the Terror, as its seat of government. Talleyrand served as the Directory's foreign minister for a time, during which period he continued to amass his fortune, primarily through bribes. Following his forced resignation from the Foreign Ministry in 1799, he helped Napoleon seize power in the coup d'état of that year.

Talleyrand made of his residence the model for a taste, a luxury, and a courtesy, the like of which now seems lost. The merits of his receptions have been attributed to his chief steward. This servant, who had started off with the Princess de Lamballe, came, it is true, from the house of de Condé;[12] but dinner at the Foreign Affairs residence was not the only thing

that drew society's elite to the minister's home; the conduct, manners, and flair found within this dwelling had a charm of irresistible attraction. With Talleyrand diplomacy was practiced everywhere, in the sitting room and at the office; his head chef was charged with the task of selecting all the cooks for the great houses abroad; this was to obtain intelligence directly from the heart of the place.[13]

Dinner, we can all readily agree, was nevertheless a serious affair for Talleyrand; every morning he settled on the menu himself with his chef. His table normally had ten to twelve settings; his service consisted of two soups, two opening dishes—including one of fish—four additional

[12] Talleyrand's *maître d'hôtel* was M. Boucher (whose original name was probably Boucheseiche) who had previously served as chef for Louis-Joseph de Bourbon, Prince de Condé, head of one of the most powerful families in pre-Revolutionary France. Boucher was a mentor to many of the great chefs of the time, including Antoine Carême who dedicated his book *Le pâtissier royal parisien* (1815) to him. Princess Marie-Thérèse-Louise de Savoy-Carignan became the princess de Lamballe when she married Louis-Alexandre de Bourbon in 1767.

[13] Carême himself was occasionally suspected by foreign governments of being the source of such "intelligence." (See, e.g., Ian Kelly, *Cooking for Kings: The Life of Antonin Carême* [New York: Walker & Co., 2003], 270–271.)

starters, two roasts, four sweets, and the dessert. We go into detail here because this arrangement became the standard rule for all the Consulate's great tables. The major contractors, the financiers of the time, persisted in their heavy excess; several feasts at Raincy, the home of M. Ouvrard, however, deserved notice and succeeded in being absolved.[14]

Seated at Talleyrand's table were not only all of those celebrated in France, but all who had made some noise in Europe and in the political world; one of the principal attractions of these meals, especially considering the private nature of some of the guests, was the conversation; the art with which these discussions abstained from any openness or spontaneity was admirable; this was a fencing match where swords crossed with surprising dexterity.

The Empire found the guidelines, rules, recommendations, and examples all in place;[15] it restored to the dinner its order and a regular and proper beauty that took nothing away from its independence and its delights, and gave to its pleasures a character that, at the same time, satisfied reason and taste. But the table at the Tuileries never had any importance; Napoleon

[14] Gabriel-Julien Ouvrard, a financier and military contractor during the Napoleonic era, was wealthy enough to lease during the first decades of the nineteenth century the Château du Raincy, a lavish country estate constructed between 1643 and 1650 by the same team of architects and designers who constructed Versailles.

[15] The first French Empire lasted from 1804, when Napoleon Bonaparte was crowned Emperor of the French, until his abdication in 1814. The Tuileries was Napoleon's official residence when he was First Consul and later served as his Imperial Palace.

pretended to pay no attention to details that were beneath him: he ate quickly and selected the simplest of foods. And

despite all the pains taken by gastronomic investigations to burden him with certain odd traits, regardless of the slanders that tried to reveal the Emperor to be as intemperate in private as he was sober in public, all that is left of these tales are his regular habits that are full of modesty, reserve, and restraint.

For the princes and princesses of his family, as well as the Empire's high dignitaries, Napoleon wanted a fifth of the annual revenues to be applied to table expenses. He cheerfully told foreign nobles visiting his court, "Do you want to dine like a soldier, then dine with me; if you want to dine like a king, dine with the Prince Archchancellor; if you want to dine like a pauper, dine with the Prince Archtreasurer."[16]

The luxury and succulence of Cambacérès' table was received wisdom under the Empire, and an opinion disseminated well beyond 1815; nothing, however, was less true than this talk so favorable to the prince's cuisine and which Napoleon himself seemed to endorse. It is an inconceivable error; it is

---

[16] *Archichancelier* and *Architrésorier* were terms in use by the Holy Roman Empire in the early medieval period and were adopted by Napoleon primarily as honorific titles. The former title was held by Jean-Jacques Régis de Cambacérès, the primary author of the Napoleonic Code and Napoleon's principal expert on juridical matters. Charles-François Lebrun helped to organize the finances of the regime and was given the title of *Architrésorier*. Both men were designated Princes of the Empire by Napoleon.

true, Cambacérès had at the head of his kitchens a skilled man; and he himself took care of much of everything concerning his table; but this was only to apply some thrift to his expenditures; he took note of the entrées that had remained intact, and he had them held over for the next day. From the regions, gifts of edibles and poultry were sent to the Archchancellor; he locked these provisions into a pantry, for which he kept the key; he gave them to his staff only slowly and sparingly, and almost always they were spoiled, and appeared on the table only when they were wilted and ruined. The indignant pages written on this subject by Carême have to be read;[17] he affirms that of all meals, the prince preferred pastry stuffed with meatballs: a heavy, dull, and stupid dish. Then, after having enumerated several miserly characteristics, he cries out: "What stinginess! What a pity! What a house!" Carême is unsparing toward certain men: he preferred Talleyrand and Rothschild in everything. According to him, Cambacérès and Brillat-Savarin never knew how to eat; in speaking of the latter, he even goes so far as to say: "At the end of the meal, he was absorbed by his digestion; I saw him sleeping!"[18]

---

[17] Marie-Antoine Carême was the most celebrated chef of the early nineteenth century, having worked variously for—along with Cambacérès—Napoleon, Talleyrand, Tsar Alexander I, George IV of England (when he was Prince Regent), and James Rothschild. He was the author of several culinary classics, but Briffault likely drew this account from *Les classiques de la table*, a collection from which he often quotes and borrows. This particular passage is drawn from a note of Carême's, published as "La table de M. le Prince Archi-Chancelier Cambacérès" (F. Fayot et al., eds., *Les classiques de la table*, 3rd ed. [Paris: Bethune et Plon, 1845], 2:512–524). The head of Cambacérès' kitchens is identified in this article as M. Grand'Manche.

[18] Jean-Anthelme Brillat-Savarin is, of course, the author of the classic *Physiologie du goût* (1825). James Mayer de Rothschild, for whom Carême worked in his later years, was the founder of the French branch of the banking family. Enormously wealthy and influential in both political and cultural spheres, he is considered the model for Baron Nucingen in Balzac's *La comédie humaine*.

And he adds: "The real eaters of my time have been the
Prince de Talleyrand, Murat, Junot, Fontanes, the Emperor
Alexander, Castelreagh, George IV, and the Marquis de Cussy."[19]
The cuisines of Queen Hortense, the Princess Pauline Borghese, Murat, the Duke de Massa, and Berthier are also mentioned with praise.[20] The King of Naples transported into his
domains the most refined of all that French art had to offer.
Carême persists in recommending the lessons of that period.
He repeats with conviction: "Adopt for your service the style
of the Empire, which was masculine and elegant." Among
bachelor dinners, those of Camerani and Corvisart were sin-
gled out.[21]

[19] Joachim Murat, a Marshal and Admiral of France under Napoleon, was named in
1808 King of Naples, where he was known as the "Dandy King"; Jean-Andoche
Junot was one of Napoleon's most active military commanders and commander of
the Peninsular campaign in 1807; Louis-Marcelin de Fontanes was a man-of-
letters who held several high positions in the French educational establishment;
Robert Steward, Viscount Castelreagh, a statesman and politician, managed
Britain's foreign policy during much of the nineteenth century's first two decades;
Louis, Marquis de Cussy, who served as chief steward (*préfet du palais*) under
Napoleon and later under Louis XVIII, was also an epicure of renown, who—
according to Alexandre-Balthazar-Laurent Grimod de la Reynière, his friend and
author of *Almanach des gourmands*—created 366 different recipes for chicken
(one for each day of the year, including leap year).
[20] Hortense de Beauharnais was Napoleon's step-daughter and wife of his brother,
Louis Napoleon, who was named King of Holland in 1806; Pauline Borghese, a
sister of Napoleon, was married (unhappily) to Prince Camillo Borghese, one of
Italy's wealthiest noblemen; Claude-Ambroise Régnier, Minister of Justice under
Napoleon, was granted the title of Duc de Massa in 1809; Louis-Alexandre
Berthier was Napoleon's Chief of Staff.
[21] Barthélemy-André Camerani had a long career as an actor and theatrical administrator
in France, but he was also a distinguished enough gourmet to have Grimod de la
Reynière's 1805 *Almanech des gourmands* dedicated to him and a very rich soup,
potage à la Camerani, named after him. Jean-Nicolas Corvisart-Desmarets was
Napoleon's primary physician and occasionally shared a meal with Brillat-Savarin.
(Briffault speaks of "bachelor dinners" in chap. 3, 55–56.)

Under the Empire, the diplomatic corps, especially the Russian and Austrian embassies, had celebrated tables; at Malmaison, the Empress Joséphine gave simple meals, although ones whose subtle delicacy was unequaled.[22] From these heights, the taste for good food and the embellishment of service won over, little by little, all of society's classes. High-ranking officials stood at the head of a trend that the bourgeoisie followed with intelligence, and dinner's fine times were brought back to life. Within the upper and administrative regions, the hour for dinner fluctuated between five and six o'clock, and everywhere else the table was set between four and five; among the thoroughly bourgeois customs, four o'clock was the time fixed for dinner.

The Empire needs to have one well-deserved verdict restored; this period allowed the bright light of a new civilization to penetrate its habitual ways; its Etruscan and Egyptian tableware, the antique form of every decoration, its Greek vases could have been criticized: we do not think that these preferences are any more singular than those that have so abruptly brought the taste for the Gothic back to us, and that foist on us today the passing fancies of the Renaissance and the *rocaille* of the eighteenth century.[23] Let us seek out with sincerity and perseverance the art of our period; but as long as we are reduced and condemned to the servility of imitation, let us not disdain the models of antiquity. For beautiful and noble inspirations, they are more fruitful than all of the others.

---

[22] Château de Malmaison was purchased by Joséphine de Beauharnais in 1799 for her husband, Napoleon, and after her divorce from him, she lived there until her death in 1814.

[23] *Rocaille* is a rococo style associated primarily with the reign of Louis XV, featuring in its architecture and decoration motifs of shells, rocks, and scrolls.

Under the Empire, something of the old liberties of past times were resumed: at dessert, there was singing at the table, sometimes drinking songs, most often popular love songs; there were also party and wedding ballads. Appearing everywhere at that time were singing dinners, bachelor dinners,

dinners among friends, corporate dinners, dinners of all kinds, and later we will turn our attention to them.

We also must place around this time the sudden and prodigious gain in momentum that took hold of the restaurant business.

And now we will show how this renaissance of the table was accepted and developed under the Restoration,[24] and what progress this same period has passed on to our present times.

Whatever might be said about it, the Restoration found, on its return to France, a highly refined society and one that fifteen years of splendor and triumph had endowed with a demeanor whose proud dignity all the courts of Europe had

---

[24] Except for the hundred days preceding Waterloo, the Bourbon Restoration lasted from 1814 to the July Revolution of 1830, when it was superseded by the July Monarchy of Louis-Philippe, who became "King of the French" (until he was overthrown in 1848). A conservative constitutional monarchy, the Restoration began with the reigns of Louis XVIII (1814–1824) and ended with the abdication of the ultra-conservative Charles X (1824–1830); both kings were brothers of Louis XVI.

admired. Perhaps some of those who came back with the hope of again seeing all things in the place where they had left them were unpleasantly surprised by the new manners, and unjustly biased against the new regime; but it truly had to be acknowledged that France was still the country of civility and elegance. From the first years, political dinners were seen to flourish; they became essential to fostering connections and conciliations; it was at the table that all the transactions were launched, carried through, and completed. These dinners, which first of all took possession of the ministerial residences, made use not only of the kitchens and offices of the Empire's ministers but also of their cooking utensils and tableware. Later, under the constitutional system, political dinners had to undergo considerable development, and Casimir Delavigne was able to have one of his characters in the *School for Old Men* say with some truth:

All's done at dinner in this century of ours
And at dinner government's empowered.[25]

At the Tuileries similar paths were followed.[26] Still, zealous courtiers had restored to favor some parts of the Old Regime's etiquette; among other curious things, there was a grand silver piece depicting a kind of a chapel that served to store the king's napkins; the head master of ceremonies claimed that a salute was required when passing before this item of furniture. The royal guard, in arms, collected and escorted serving dishes

[25] Casimir Delavigne was a popular poet and dramatist, whose song "La Parisienne" became the anthem for the July Monarchy. His comedy *L'école des veillards* (1823) led to his election to the Académie française in 1825.

[26] The Tuileries was the royal residence in Paris during the Restoration, as it was also during the July Monarchy.

from the kitchen; the royal family dined alone, and even during the galas in the Gallery of Diana,[27] it kept its setting separate from the other tables; the king acted as host for his guests only at breakfast. Louis XVIII has left a reputation for gluttony that, in fact, seemed to be hereditary within the senior branch of the Bourbons. In her memoirs, the Princess Palatine said: "I have often seen the king [Louis XIV] eat four platefuls of different soups, an entire pheasant, a partridge, a large plateful of salad, some garlicky mutton in gravy, two thick slices of

ham, a plateful of pastries, and then still some fruit and preserves."[28] For a long time, Louis XVIII kept the doors to the dining hall open during the royal family's dinner; but toward the end of his reign he always ate behind closed

doors, and what follows was the reason for this change. M. Portal, the king's chief doctor, had forbidden spinach, which he liked very much, to be served to him.[29] At dinner, the king

[27] The Galerie de Diane is the largest room in the royal palace at Fontainebleau.

[28] Elizabeth Charlotte, Princess Palatine, was the second wife of the younger brother of Louis XIV, Philippe I, Duc d'Orléans. Her correspondence and memoirs provide an intimate portrait of the court of the Sun King, and the above passage can be found in her letter of December 6, 1718 (M. G. Brunet, ed., *Correspondance complète de Madame Duchesse d'Orléans* [Paris: Charpentier, 1863], 2:37).

[29] Antoine Portal was the founding president of the Académie nationale de médecine as well as *premier médecin* to both Louis XVIII and Charles X.

asked for his plate of spinach: the Duc d'Aumont, first gentle-man of the bedchamber, approached to tell him that there was no more spinach;[30] the king insisted that some be found for him, adding that if there was none in the palace, it should be sought for at the caterer's. Extremely angry, he cried out in fury, swearing royally: "What, I'm King of France, and I can't even eat some spinach?" At these words, a great outburst of laughter was heard from the neighboring room, where the royal guard was stationed. The king had the doors closed and ordered the entire shift to be placed under arrest. From that time on, dinner at the Tuileries was behind closed doors; but history does not say whether the King of France got to eat some spinach.

Under the Restoration, particularly during the first years, there were only two kinds of political dinners: those at the palace, where the first gentleman of the bedchamber did the honors, and the ministers' dinners. A few receptions hosted by the heads of the courts and legislative chambers and the din-ners of the military and administrative leaders completed the set. During that period, the diplomatic dinners put on a con-siderable show to distinguish themselves from what was called the common crowd. In the Saint-Germain district, bad food was being served almost everywhere;[31] there were many ser-vants behind the chairs and few worthy dishes on the table.

---

[30] The *premier gentilhomme de la chambre* was an office revived from the Old Regime, held primarily by a noble who waited on the King in all of his private matters, including presiding over his meals. For some two centuries, this was a hereditary role for the Ducs d'Aumont, and Louis-Marie-Céleste d'Aumont held the position under Louis XVIII.

[31] During the Restoration, the faubourg Saint-Germain was the center for the royalist party and, as it was during a good part of the Old Regime, the home for much of the higher nobility.

The bankers' dinners did not come along until later: M. Lafitte was the host for the opposition; M. Thiers was the giant at M. Lafitte's table;[32] Talleyrand's home, the mansion on rue Saint-Florentin, was neutral territory, where everyone was put to the

 test.[33] A deputy from the center was given responsibility for dealing with his colleagues in order to provide a little relief to the ministers' tables. M. Piet's table, on rue Thérèse, became one of the annexes of the elected assembly.[34] At this time, a compliant deputy, to control the ordering of his invitations, kept a weekly calendar where the seven days of every week ended up with the same table settings being periodically fixed and allocated.

[32] Jacques Laffitte was a banker and a liberal deputy who eventually became Président du Conseil during the July Monarchy. Marie-Joseph-Louis-Adolphe Thiers, like Laffitte, was hostile to the Restoration; he would serve several times as Prime Minister under the July Monarchy, one of the many offices he held in his long political career, which continued until his death in 1877. His small stature was a frequent object of comment.

[33] The Hôtel de Saint-Florentin, built in 1769 at the northern edge of the Tuileries Garden, was purchased by Talleyrand in 1812, and he died there in 1838.

[34] Jean-Pierre Piet-Tardiveau, a member of the Chamber of Deputies from 1815 to 1819 and 1820 to 1827, regularly hosted dinners at his home on rue Thérèse, where the Royalists met to discuss policy: "One [deputy] sent him a roe, another a boar's head, and a third a truffled turkey. An anonymous purse provided for everything else so that twice a week the honest fellow had the pleasure of inviting twenty of his colleagues to a very good dinner, at the close of which they formed themselves into a miniature Chamber" (François-Auguste Fauveau de Frénilly, *Recollections of Baron de Frénilly*, trans. Frederic Lees [New York: Putnam, 1909], 813–814).

The clergy, which, under the Imperial government, had grown accustomed to viewing the world with an entirely philosophical tolerance, also had its dinners; it even took considerable care in choosing meatless days to provide its cooks with opportunities to distinguish themselves. These particular sorts

of dinners served by the Grand Chaplain of France, in the Tuileries, had a considerable reputation. About one of these meals, on the occasion of the presence of a monstrous turbot, this anecdote was told:[35] Cardinal Fesch had received two

turbots, equally beautiful, equally prodigious. What to do about this twofold wonder? To give away one and keep the other would run the risk, at the very least, of a needless competition; eating both of them would be an impossible task; wasting one would have been a

real shame. While all searched for a solution, the chief steward exclaimed he had found a way to put each of the turbots to good use, without causing any embarrassment. The cardinal

[35] The *grand aumonier de France* was another office from the Old Regime, one usually filled by a bishop or cardinal who directed the religious affairs of the Imperial or royal household. Joseph Fesch, who was an uncle of Napoleon, held the office during the Imperial period. The source for this anecdote may have been Louis-Antoine Fauvelet de Bourrienne's *Mémoires* (1831) of Napoleon. See, e.g., *Memoirs of Napoleon Bonaparte*, ed. R. W. Phipps (London: Bentley, 1885), 2:11–12.

and the persons he had invited sat down at the table; when the soups had been served, they watched as a turbot—whose proportions aroused a cry of astonishment from the attendees—arrived, carried with great pomp on an immense tray. At the height of their admiration, the tray wavered, they heard the fearful noise of its fall, and the turbot could be beheld ignominiously broken into segments strewn across the floor; at that pitiful sight there was a grievous outcry. The steward promised that at that very same instant he was going to repair the damage; at a given signal, through another door, another turbot, in all things similar to the first, with all the same trimmings, made an appearance. This one was served, and the guests, while eating its softly resistant white flesh, were astonished that two fish, so equally magnificent and so equally delicious, could be found in the sea.

The Empire had rehabilitated meatless days; at Murat's home, especially during Lent, a splendid meatless meal was prepared. The celebrated cooks of that time emphatically boasted about having restored "fine meatless meals" to the Church.[36]

In 1830, dinner was served the day after the revolution. For three days Paris lived in the streets, in camps, or by chance; like the Janissaries in revolt, the Parisians had overturned their stewpots.[37] However, on the Place de la Bourse, the headquarters

[36] Briffault seems here to be drawing from the Marquis de Cussy's contribution to *Les classiques de la table* where he cites Carême: " '[During the Empire] the Eastern abstinence was seized on as an occasion for gourmet feasts full of charm and sparkle. The fine meatless meal first reappeared at the home of Princess Caroline Murat. This was the sanctuary for fine fare' " ("Chapter IV," *Les classiques*, 3rd ed., 1:265). Caroline Murat, Napoleon's sister, later became Queen of Naples as the wife of Joachim Murat.

[37] To prevent being disbanded for corruption in 1826, the Janissaries, an elite corps of Ottoman soldiers founded in the fourteenth century, overturned their pots, a traditional sign of revolt, and mutinied. (The rebellion was quickly suppressed and

for the first two days, in the Théâtre des Nouveautés—today occupied by the Théâtre du Vaudeville—the manager kept a table.[38] Everything seasonal that was most appealing—fruits, fresh fish, and iced wines—was offered there for those who were going off to the task at hand or were returning from it. This was one of the July Revolution's most eminently Parisian scenes; this refined and carefree way of life, amidst such formidable deeds, presented a striking contrast.

After the victory the first moments of exuberance led to numerous enthusiastic outbursts; dining was heavy and frequent, but never well done; unrest was widespread, and everyone, before turning the table back upright, preferred waiting for calmer times.

There was then a certain bourgeois manner or rather a deep humility on the part of our feminine citizens. Those obliged by their position to host meals took this primitive artlessness at its word, and all the dinners, even at the highest level, felt the effects of this modesty. The "so-much-per-head" dinner even made its appearance in dining rooms that should never have been tarnished by its presence.[39] So, official dinners

they were eliminated as a military force.) The "revolution" was, of course, the July Revolution, which in "three glorious days" overturned the Bourbon Restoration and installed Louis-Philippe as King of the French.

[38] The director of the Théâtre des Nouveautés—which stood across from the Palais de la Bourse—was Cyprien Bérard, who founded it in 1827 and closed it in 1832, when it was replaced by the Opéra Comique and then by the Théâtre du Vaudeville in 1840.

[39] Dinners that were served or prepared (often by an outside caterer) at *tant per tête* (so much per head) were associated with *tables d'hôte* and often had a bad reputation for quality and quantity: "But especially watch out for those great food

multiplied to the greater detriment of both taste and elegance. Other kinds of dinners were rare; all of society had dispersed; Paris no longer dined in town.

Order was restored first; then there was a resurgence in the arts; fine dinners became frequent; progress shone with a brilliance thoroughly characteristic of our time and over which the observer's gaze now settles with indulgence.

Our good ancestors regularly had four meals, and they continued throughout life the customs of their childhood: such was the case at least in most of the provinces. Some countries still retained breakfast, dinner, the late snack, and supper. Recently, a young Danish prince, who could in the same day double and even triple these four meals, was mentioned with a good deal of praise; this is a majestic stomach that offers the highest of hopes. Paris has retained only two meals: breakfast and dinner.

For the entire Parisian population, dinner is the most interesting business of the day; and it is with dinner we have to begin this trip around the table.

However numerous the varieties of the Parisian dinner may seem, we think that, in reference to individual persons, they can be reduced into two principal divisions: the people who take dinner and those who do not.

establishments that put together dinners at so-much-per-head or per plate. They will always serve you a stupid dinner that will not satisfy your purpose" ("Rêvasseries d'un gourmet," *La vie parisienne* 5 [May 4, 1867]: 31).

Let us first discuss what generally has been called fine dinners, and then we will arrive at the good dinners; finally we will travel through the lower circles down into the more distressed regions.

Today, the royal dinner is no longer a mystery to the greater public; contact with the royalty has been so frequent that the palaces are like glass houses. Formerly there was a luxury that by its very nature—abundant, splendid, and majestic—belonged to the pomp of monarchy. The conditions of this magnificence were such that its wealth dispensed with good taste and gracefulness; too often heaviness overwhelmed everything, leaving no room for art and beauty. The royal tables buckled beneath the weight of the ornamentation.

This is no longer the case; without rejecting a splendor that is appropriate to them, these tables seek out and adopt everything ingenious and perfect produced by art and labor. The price of the material is no longer the principal worth of an object, and some fashioned in bronze are more valuable than the gold or silver ones poorly crafted. The tableware in precious metals, the porcelain, the crystal, all that contribute to the brilliance of a meal, conform to this shift toward intelligence. The reception halls, where governing takes place, have been unable to avoid a certain need for ceremony; but wherever taste has been able to penetrate, it has been welcome. The royal table, on formal occasions, thus presents a resplendent picture; the centerpiece,[40] the flowers, the crystal, the vases, the candelabra, the brightness from the candles, the wonders

---

[40] The term here is *surtout*, which was indeed a "centerpiece," but one that was usually highly elaborate and distinctive, often containing candelabra, mirrored surfaces, and accoutrements adorned with carved fruits, foliage, and even hunting scenes. (See also n. 47.)

of incised metal, contribute to a dazzling spectacle. Everything conforms to this beauty whose harmony is undisturbed by a single detail; but within these arrangements can be sensed a certain gravity that allows little entry for fancy, imagination, or charming leaps of the imagination. Such attractions, frightened away by grandeur, can be found in receptions more ordinary and less imposing than those for formal occasions.

As for the dishes served, it is always pretty much the same thing; the royal menu is one that does not vary; it marches forward regularly from season to season, flanked by its officiating staff. As for the service personnel, the annoying crowd has wisely been cleared away. However, we will admit that the variety of uniforms that surrounded the royal table during the Restoration, with their brilliant colors and silver and gold embroidery, had an admirable effect and one we cannot help but miss. What was then called the "great table display"[41] was

something magical, like an oriental fairyland. In short, it is now conceivable for a private individual's opulence to attain the splendor of the royal home; the line that separates the luxury of kings from the efforts of any of the great fortunes no longer exists. We are speaking only of what is happening in Paris; we know that nothing can

---

[41] This *grand couvert*, another tradition restored from the Old Regime by Louis XVIII, had been a very formal public dinner served to Louis XIV in Versailles' Antichambre du Grand Couvert, at a table surrounded by large numbers of servants and courtiers.

equal the wealth existing at the English court, spoils stripped from the land of gold and precious gems.[42]

Sometimes, the sight of the royal opulence first causes a fatigue that then leads to sadness; we know of only one place where this impression can be entirely avoided, and that is Neuilly. Neuilly is, it is true, more of a family estate than a courtly residence. At Neuilly, taste is endowed with absolute power; it is custodian of both buildings and gardens; it presides over interior design; it is chief steward and master of ceremonies.[43]

The details of the lives of the great have always drawn considerable curiosity; this curiosity has quite often been disappointed by the vulgarity of what it finds; where there is nothing particularly remarkable of note, good sense and propriety demand restraint.

The palace life is austere; but, head of a young court, the Royal Prince—so cruelly snatched from our future—had a lofty understanding of the intimate alliance luxury should establish with the progress of a work. He saved his highest enthusiasms

---

[42] This "pays de l'or et des pierreries" is likely a reference to India: "That country of diamond mines and fabulous riches…those gates of the sun all of gold and precious gems" (Adolphe Dubois de Jancigny and Xavier Raymond, *Inde* [Paris: Firmin Didot, 1845], 445).

[43] Built in 1751, the Château de Neuilly at Neuilly-sur-Seine was purchased by the Duc d'Orléans, the future Louis-Philippe, in 1819 as his summer residence. It was later destroyed during the revolution of 1848. The "taste" in this paragraph likely belonged to Ferdinand-Philippe—named specifically a few paragraphs below— who was the eldest son of Louis-Philippe and the Royal Prince during the July Monarchy. The Prince was popular among the French, and it was a huge blow to the regime when he died in a carriage accident at the age of thirty-two in 1842. Briffault wrote a short laudatory biography of the Prince the year of his death, praising, among other qualities, his patronage of modern artists and designers: "He entrusted to their talents his tableware, his furniture, the decoration of his residences…all the adornment of his princely existence" (*Le Duc d'Orléans: Prince Royal* [Paris: Ildefonse Rousset, 1842], 51).

and his generosity for the encouragement of art and industry. Whether the materials were humble or precious, he wanted the work always to be estimable. A table service, whose implementation the Prince wanted to direct but which remained an incomplete project, was much talked about.

This service was supposed to extend over a table around thirteen meters in length and about two meters in width, and devised for fifty settings. Gold, silver, and gemstones were reserved for the design of the centerpiece; rubies and diamonds were excluded. All parts of the service, from the forks to the coffee cups, were supposed to be in harmony with the elements of this centerpiece. Its design was spoken of as if it were a concept whose execution would surpass all art created by both the ancients and the age of Louis XIV. Princess Marie and the Duc de Nemours put together the groups;[44] celebrated artists, those the Prince loved to have around him, worked on it, but the secret of its final composition was known only to a few devoted persons.[45]

The cost of this work was estimated at three million, and considerable pride was taken in eclipsing the famous centerpiece of M. Pozzo di Borgo,[46] which cost only 100,000 francs, but which, nevertheless, was admired for its taste and proudly displayed for a long time by the diplomatic corps. This splendid service of the Duc d'Orléans had been taken almost

[44] Marie d'Orléans, Louis-Philippe's daughter, was an accomplished sculptor, but she, like her brother the Royal Prince, died young. Louis d'Orléans, Duc de Nemours, was the second son of Louis-Philippe.

[45] The source for the details for this service was probably the Marquis de Cussy's article "L'art culinaire" in *Les classiques de la table* (3rd ed., I:278–279).

[46] Carlo Andrea Pozzo di Borgo, born into a noble Corsican family and a fierce opponent of Napoleon, eventually entered the Russian diplomatic service, although he was also a peer of France and spent his last years in Paris, where he died in 1842.

to the three-quarters stage under the care of Chenavard and Barye.[47]

There is an opinion, quite widely accepted, that to dine at court is to dine poorly, or, rather, not to dine at all. We can confirm that there are many persons who, when they are invited there, have a fine time at the royal table, people of healthy appetites who leave quite satisfied with whatever they find of substance at these ceremonies. Nevertheless, the sovereign's cuisine, with just a few exceptions, and certainly not outside the smaller apartments, has never had nor merited an illustrious reputation.

The first dinners recently given by the Duc de Nemours have displayed both luxury and good taste.

---

[47] Claude-Aimé Chenavard was a decorative painter, draftsman, and author of several books on interior design. Antoine-Louis Barye was a sculptor, celebrated for his depictions of animals. The *surtout* (centerpiece) mentioned here has an exceptional history of its own. Chenavard designed the ensemble and the ornamentation, and although Barye modeled the sculpted groups, several other sculptors worked on it. Reportedly, the Prince wanted only a modest piece, but Chenavard considered it to be his *magnum opus*, and when the first model was displayed, the table collapsed under its weight. Undeterred, Chenavard had a table constructed large enough to sustain the piece, but when it was moved into the intended dining hall in the Tuileries palace, it did not leave sufficient space for chairs, guests, or servants. Chenavard lobbied to have the walls of the dining hall moved back, but the royal architect refused, and it was said that Chenavard died of despair at the thought of never seeing his masterpiece finished. Work on the *surtout* continued up to 1848, but with the change in regimes, the project was ended, and the piece was eventually divided into parts and sold as separate sculptures. For a more complete version of this "poème-héroico-burlesque," see Emile Lamé, "Les sculptures d'animaux: M. Barye," *Revue de Paris*, 30 (Feb. 1, 1856):204.

Poor fare is generally found at the homes of the ministers; but it is almost always extensive and abundant, and with a little something to appeal to gourmet appetites; the ministerial tables of all regimes resemble each other; they have the look of restaurants; however, we have heard some diplomatic gourmets praise the dinners at the Ministry of Foreign Affairs. Generally, within the official mansions, everything is old, frayed, worn-out, and secondhand; it all has the feel of a furnished room: it looks as if it is all rented, and no one seems to be at home, not even the head of the household. This characteristic can be found, from top to bottom, in almost all government residences. Here is a story Addison tells, in *The Spectator*:

"A Dervish, travelling through Tartary, being arrived at the town of Balk, went into the king's palace by mistake, as thinking it to be a public inn or caravansary. Having looked about him for some time, he entered into a long gallery, where he laid down his wallet, and spread his carpet, in order to repose himself upon it after the manner of the eastern nations. He had not been long in this posture before he was discovered by some of the guards, who asked him what was his business in that place? The Dervish told them he intended to take up his night's lodging in that caravansary. The guards let him know, in a very angry manner, that the house he was in was not a caravansary, but the king's palace. It happened that the king himself passed through the gallery during this debate, and smiling at the mistake of the Dervish, asked him how he could possibly be so dull as not to distinguish a palace from a caravansary? 'Sir,' says the Dervish, 'give me leave to ask your Majesty a question or two. Who were the persons that lodged in this house when it was first built?' The king replied, his ancestors. 'And who,' says the Dervish, 'was the last person that lodged here?' The king replied, his father. 'And who is it,' says the Dervish, 'that lodges here at present?' The king told him, that it was he himself. 'And who,' says the Dervish, 'will be here after you?' The king answered, the young prince his son. 'Ah Sir,' said the Dervish, 'a house that changes its inhabitants so often, and receives such a perpetual succession of guests, is not a palace but a caravansary.' "[48]

How many people, with far less simplicity of heart, drop in on the homes of the great as if it were an inn where they are always ready to flatter the owner!

Winter is, in Paris, the season for fine dinners;[49] ordinarily, the signal for these celebrations does not come from the political world; it is given by the Bank: it sets out from the Chausée-d'Antin and the neighboring buildings. From there it hurries to awaken the Saint-Honoré district, which is sleeping beneath its high-paneled wainscoting; it reaches the core of the city, the working city and also the city of leisurely pursuits; it halts at the Saint-Germain district, where the empty mansions still await the noble families detained in the country-side.[50] The political and government dinners precede by a few

[48] Joseph Addison was an English writer known especially for his essays in *The Spectator*, a daily journal that he cofounded with his co-contributor Richard Steele, and which was published from 1711 to 1712. The extract, cited here in its original English version, is from issue no. 289 (Jan. 31, 1712); it is drawn by Addison from the travels of Sir John Chardin. The French translation that Briffault cites originally appeared in *Le Spectateur, ou le Socrate moderne*, published in six volumes from 1711 to 1726. This same translation reappeared in *Réduction du Spectateur anglois* in 1753, for which the theologian Marie Huber is usually given credit.

[49] "Winter will soon be here, the season for balls and dinners!" are the first words spoken by Frédéric Moreau (in September 1840) to the woman of his dreams, Madame Arnoux, in Chapter 2 of Gustave Flaubert's *L'éducation sentimentale* (1869).

[50] During Briffault's time, rue de la Chausée-d'Antin was associated with the haute bourgeoisie, the retail trade, and bankers and financiers, such as Balzac's fabulously wealthy Baron de Nucingen. The district was in competition with the faubourg Saint-Germain, a neighborhood associated with the old aristocracy: "Birotteau

days the opening sessions of the legislative chambers; at this moment, Paris is the center of what is most active and lively in French society. The artists, the entire nation that makes a profession of intelligence, wit, and imagination, return at the same time as the aristocracy, a time when winter has already taken up residence, and only in the last days of January is society fully present, with all its entertainments, luxuries, and pleasures in place.

It needs to be said that French society is now far removed from the witty urbanity, the polished sensitivity, and all the amiable qualities that had brought its reputation so high and so far: our diners were conversationalists, they have become prattlers; they chatted, currently they chatter; they discussed, now they quarrel. Conversation struts about and shows off; there is no longer candor or innocence in the talk; it is stiff, vain, and far worse than malicious. Formerly, the roast patiently awaited the end of a well-told tale; now discussion is ill-tempered and discourteous; it shouts and it fatigues rather than charms; to escape the noise, refuge is sought in the cup and on the dish.

Here is how the masters of the art of eating have, from experience, arranged the principal points of dinner:[51]

presented himself three times at the hôtel of the famous banker, the Baron de Nucingen, but in vain. The opening of the year, with all of its festivities, sufficiently explained the absence of the financier.... [He] crossed the sumptuous rooms, which helped to make Madame Delphine de Nucingen famous in the Chausée-d'Antin. The baronne's ambition was to rival the great ladies of the faubourg Saint-Germain, to whose houses she was not as yet admitted" (Honoré de Balzac, *Rise and Fall of Cesar Birotteau* [1837], trans. K.P. Wormeley [Boston: Robert Bros., 1890], 285–286). Faubourg Saint-Honoré was also the home of the wealthy, government officials, and nobility.

[51] Briffault probably drew many of the details and observations in the next three paragraphs from the introduction "Quelques explications preliminaires" of *Les classiques de la table*. (See, in particular, 3rd ed., I:xiv–xviii.)

"The linen must be very white, it is the background for the décor; today it is adorned with graceful patterns, and covers the table down to two-thirds of its height. Fine linen is very soft to the touch. Saxony damask, which French art is beginning to displace, is still the linen most sought after.[52] It is in good taste, as in Germany, for the pattern of the napkins to repeat that of the tablecloth or to be complementary to it; we have seen in Dresden a cloth depicting a view of Cologne, and on each napkin a reproduction of one of that city's monuments. Under the tablecloth, and to soften the touch, a light woolen mat is placed; in Germany, a deerskin is put beneath the tablecloth. We cannot approve of woolen or silk tablecloths, in damask or in brocatelle;[53] white linen enhances the entire service, brightens it, and accentuates the finery of the table; it is fresh and appealing to the eye; the other colors cannot, like white, serve as background for all the nuances and sheen."

A great deal has been said about the conditions for an ideal dining room; without worrying too much about its dimensions and presentation, we think that the meticulous attention to its requirements have been pushed too far; we will expect it to be high, spacious, and well lit; cool in summer, well heated in winter. We would like its temperature to be whatever leads to an impression of intangible well-being; no stoves, but heating elements; no fans, but a garden's fresh air.

A dining room that expects to be considered seriously is constructed of stucco or marble: the first should assume the pale yellow color of Siennese marble; the second, a soft and

[52] Saxony, in eastern Germany, had a large textile industry in the nineteenth century and was well known for its damask, or patterned, table linens (woven from flax).
[53] Brocatelle is a variant of damask and is usually stiff, heavy, and patterned.

milky white; the hues of the walls must not shout. In winter, the guests should settle their feet gently down on a soft rug; in summer, a Chinese mat will be placed over the marble surface, which we prefer to all others, even mosaic; around the table, at all times, a strip of carpet will predominate, with one extension leading to the entryway. This measure has a dual purpose: it should soften the noise from the tread of the serving staff, and during the meal, it should prevent the guests' feet from getting the least bit chilled. We have seen other dining room schemes that affect a medieval style; our dwellings are too narrow to support Gothic devices; in the home of the Marquis de Custine, the sideboards of Charles the Bold are cumbersome.[54] We think that the imagination, when straying from a beautiful and regular arrangement, runs the risk of tumbling into a restaurant dining hall or a refectory.

If we are to believe an English doctor, whose highly practical book we have just read, the ailments following a fine dinner do not derive from the guests having taken in more nourishment than their constitutions require, but rather from the contamination of the air that occurs after some time in the banquet hall. A populous philosophical society, meeting in Edinburgh,

---

[54] Astolphe-Louis-Léonor, Marquis de Custine, is remembered primarily for his travel writings, but he was also well known enough as a connoisseur of medieval furnishings to be cited by Balzac in *La fausse maîtresse* (1843): "The dining hall, which had no rivals in Paris other than that of the Marquis de Custine, was at the end of a small gallery with ceiling and decoration in medieval style" (*Oeuvres complètes* [Paris: Hebert, 1874], 1:357). The cumbersome "sideboards" here are *dressoirs*, large, sumptuous cabinets often displaying family treasures. The elaborate *dressoir* of Isabella de Bourbon, second wife of the fifteenth-century Duc de Bourgogne, Charles "the Bold," is described in Aliénor de Poitiers' *Les honneurs de la cours*, written between 1484 and 1491. Three of these sideboards can be viewed in the lithograph "Meubles d'une salle à manger chez M. le Marquis de Custine," *Journal des gens du monde* I [Dec. 1835]: planche 26, between 148 and 149.

was able to ingest, without realizing it, more than double the wine and foodstuffs normally consumed, and no misfortune resulted, because the banquet took place in a well-ventilated

hall.[55] According to the same author, in factories where adequate ventilation was installed, the workers asked for higher wages on account of the increase in their appetites.

The table will be of mahogany or rosewood, with oaken leaves, which attach and join together better than any other wood. Tall sideboards and wide buffets should be placed against the walls and packed with fine tableware to complete the opulence of the service. One thing that will need to be carefully supervised is the absence of all confusion and clutter. What should be deposited on the table's surface—centerpiece, candelabra, dishes, hors d'oeuvres, accessories, vases—also

[55] The book referred to here is *Illustrations of the Theory and Practice of Ventilation* by the Scottish doctor and chemist David Boswell Reid who, for a time, served as a ventilation engineer for the Houses of Parliament. The anecdote mentioned by Briffault, regarding a club of the Royal Society of Edinburgh, can be found on pages 180–181 of the first English edition (London: Green & Longmans, 1844).

will need to be considered when calculating the number of guests. We censure wholeheartedly the new fashion of serving wines in crystal carafes. Whatever may be the charm of these objects, they remove some of that venerable old age from the bottles and that dust of antiquity that is the pride of the ban‐

quet. The servants pouring the drinks are of high standing; to us they are quite displeasing. We recommend, for every season, two important things, piping hot plates and iced water, whose carafes should be set within the reach of all the guests; one little known prac‐ tice is to place, at the right of each guest and a little forward, a salt-and-pepper cellar—trim, small, light, and taking up the least space possible; those who have experienced the annoyance of asking for and passing salt and pepper to their neighbors will appreciate this consideration. Concerning those devices for English seasonings, we would like them to remain permanently on the table.[56]

It is necessary to be generous with the lighting, whether a chandelier hangs from the ceiling, lighting fixtures sprout from the walls, or tall candelabra with multiple branches illuminate and make the service shine; candles everywhere, and oil lamps nowhere. Candles are the table's sunlight.

Parisian manufacture is at the head of the industry that decorates the table; the services that adorn the royal tables of

[56] In Balzac's 1839 novel *Beatrix*, his hero Calyste is fond of "those English seasonings that are served in cruets...[and] all sorts of hot condiments," and he compels his wife, Sabine, to purchase "the English cruet set and its scorching flasks" (*Oeuvres complètes* [Paris: Hebert, 1877], 4:42).

St. Petersburg, Vienna, Berlin, Munich, and Madrid are shipped from Paris.

All the wonders of the table service should be placed with a perfect regularity and the most exact symmetry. Four glasses are set in front of each guest: the crystal called "mousseline" is the prettiest and most precious of its kind, especially when a foliage of grape vines has been made to coil around its diaphanous and very fragile surface.[57] These four glasses are reserved for the Madeira, the table wine, the champagne—with its iced buckets placed at the ends and middle of the table—and the Bordeaux. Each time the wine is changed, it is a strict matter of principle to change the glass.

We do not agree with perfuming the air of dining rooms; disturbing the sensations from the meal with artificial effects or impressions should be avoided; but a dining room should have two doors, one for the service, the other for the guests.

As for the operation of the service, it has its rules and precepts; gastronomy has enacted its laws. Formerly, only the great houses had what was called a "carver" and a staff for serving. Elsewhere, the master and mistress of the household, with the help of friends, did the honors at the table; there was in this continual exchange of courtesies an occasion, both mutual and recurrent, for cordial relations that the intervention of servants removed. The use of carvers and servants has descended into the middling regions, and

---

[57] "Mousselines" are made of fine frosted glass, inlaid with transparent designs to mimic mousseline fabric.

more than one bourgeois homeowner believes to have assumed gentlemanly airs by taking on a retinue that is loudly
vilified by Martine, Nicole, and Madame Jourdain, who understand nothing about this surfeit of people whom they are
only too willing to view as thieves.[58]

Lady Morgan, in the account of one of her trips to Paris,
tells the story of two dinners, one at the home of the Comte de
Ségur, the other at the home of M. de Rothschild, at his
Château de Boulogne; she calls them "very fine" and "very notable" dinners.[59] At the Comte de Ségur's event, she related
only an anecdote about Napoleon. She retained other memories of Boulogne, portraying with great delight "the dinner
served among orange trees, in a hall shaped by a pavilion in
white marble, where the air was refreshed by the proximity of
small fountains spraying pure and shimmering waters. The
middle of the table, with service *en ambigu*,[60] was set with a
dessert of admirable elegance. The crystal-clear day was ever-
present in the thousand rays of the setting sun; the silverware
gleamed with even greater brilliance; the porcelain, more precious than gold or silver because of the perfection of the work,

---

[58] Madame Jourdain and the family maid, Nicole, protest vigorously against the
aristocratic pretentions of M. Jourdain in Molière's *Le bourgeois gentilhomme*
(1670). Nicole is occasionally compared to Martine, who is in a similar position
vis-à-vis the pretensions of her mistress in Molière's *Les femmes servantes* (1672).

[59] Lady Morgan, née Sydney Owenson, was known for her novels, travel writings, and
essays, particularly those in support of Irish causes. Philippe-Paul, Comte de
Ségur, served as a general under Napoleon and was author of a popular history of
the Russian campaign. The Rothschild referred to here is James Mayer de
Rothschild, the founder of the French branch of the family and one of the
wealthiest men in the world at that time. Château Rothschild was in Boulogne-
Billancourt, a western suburb of Paris, and Marie-Antoine Carême, his chef for a
time, presided over many of the Château's dinners.

[60] *En ambigu* refers to a service where the dishes, often all cold, are displayed together,
with the dessert usually given prominence.

depicted domestic scenes. All the details of the service proclaimed the science of life's finery, an exquisite simplicity. "The entrées were placed around this beautiful dessert. The display and the dinner all proclaimed Carême; this was his shining merit, his measure of perfection. No more English spices, no more black sauce: quite the opposite, delicate flavors and the aroma of truffles; we were in the month of July and we could have believed it to be January. This setting aroused universal satisfaction, and at any given moment, we were showering with praise some delicious dish. The vegetables still had a vibrant hue; the mayonnaise seemed to have been whipped in snow, like the heart of Madame de Sévigné;[61] the *plombière*,[62] with its sweet freshness and the taste of its fruits, took the place of our bland English pudding."[63]

[61] This is actually a reference to the heart of Charles de Sévigné, the son of Marie de Rabutin-Chantel, marquise de Sévigné, who, in her letter of April 12, 1671 (#159) to her daughter, quotes the accusation of her son's lover (Ninon de l'Enclos) that he had "a soul of a bowl of mush, a body of wet paper, and a heart of pumpkin whipped (*fricassé*) in snow."

[62] A *plombière* is an elaborate ice cream dessert, usually formed in a mold of lead (*plomb*).

[63] Briffault is probably citing here from the extract published in *Les classiques de la table* (see, e.g., 3rd ed., 2:509–513), which is, in fact, quite different from the version of these dinners that appeared in the original edition of Lady Morgan's *France: 1829–1830* (London: Saunders & Otley, 1830, 2:267–268) or its translation by A. Sobry (*La France en 1829 et 1830* [Stuttgart: Hoffmann, 1830], 2:267–268).

• III •

DINNER IN THE CURRENT AGE

The dinner in the current age has, more than those that have preceded it, its own distinct character; it has proven to be highly sophisticated regarding its own well-being. The Empire's dinner tables and those of the Restoration tried to connect with former times; our table, with greater independence and reason, has proven to be freer and more ingenious than what it had been formerly. Under the Empire and the Restoration, the service and the cuisine had neither enough invention nor novelty; they restored and followed the old traditions, and were unwilling to see that there were useful directions elsewhere than in France. Today everything is ventured, and we take openly from foreign lands whatever we find to be good and pleasing in their practices.

The special character of our table is a cosmopolitanism unknown to others.[1]

Remember that a few years before 1830, land speculation,[2] compensation for the émigrés, and certain military procure-

---

[1] In Gustave Flaubert's *L'éducation sentimentale*, Frédéric Moreau attends a dinner in the early 1840s given by the publisher Jacques Arnoux that consists of Spanish gazpacho, curry, Corsican blackbirds, and lasagna, accompanied by German and Hungarian wines (part I, chap. 4).

[2] For the economic boom in the early 1820s that led to intense speculation in stocks, bonds, and Parisian property, see Philip Mansel, *Paris between Empires, 1814–1852* (London: John Murray, 2001), 185–190.

ments lent a feverish bustle of activity to what we call "the floating fortune"; the conversion of interest rates conveyed, over this shifting and scorching ground, what had, up to then, seemed to have been the most stable and untroubled fortunes.[3] The imaginary credit and fanciful hopes—about which article 405 of the penal code speaks with such disrespect—were then very much in favor.[4] Luxury, not only that which is displayed outwardly for one's own gratification but also that which is shared with others, has always been one of the most powerful means of seduction. What fraudulent disasters were concealed behind dinners and balls! What failures, bankruptcies, deceits, breaches of trust, and embezzlement of funds were discovered the day after a celebration! When these financial crises shake up a country, dining is practiced with a fury. The most timid leap fearlessly forward; each spends what he has and what he doesn't have. Life is lived sumptuously on credit; in anticipation of profit, hopes are devoured; the appearance of wealth is necessary, no matter the cost; everyone gives dinners. That initial euphoria— which troubled wiser heads and brought to our furnishings and tables an affectation for opulence and prodigality beyond all measure—has to be traced back to the time of that effervescence. The profusion of these catastrophes is well known; it was a moment when the whole of society was bankrupt.

[3] In 1825 a law was passed to raise more than one billion francs to compensate needy émigrés (whose property had been confiscated during the French Revolution), to be funded by the conversion of interest rates for government bonds from 5 percent to 3 percent, an action leading to a great deal of uncertainty and financial speculation.

[4] Article 405 of the penal code of 1810 outlaws fraudulent practices leading to "belief of false speculation or of imaginary means of credit."

Something similar to that excessive situation is happening now.[5]

The mania over limited partnerships,[6] the striving, the political fortunes, the corruption, and the scandal produced in Parisian life a boiling ferment that egoism, greed, and the worship of self-interest and material pleasure intensified remarkably. In this second outburst, we went much further than in the first; our dinners marched to the front rank of that senseless pomp.

So, this luxury we have described above spread everywhere, and became in some ways a normal condition; what had been the privilege of Fortune's elect descended into the middle classes, forced to follow the headlong rush of those adventurous spirits who set the course for our life and its business. It has been alleged that this inflammatory disease has subsided, and that society has resumed its normal bearing and detests today what it loved with so much force. We want to believe in this reversion; but these convulsions left such deep scars, they changed the very character of our manners.

Tourism exerted another influence over our dinners. Throughout all of Europe, vast travelers' inns were established, veritable palaces that adorn our cities, and line our roads and rivers with splendor. The steam engine shook up the world, and the longest voyages no longer frighten anyone; distances

---

[5] "In 1842 a national [railway] network was approved in the Chamber of Deputies, prompting railway fever on the Bourse as frenzied as the property fever of the early 1820s" (Mansel, *Paris between Empires*, 385).

[6] In order to stimulate economic activity, the July Monarchy enacted several measures after 1835 to authorize and simplify the creation of limited partnerships (*sociétés en commandite*), resulting in a proliferation of such structures in a variety of sectors. (See, e.g., Chapter 12: "La mise en place d'une économie moderne" in Gabriel de Broglie, *La Monarchie de Juillet* [Paris: Arthème Fayard, 2011]).

vanished, and peoples visit one another as country neighbors did once before. Manners intermingled; thanks to living together and speaking all languages, we became familiar with all traditions, and each brought home the best of what had been seen in the homes of others. The French, so scornful of foreign practices and so vain about their own superiority, have from their eagerness to import exotic customs perhaps gone astray. That being said, before traveling through the world of Parisian diners, we have had to acknowledge the two principal features of our current table: exorbitant luxury and extravagant cosmopolitanism.

Below the very heights, distinctions have become difficult to establish formally. Dining is almost the same everywhere; however, there are nuances that the trained eye can still capture.

When our ministers wish to assume a royal air, you will see the poverty of the service in the fatigue and clumsiness of the servants as they strive to duplicate themselves. A few great houses—those under the names of Noailles, Montmorency, and La Trémoille, ambassadors who aim to prove worthy of their rank, name, and country—can achieve true superiority;[7] but they are not seen as elevating themselves inappropriately;

---

[7] These three families date back to the tenth or eleventh centuries. Members of the Noailles and Montmorency families served as ambassadors during the Restoration.

this fault still belongs to all those who have been recently exalted by political events; their table never offered more than a clumsy and grotesque bounty, concealing poorly their commonplace and parsimonious ways.

Within the higher ranks of trade, banking, and among the winners on the stock exchange, there was greater taste and discernment; but all the conditions for good sense, elegance, and urbanity were not entirely fulfilled; there is, even upon those tables most deserving of it, a brand new luxury displayed by those unaccustomed to it. However, it still needs to be recognized that, in this respect, the newest opulence made an honest effort; but we persist in thinking that the bankers and brokers acted too much like little princes, in such a way that they remained quite a distance from the great nobility.

The highest commercial rank had instincts more certain and more straightforward; in its constructions, its little palaces, its houses in town and country, it was, quite simply, enveloped in an enormous luxury and the most sumptuous abundance. Often, in the depths of the provinces, it displayed a pomp that would astonish even Paris.

You generally dine well enough among the professions, at the homes of those notaries, barristers, and doctors who, as a result of their influence and the presumption of their worth and expertise, are placed so close to the leading lights of society they are sometimes mistaken for them; at some you even dine wisely, but with a gravity that makes things safe and sure, priding itself neither on its frivolity nor its capricious fantasy: the sweet tooth is not always satisfied there, but the stomach is

---

Also during the Restoration two of the La Trémoille brothers served in the position of *lieutenant-général* (an honorific representative of royalty).

content. These dinners usually have certain customs, where the transfer of commissions and clientele plays a considerable role.

Solicitors generally have livelier styles; even at the homes of the oldest ones, especially in regard to revelry at the table, they retain something of the clerk;[8] their fare is, generally speaking, youthful and sensual, but only on good days: their usual meals are almost always detestable.

In Paris there is a kind of succulent dinner almost beyond reproach: these are the ones given by single men of leisure, persons withdrawn from the world and comfortably placed, who quietly pass the better part of their lives in an exchange of genteel gourmandizing.

[8] For a brief description of the various titles within the legal profession of the time, see chap. 6, n. 13.

These meals are called bachelor dinners. They are usually put together with infinite art, and their execution is overseen with loving care. At these tables a perfect decorum is the only luxury, which, in fact, does much for the sheer joy of those for whom such meals are suitable; the excellent quality of all the dishes and of all the preparations is the host's pride. These dinners have two separate characters: the one, engaged, almost studious, frugal in speech, and attesting to its happiness through an expressive pantomime, rigorously tied to the rules, and taking a serious pleasure in the joys of the table; the other, animated and joyful, little concerned about etiquette, downright boisterous, eating and drinking to excess, with radiant features and a bright and open look.

Youth and women do not like being in such company; mature years and a vigorous old age find considerable delight

there. It is not rare to see these amiable meals favor one or two choice morsels— a fine fish, a marvel of a chicken or an extraordinary roast of game, a renowned fish stew or a perfect pheasant in sauce, or some celebrated spring vegetable— bearing the brunt of the cost for a dinner where all the honor belongs to them. Married men, out on a fling and far from the conjugal *pot-au-feu*,[9] also love

---

[9] *Pot-au-feu* usually consists of a piece of beef poached with vegetables and served separately from the broth in which it is cooked. It comes as close as any other preparation to being a French national dish, at least for the lower and middle classes. It is the first dish mentioned by Brillat-Savarin in his *Physiologie du goût* (1825) and by Carême in his *L'art de la cuisine française au dix-neuvième siècle* (1833), and later in this chapter Briffault calls it "the most basic item of the Parisian dinner," declaring that "in most of France, the convention of soup and beef is a national tradition."

and cultivate fine fare. These tables have a motto that exactly sums up their tendencies and preferences; upon sitting down, the diners say to each other: "Let's go slow and easy, and eat everything."

We have never been fooled by what has been said about the tables of famous artists. Talma and Mlle. Mars had dinners that were praised without conviction, but the prize attached to being admitted into the company of these famous people was the best seasoning for a meal reported to be full of wonders.[10] Mlle. Mars always had a well-appointed table, but without any real distinction; at her place a certain conventional spirit prevailed that smacked far more of the clique than of the world; words were spoken there that were immediately put into circulation outside. A detestable habit! Regular guests rule in these houses; with manner and look they tyrannize newcomers, whose presence seems to disturb them. During the last years she spent in the theater, Mlle. Mars surrounded herself with girls and young women; once retired from the scene, she continued with these preferences, giving to her dinners the air of a boarding-school tea and to her drawing room the look of the school's vestibule. The age of Mlle. Mars, like that of Mme. de Maintenon, turned it into a St. Cyr.[11] Several reputations for wit emerged from this table and the venerable drawing room of Mlle. Mars.

[10] François-Joseph Talma, a friend of revolutionaries and Napoleon Bonaparte, was one of the most renowned actors during the first two decades of the nineteenth century. Mlle. Mars, Anne-Françoise-Hyppolyte Boutet Salvetat, Talma's contemporary, was a primary interpreter of Molière and Beaumarchais during a long and celebrated acting career.

[11] A boarding school for the daughters of impoverished nobility was founded in St. Cyr by Louis XIV in 1685 under the patronage of his second wife, Mme. de Maintenon.

Mlle. Contat gave her name to a soup;[12] formerly, the great nobles were fond of such baptisms.[13]

At Talma's we will have said everything about its master, his table, and the company when we write these few words: "Good times were had there by all."

Mlle. Duchesnois prepared and offered fine fare; she was ruined by it.[14] Mlle. Bourgoin was kindness personified; her house was open to all comers, welcomed by her smile, her beauty, and that grace that was hers alone.[15] There was much there for pleasure, perhaps too little for taste and wit. Mlle. Bourgoin received persons of considerable substance, Marshals of France: it was at her place that the Spanish loan was concluded. At the dinner she gave to celebrate this occasion, she

---

[12] Émilie Contat was an actress for the Comédie-Française from 1784 to 1815, where, cast primarily in secondary roles, she remained in the shadow of her more popular sister, Louise. According to Christian Guy, *potage à la Contat* was a practice, suggested by the actress, rather than a soup, whereby the course was served before the guests were seated at the table to avoid spills hazardous to expensive wardrobes (*La vie quotidienne de la société gourmande en France au XIXe siècle* [Paris: Hachette, 1971], 114).

[13] This particular "baptism" may be a reference to the custom of strengthening a dish with a dash of wine (or stronger beverage). Briffault did not disdain puns, and the accompanying illustration is a good example of Bertall fortifying the text in the same way the "grand seigneur" is fortifying the soup.

[14] Catherine-Joséphine Duchesnois was active at the Comédie-Française from 1810 to 1829.

[15] Marie-Thérèse Bourgoin made her debut at the Comédie-Française in 1799 at the age of fourteen, acting there until her retirement in 1829. She also was on stage for a short time at the Théâtres Impériaux in St. Petersburg, and, a close friend of Napoleon's, she was rumored to have been the lover of Tsar Alexander I.

found under her napkin 100,000 francs presented to her by
M. Toreno.[16]
During this period, a cordial and fraternal linkage existed
among all the great intellects: writers, painters, artists, musi-
cians, and actors, all who were involved in the work of mind
and spirit, from near or far—as well as those who were attached to the arts, to literature or to the theater by their taste,
their cooperative nature, their affections, their relations, and
by their good will—were affiliated with the intellectual family.
They gathered everywhere, and dinners multiplied where
each brought along a spirit devoid of envy but ready for those
battles given such sharp rivalry by self-esteem.

Critics of some substance had their tables set almost everywhere, especially at the homes of the theater's illustrious sub-
jects; this was the time when men who were sought out for the
appeal of their conversation were similar to Fontenelle, who
never dined at his own table.[17]

At the Opera, you had dinner only at the homes of Mme.
Branchu and Mme. Clotilde:[18] song and dance received their
friends at supper.

---

[16] José María Queipo de Llano, Seventh Count of Tereno, was in and out of power
frequently in Spain, and he occasionally took up residence-in-exile in Paris where
he died in 1843. Since during the 1820s he was also thought to be Mlle. Bourgoin's
lover, it is likely that the 100,000 francs mentioned above was for something other
than assistance with the many loans Spain was arranging at the time. (See
F. Martínez López, J. Canal, and E. Lemus, eds., *Paris, ciudad de acogida* [Madrid:
Marcial Pons, 2010], 47.)

[17] Bernard Le Bovier de Fontenelle was an Enlightenment scientist, man-of-letters,
and gourmet who attributed his long life to the consumption of strawberries (he
died in 1757, a month before his hundredth birthday).

[18] Alexandrine-Caroline Branchu was the leading soprano at the Paris Opera in the
first quarter of the nineteenth century and was reputed to be Napoleon Bonaparte's
mistress for a short time. Clotilde is likely the dancer Clotilde Farcy who is
mentioned in contemporary reviews and histories of the ballet. (See, e.g., Judith

Today, the kings and queens, the princes and princesses of the theater sometimes give a surprising dinner, on occasion a splendid ball with a meal at night, or even a few concerts bursting with camaraderie. But when the actresses have, in one evening, dissolved Cleopatra's pearl,[19] when the actors have spent, in one night, half the receipts from a benefit performance, all is said and done: it is a debt paid off once a year; you go to their homes out of curiosity. Between the theater and the world there is nothing else in common; the stage knows nothing else of the world; the world understands nothing else of the theater.

Mlle. Rachel has a mansion in Paris and a pavilion in Marly:[20] in the winter, in the city, crêpes are made or chestnuts are eaten, and you drink cider; in the summer, in the country, fruit from the garden is eaten, and you drink beer. On the quai Voltaire, lotto[21] is played in the drawing room; at Marly, hide-and-seek is played. The games and pleasures of children that, later, seem absurd.

Chazin-Bennahum, *The Lure of Perfection: Fashion and Ballet, 1789–1830* [New York: Routledge, 2005], *passim*.)

[19] The story of Cleopatra dissolving a pearl in a beaker of vinegar as a display of her extravagance and arrogance can be found in Pliny the Elder's *Natural History* (9).

[20] Rachel was the stage name for Elizabeth-Rachel Félix, perhaps the supreme tragedienne of Briffault's time. She was also the mistress of Napoleon's son, Count Alexandre Colonna-Walewski, and she gave birth to his son at Marly-le-roi in 1844.

[21] Lotto is a board game similar to bingo.

In general, actors and artists, by their very position, are delivered over to a kind of female steward who almost always replaces the master's intentions with her own narrow interests; also, in these dwellings, a certain discomfort caused by disorder can be seen peeking out from behind the luxury: there is abundance and distress.

There is nothing finer nor more delicate than the table of the well-off Parisian bourgeoisie; we do not hesitate to assert that a certain degree of perfection is found in this middle range. The sparseness of its service was once thought worthy of reproach; and the gluttony of some provinces was very much amused by what it called the small plates of Paris. Despite these admonitions, it is still unnecessary to look much further than the affluent bourgeoisie for the perfect example and real charms of the Parisian dinner.

The dinners we are talking about are those that homes, which are enjoying good fortune and experiencing some progress in business and interests, give once a week for guests who, in number, should never be less than five nor more than twelve. Ordinarily, these meals are prepared by a woman cook. Those who assume some disdain for the feminine kind in matters of cooking are unaware of the superior levels these women have reached through their merit, to which tradition still assigns the name of "blue ribbon."[22] It is impossible to bring greater

---

[22] The term "cordon bleu" derives from the blue ribbon on which hung a cross symbolizing L'ordre du Saint-Esprit, established by Henry III in 1578 and the highest order of chivalry under the Bourbon kings. Along with its association with excellence, the term probably became connected with culinary skills from the lavish banquets held in honor of its recipients. A clear sign that its association with cooking (and, in particular, the efforts of women cooks in bourgeois kitchens) was well established in the nineteenth century was the publication in 1827 of the cookbook *Le cordon bleu, ou nouvelle cuisinière bourgeoise* by Mlle. Marguerite

care, greater delicacy, greater taste, and greater intelligence than what they apply to the choice and preparation of dishes. A good Parisian cook who has been allowed real freedom of action is a person whose talent can contend with that of the celebrated chefs, with the exception only of the fashioning of the great centerpieces and grand dessert confections;[23] but in the matter of refined delicacies and morsels prepared with scrupulous care, a good cook yields to no one. Place beside her a lady of the house who manages without badgering her, who

guides and enlightens without tormenting her, and from that happy alliance, you will see engendered those exquisite meals whose memory is never lost once they have been experienced.

No luxury, nothing exorbitant is seen on the bourgeois tables; but there is the utmost decorum. The serving implements do not exhibit, as elsewhere, the latest styles; perhaps even the form of these objects has been outdated, but

[Horace-Napoléon Raisson], which went through several editions. The Cordon Bleu cooking school, incidentally, was founded in 1895 by the publisher of *La cuisinière cordon bleu* magazine.

[23] This is no small exception, however, since the great dessert centerpieces, prepared with the vision of an architect and the hand of a sculptor, were often the high point of a banquet display. Carême, who began his career as a pastry chef, gained renown through his great *pièces montées*, and even the bourgeois table often required outside help for important events. The three-tiered confection at the Bovary wedding dinner in Chapter 4 of Gustave Flaubert's *Madame Bovary* (1856)—with its temple, fortifications, statuettes, and lakes of jam, all of which elicited cries of delight—was prepared by a confectioner from Yvetot seeking to make a name for himself. For more on this topic, see Maryann Tebben, "Seeing and Tasting: The Evolution of Dessert in French Gastronomy," *Gastronomica: The Journal of Critical Food Studies* 15, no. 2 (Summer 2015): 10–25.

everything there has an accommodating air. It seems that on these tables, the mark of a stable fortune can be found; the extent of the family's luxury is reflected in the very date of the dishware's length of service. This material comfort, which has not come overnight, is appreciated, and that modesty of the old hearth pleases just as, in other places, the opulence of the genuine aristocracy surprises and seduces. At these dinners, the dishes are not numerous, are in no way abundant; but the excellence of the quality makes it easy to forget what might be lacking in quantity. One of the merits of these meals is the kindly and attentive courtesy that presides over their management. The guests are not abandoned to the serving staff; the master and mistress of the house, their closest friends and relatives are united in a common concern that reaches out to all desires, anticipates every wish, and is never intrusive. These happy meals are quite often enlivened by the openness of the talk; perfect wines, which are a credit to the better homes, support the gaiety of a conversation less noisy, without a doubt, than the deafening discussions of more pretentious tables. But the wit there is gentle, easily approachable; it does not stifle the dinner, it adorns it, embellishes it, and leaves a little space for other pleasures besides that of being heard.

The length of these dinners is carefully calculated: you should not be at the table for less than two hours, you should not spend more than three hours there. The best guideline to follow is never to hurry or accelerate anything, and especially to make sure that, without any rush, the guest is always occupied: that is the height of good taste and true courtesy.

How very much we prefer these dinners, these celebrations of the Parisian bourgeoisie, to those great meals, ablaze with splendor! How much we place them especially above those brawling mob scenes that substitute fatigue for pleasure, and those dinners structured and stiffened by etiquette and the chilly requirements of the ceremonial.

We have one particular compliment to direct to the dinners of the Parisian bourgeoisie; they have shaken off the yoke of culinary routine: they have sensibly removed from their tables some of those dishes eagerly sought after in the past. Of this type we know of no more resounding and deserved fall than that of the *fricandeau*,[24] formerly so honored and now found no more except among suburban cook-caterers and on a few tables in the Marais.[25]

In Paris, the true bourgeois dinners were exempt from the passion for progress and the fury with which, in the higher regions, foreign habits were wildly pursued. They have embraced cuts of meat and fish roasted and boiled in the English manner; but they sensibly renounced those improvised preparations that can enhance tasteless dishes only by scorching the palate. The bourgeois dinner did not allow its table to be invaded by the monstrous puddings that so ineptly stuff French stomachs; but they diminished the abuse of sauces, various in the extreme, and that chemistry of spices that for so long made French cuisine a threat to health.[26] It's not impossible that we have just expressed a series of gastronomic blasphemies, but

[24] In Alexandre Dumas' *Grand dictionnaire de cuisine,* after describing *fricandeau* as "a larded and glazed filet or slice of veal," he quotes a couplet he attributes to Beaumarchais: "In restaurants that are new,/ all your dishes are ideal,/ and yet those fricandeaux/ are always the same meal" (Alexandre Dumas, *Grand dictionnaire de cuisine* [Paris: Alphonse Lemerre, 1873], 571–572).

[25] By the mid-nineteenth century the Marais had been largely abandoned by the moneyed classes, becoming a district of large homes converted to tenements, apartments, and ateliers.

[26] "There is no need to spice our food. Nevertheless, even at the reign of Louis XIV our cooking was still too spicy, as it was during that of Louis XV'" (Antoine Carême cited in Philip Hyman, "'Culina Mutata: Carême and l'ancienne cuisine," *French Food on the Table, on the Page, and in French Culture*, ed. Lawrence A. Schehr and Allen S. Weiss [New York: Routledge, 2001], 72).

we are sure we have on our side the sense, spirit, and taste of honest folk.

Before going into the common generalities about the Parisian dinner, and after having said what we know about the best, we ought to say what we know about the worst.

This is the dinner of the upstart social climber.

In Paris, this is one of those tables given a reputation by parasites, one that, furthermore, has never transcended the boundaries of a space that is absolutely foreign to the rest of the world.

The art of giving a dinner cannot be learned while living at the cook-caterers or in the cabarets, as our Young Turks were declaring. Allow a man, suddenly favored by good fortune, to think about setting a table, and you will glimpse in his receptions those impudent and grotesque absurdities that encumber the entire person of a moneyed lout. You will see at once that he very seriously believes he has the right to entrust the happiness of those he has invited to his lackeys. At first sight, his table will resemble a silversmith's shop; and within that confused mass of objects, of utensils, and of vases and vessels of all shapes and sizes, where nothing reveals its function, you are embarrassed, flustered, and without guidance. Do not ask the master of the house the purpose of all these things he has piled up, and

 in such a manner that one cannot be touched without upsetting all the others; he personally knows nothing about it; it has all been packed off to him like trinkets for the natives. Dinner is more of the same; it comes from the most famous caterer, but it arrives cold, in no particular order; those serving it barely understand how to serve the general public. They come on time, rush the guests, hurry the service, get everything out-of-order, and thereby manage to combine all the drawbacks of a restaurant without any of those privileges that, in such places, can redeem everything.

To know if the dinner he gives is good or bad, the upstart has only one standard, the price the meal will cost him. Concerning everything that could increase his guests' pleasure through the civility of their mutual interactions, this man has never even thought about it; he is not giving you a dinner for you, he is giving you a dinner for himself. Do you still remember that he has relegated your happiness to his servants!

The only attention he sometimes shows is to ask you bluntly if you are satisfied. He is used to being paid with a thankful tribute by the core of those he feeds, as they leave the table.

What this sort of person overlooks the most is that dinner is not done with the last mouthful eaten and the last swallow of a drink; beyond the dining room there are considerations and a thousand delicate touches of immeasurable charm, delectable details that complete the pleasure. The higher precincts do not have the leisure to think about that. A gala dinner abandons

its guests upon the exit from the table; but a truly fine dinner accompanies them in all the small joys that follow in their footsteps after the dessert. As for the upstart, he lets his people put out the candles, his guests search for their hats, and he runs to digest his meal publicly in his box at the Opera, to let everyone know he has dined copiously; neither his face, nor the tone of his voice, nor his mannerisms leave any doubt of that.

There will be no lack of persons to repeat in all places that this table is one of the finest in Paris, and the upstart will take them at their word, without suspecting the cruel and savage irony in such praise. He does not hear these lines from *The Misanthrope*, muttered under one's breath on rising from the table:

> He is, in my book, quite a nasty dish, this lout,
> Which spoils every dinner given in his house. (Act II, v)

Not all the tables of the Parisian bourgeoisie have the same merits; we need to go step by step from the delights we have just described down to the mediocre, almost down to the poverty-stricken. No populace is more inventive about the pleasures, resources, and the necessities of domestic life than that of Paris. Following the affluent bourgeoisie, whose existence borders on the opulent and the aristocratic, come the more modest classes, and we arrive at the office clerks and those living off of small incomes and mediocre pensions and the most narrow of profits, off of uncertainty and the most slender of means. And still, at every level, to the degree that well-being diminishes, you see the care, the solicitude, the effort, and the intelligence increase; the slightest dish is prepared with infinite art. The aroma of a certain lamb stew has made the wealthy man, who has just passed in front of the porter's shed on his way to eat a truffled turkey, quiver with desire and delight; it needs also to be said that no other city offers more resources to the smaller fortunes and to the discretion of those who wish to hide their thriftiness from sight, than Paris. The number of these small dinners, composed sometimes of a single dish, makes up the majority of the modest meals homemakers prepare with as much zeal as if it

were the finest cuisine. In such diminished diets, there is nothing neglected, nothing shoddy. When not intemperate, the Parisian is strangely sober; women especially live off of little.

Rich or poor, comfortable or uncomfortable, the Parisian has one compulsion we do not have the boldness to fault: he is mad about hospitality.

"What day are you coming to have dinner with us?" "When can we expect you?" "Your place is always set." "Come and have some soup with us."

All of these expressions are, for him, a part of common civility, and still they are not empty phrases. When the Parisian entertains or receives, he wants to gain a certain amount of credit from those he has invited. For that he spares nothing, he knows how to conceal his adversity: and it is not rare, when vanity or self-interest is at stake, for an embarrassed household to roll out a luxury purchased on credit, bringing along with it, as a consequence, extended grief: but for a couple of hours, a veil has been thrown over a poverty that modern manners have made almost into a crime, and for the moment that is good enough. To give a dinner sufficient to establish a reputation for opulence, there are houses willing to fast for entire months, and, for one day of luxury, endure long and oppressive deprivations. These foibles, that breed vanity at the higher levels, reach the lower regions only in rare and weakened forms. A woman, about to leave for the ball, brilliant in diamonds and lace, dines with her maid; namely, by dunking, in turns, a sliver of bread into a soft-boiled egg.

The merchant's dinner is never an object of particular concern. Industry, business, trade, whatever they are doing, they dine only on the run. Stores of some significance do not look down on good everyday fare; but they do not have the leisure or the necessary peace of mind to enjoy these resources. The meals at the major establishments where the clerks are fed are almost always outrageously simple; there are few exceptions to this rule. These dinners take after the dietary programs of schools and boarding houses. Within these industrial communities, women are still more poorly treated than men. The houses

that look after their workers are few in number, and there is one particular establishment, whose magnificent exterior astounds the passerby, that allows the young women who labor in its workshops literally to die of hunger. If the secret of this shameful stinginess were known, the excessive appetites of these young ladies when they were dining out on the town would be less surprising.

As for the shop, everything is done at once and in haste; at dinnertime the bourgeois wife and her maid go to the nearest market and hastily buy whatever food can be cooked in a few minutes. And, what a dinner! A morsel cut into without any assurance it can ever be finished: eye and ear on the watch, ready to get up and leave at a moment's notice, that's how the Parisian storekeeper dines. There are grocery clerks pestered incessantly by the mischief of the Parisian urchins; these un-

fortunates cannot lift a fork without a buyer coming in to rouse them up, and it is always about a penny purchase. Never enter a barber-shop at the dinner

hour; the help, upset about leaving the table, will take out their displeasure on your head or chin.

The worker who has his own household and eats his own cooking dines quickly, sometimes on what is brought to him from home, sometimes on what he has carried with him that morning. Evening is his time for a meal at his own place; we will come back to him and his family for that moment. The most basic item of the Parisian dinner is the *pot-au-feu*. In most of France, the convention of soup and beef is a national tradition.[27]

In traveling through these different regions, in visiting and searching through instances so diverse, we see popular customs altering in a thousand ways; under observation, these variations seem to grow in number.

An entire class of laborers dines out in the open; they can be found on the quays, on the bridges, in the squares, and on the streets, near buildings under construction. The workers who adopt this way of life are generally the most frugal; they eat while walking, in groups, sitting down or reclining like the Neapolitan *lazzarone*,[28] the cooked and cured meats still sizzling, having been lifted right off the pan of the peddler, whose counter is a dripping-tray: these portable, walking kitchens are common only in Paris.[29] The women who practice this trade are the worker's salvation, and quite often when he is in search of work, or sitting on his hands from lack of a job, he is fed by a dinner where the security for its price is the prospect of better days.

---

[27] For *pot-au-feu*, see n. 9 above.

[28] Italian for "rascal" or "idler."

[29] "I am sorry to have forgotten the locomotive cook; I mean a woman with an *appareil de cuisine* about her neck, having meat and fish hung, by hooks, on both her haunches, and sausages, or fish, or potatoes, hissing in a frying pan.... She haunts, usually, the Pont Neuf and its vicinity, and looks like gastronomy personified" (John Sanderson, *The American in Paris* [London: Henry Colburn, 1838], 1:262).

And let's not forget that young man whose elegance is beginning to look a little threadbare; he carries his dinner in his
pocket: a small roll that he crumbles, swallowing each mouthful on the sly, with a turn of the head.

Given such matters, Sunday joys and the
licentiousness of the seventh day should be
viewed without surprise; for this entire laboring populace, burdened by work for six
days, and on whom such harsh privations are
imposed, a few hours of free pleasures are
a gift from heaven. If the circumstances in
which these masses of workers are placed
were considered, less severity for their rec-
reational excesses would be shown.

There are, for dinner, some general prin-
ciples, and among others, we will readily recall those directed
far more to the mind than to the stomach.

The right choice of and the balance among the assembled
guests are some of the most important conditions for a fine
dinner; it is here especially that this quality of taste, which
seems in itself to encompass all the elements, ought to be recognized; and it is called "tact."

"A man who knows how to live eats and drinks little at his own table."[30]

"A subtle innovation, an intelligent adaptation of current customs to our revised ideas, almost always enchants. Real elegance is innovation under restraint, a transition well arranged. Its secret is in these words: 'Enough: never too much.'"

In Paris, the bourgeois dinner has its absurdities, its tribulations, and its difficulties. The number of guests—which needs to be balanced with the demands of interpersonal relationships, the dimensions of the apartment, and the resources of the household—is, of itself, a subject for grave concern and contention. The issue of precedence and petty considerations, of self-esteem and incompatible temperaments, is neither less lengthy nor less exhausting. The more mediocre the social position, the more relentless and arrogant are the pretensions.

Here is a model for the lady of the house that we recommend to all women, one also that more than one man can study with profit.

Mme. De Fontanes had such a reliable sense of tact her husband never had any need to point out to her the degree of favor, familiarity, or frigidity she ought to be using regarding

[30] This citation is taken from a piece, "Dîner," written by Frédéric Fayot for *Encyclopédie des gens du monde* (Paris: Treuttel et Würtz, 1837), 8:233, and reprinted in *Les classiques de la table*. Several observations in *Paris à table* are drawn from this piece.

one or the other of their guests.[31] Always well versed on the
latest appointments and university-faculty promotions, thoroughly knowledgeable about the merits of the foreign scholars
visiting Paris, taking care to be well informed about the literary successes of the day, she knew which man ought to be the
evening's guest-of-honor, to whom she could not avoid offering her hand during the passage from drawing- to dining-
room, those also who ought to be placed to her right or her
left, and, finally, those she could, without wounding, relegate
to the lower ends of the table. Such subtle and skillful atten-
tions from the mistresses of the great houses are possessed
by few of today's great ladies in any higher degree; yet it is
still one of the powerful paths to success in the administrative and political realms. Mme. de D. won more friends for
M. Talleyrand than all the wounded vanities his sharp wit had
alienated.[32] To welcome and treat people according to their

recognized merit or the success
they have just obtained; to avoid
irritating rival self-esteems by
clear and sustained preferences; to
prompt, for some, the tale of the
previous night and, for others, the
anecdote of the day in order to
make those who tell the best sto-

---

[31] Geneviève-Marie-Faustin-Chantal de Fontanes was the wife of the poet and man-
of-letters Louis-Marcelin de Fontanes who held several high positions in French
educational institutions in the first two decades of the nineteenth century.

[32] Married to Talleyrand's nephew, Dorothea von Biron was also known as Madame de
Dino after her husband was named Duc de Dino in 1815. An accomplished
hostess, she was Talleyrand's companion for several years and said to be his
mistress, although she was also known to have younger lovers. "Parisians remarked
on the inappropriateness of her new title. The new Duchess of Dino was not
accustomed to say no" (Mansel, *Paris between Empires,* 139).

ries shine; to lead deftly into the fray the man who has only some knowledge of a field of study; to force a serious conversation to turn toward the arts, enabling an artist, up to then silent and neglected, to make a case for his specialty; and with all that, while at the table, ensuring the circulation of the choicest morsels and, upon return to the drawing-room, of the most gracious words: that is a very precious talent and one almost lost in the hurly-burly of our banquets.

The Boileau satire on his anger over a bad dinner[33] is gentle, benign, and indulgent if compared to the cruelty of the sarcasms that nowadays hound a disagreeable and displeasing dinner. For this malfeasance, for this crime of lèse-hospitality, the world has no pity.

Several examples of these entertaining outbursts could be quoted. We will report on the most ludicrous ones.[34]

It was at the home of a woman who was very distinguished and usually very good company, but unaware of Parisian gastronomy's thousand affectations. It was in June; the water in the carafes was not iced. "Ah, warm water!" cried out one of the guests. "François, go find me some ice; I'm sorry to say, tepid water makes me sick, I would not be able to eat dinner." The mistress of the house was embarrassed. A moment later another guest cried out, "Oof, some fish! If the water's not fresh, the fish is no longer fresh, they're in tune together." "Oh, look,

---

[33] See chap 2, n. 1 for more on Nicolas Boileau's "Le repas ridicule."

[34] The following four anecdotes are indeed "quoted," having been drawn directly, often in the same language, from letter 18 of December 7, 1840, written under the pseudonym of Vicomte Charles de Launay by Delphine de Girardin for the series "Courrier de Paris," published in her husband's newspaper *La presse* from 1831 to 1848, and later collected in several editions including Girardin's complete works. (See Vicomte de Launay, *Lettres parisiennes* [Paris: Michel Lévy Frères, 1857], 3:134–137.)

it's Bilboquet's carp you're serving us here," another comic voice replied in turn. "Passing through the market, I saw a superb carp; two weeks from now, I'll haggle for it." (See Odry et *Les Saltimbanques*.)[35]

This sharp reference was greeted with merciless outbursts of laughter; the mistress of the house could hardly breathe. Champagne was served. "Ah, this," said an old bon-vivant to the lord of the manor. "Are you the one, my friend, who makes his own champagne himself? It's not bad, but it's missing just one thing to be excellent. There's simply not enough tarragon."

The outbursts of laughter intensified: the mistress of the house turned red with shame, her husband purple with anger; but they kept their composure. The water-cure, the boot, the rack, the wheel are tortures that had been abolished; these torments were nothing compared to those endured by these martyred hosts; and so it was for the entire length of the dinner,

witticisms for every wine, epigrams for every dish. At last, all rose from the table; and a final word put a proper end to that sad celebration: "Ah, I'm so hungry! I'm so hungry!" cried one of the guests loud and clear upon leaving the dining room. "Sirs, I'm inviting you all to sup with me tonight at the Café Anglais!"

To soothe the reader's indignation, we will talk about one of the characteristics that does most honor to the venerable tradition of French courtesy.

[35] *Les saltimbanques* by Théophile Marion Dumersan and Charles Voirin, was produced with some success at the Théâtre des Variétés in 1838. In the play, the popular comic actor Jacques Odry was celebrated for his portrayal of Bilboquet who speaks in Act II, scene iii, a line similar to the one referred to here.

In England, at the time of the French Revolution, the Duke of Bedford offered the émigré Duc de Gramont a splendid meal, one of those quasi-royal celebrations that the great English lords give to heads of state to display their pride and offer to exiles to show their good taste.[36] At dessert a certain bottle of Constantia[37] was produced, a marvelous wine, peerless, ageless, priceless. It was liquid gold inside sacred crystal; a molten treasure that was a privilege to taste, a beam of sunlight sent down into your glass: it was the ultimate nectar, Bacchus' final word. The Duke of Bedford wished personally to pour this divine liquor for his guest. The Duc de Gramont took the glass, tasted the alleged wine, and pronounced it excellent. Bedford, to match him, wanted to drink to his health in turn; but hardly had he brought the glass to his lips when he cried out in horrid disgust: "Ah, what in heaven's name is this?" He was quickly surrounded, the bottle examined, the aroma investigated: it was castor oil. Gramont had swallowed that detestable medicine without raising an eyebrow. This sublime characteristic did great honor to the nobility of France; where courtesy approaches heroism, a lofty notion of a country can be imagined.

The sensitivities of the petite bourgeoisie can be great fun; they are extreme, although those of the aristocracy yield nothing to them; they are as haughty as those of the other are petty.

---

[36] The Duke mentioned here is probably Francis Russell, the fifth Duke of Bedford, and Gramont is likely the eighth duke, Antoine-Louis-Marie de Gramont, who emigrated during the Revolution.

[37] Constantia is a South African dessert wine that was a favorite of nineteenth-century European royalty. Napoleon had thirty bottles a month shipped to Saint Helena for solace during his confinement.

At the home of a rich banker, a man known for his urbanity was taking some coffee after dinner: at the very moment he was about to savor this delicious brew, a young and very pretty woman approached him, rolling an enormous piece of sugar about her fingers. "Sir," she said to him with the most gracious of smiles, "would you allow me to dunk my sugar?"

This odd familiarity disconcerted him to such a degree that he turned pale, trembled, and dumped the contents of his cup over the white dress of the sugar lady.

A German countess poured some tea; a German baron, instead of using tongs, took some sugar with his fingers. The countess marched over to the window, opened it, and tossed out the sugar bowl; the baron quietly finished drinking his tea; when he was done, he also went over to the window, opened it, and threw out his empty cup. Two months after this scene, the baron married the countess.

We have made the particular features of the Parisian dinner's character and several of its singular habits the object of this specific study.

It is perhaps within the postscript where the thinking behind everything preceding it needs to be sought.

We end with an aphorism: "The disposition of a dinner must be like the machines behind the Opera, where the effect charms and the strings are never seen."[38]

---

[38] This quote is very similar to one attributed to Suzanne Curchod, the wife of the Swiss financier Jacques Necker and hostess of one of the *Ancien Régime's* most brilliant salons, although her reference is to "The disposition (*l'ordre*) of the house (*maison*)..." rather than to the "*dîner*" (*Mélanges extraits des manuscrits de Mme. Necker* [Paris: Pougens, 1798], I: 241).

VARIETIES OF DINNER

The Empire endowed all things with gigantic dimensions; for its soldiers it held meals that left all memories of past times well behind them; its military celebrations had a Homeric character. On the return from the Prussian campaign, Napoleon entertained his Imperial Guard in the Tuileries Garden; in 1815, before Waterloo, with glass in hand, he allied them with the Parisian National Guard on the slopes around the Champ de Mars.[1]

The taste for arts and letters—and for everything else that restored a polished and enlightened civilization—led the revival for gatherings at a table where wit fraternized with gaiety. This was a tribute paid to those dinners that had brought the reputation of our society to such a high level.

Singing societies, under different names, rose up everywhere;[2] and from the dinners at the Cadran Bleu and the

---

[1] The Grand Entrance of the Imperial Guard into Paris on November 25, 1807, after Napoleon's successful Prussian campaign passed through the Tuileries Garden before culminating in a banquet for 10,000 of the soldiers on the Champs Élysée. On April 2, 1815, an even grander banquet, for 15,000, was held on the Champ de Mars (a public green space in front of the École Militaire), the Imperial and National Guards uniting to celebrate the return of Napoleon from Elba. (See, e.g., John Grand-Carteret, *XIXe siècle: classes, moeurs, usages, costumes, inventions* [Paris: Firmin-Didot, 1893], 580–581.)

[2] *Sociétés chantantes*, popular during the nineteenth century, were gatherings whose members met regularly to create, sing, and critique songs, often of a ribald or

Rocher de Cancale to those at the humblest of cabarets, drinking and singing were joined.[3] We ask all those old luminaries kindly to pardon us for never having taken their epicurean songs and Bacchic refrains seriously; but in the matter of good wine and fine food, their love was only platonic; they sang of the delights and intoxications of the table like the poets who adore and celebrate in their verse an imaginary beauty. These singing societies have never held a good dinner; the restaurateurs whose reputations they have enhanced have always treated these false epicureans as veritable fools infatuated with something they know nothing about. We will add that the gaiety and fraternity of the singing societies have only been fictions; they tear each other apart there with their teeth, and beneath the frivolity of song lurk the resentments of self-esteem. We have every reason to believe—and that from contemporary accounts—that these gatherings did not reckon on true fellowship within their ranks; they had only a replica of it.

Two or three *caveaux*, more or less modern, and two or three *gymnases*, more or less lyrical, still, perhaps, exist.[4]

political nature. Some of the most celebrated songwriters were active in these societies, which occasionally published collections under their imprimatur. For more about these societies, and particularly their ribaldry, see Marie-Véronique Gauthier, "Sociétés chantantes et grivoiserie au XIXe siècle," *Romantisme* 20 (1990): 75–86.

[3] For these two restaurants, see Chap. 10. Translated here as "cabaret," the word *goguette* can be used both for a particular kind of singing society and its site.

[4] "Le Caveau" was the name of one of the first singing societies, and although it lasted only from 1719 to 1739, the name was adopted by various other *goguettes*, including Le Caveau Moderne, which was active from 1806 to 1817. Founded in 1824 and based on Le Caveau Moderne, Le Gymnase Lyrique was active until it was eventually torn apart by internal dispute and discontinued in 1841: "In 1838 the wounded self-esteem of some members...led to a most lively discussion, at the end of which there was a split" (Théophile-Marion Dumersan, *Chansons nationales et populaires de France* [Paris: Garnier, 1866], 1:xxxviii–xxxix. See also Achille

A few years ago they quarreled over their predecessors' inheritance; but from that legacy, they reaped only the privilege of dining poorly.

The true cabaret societies, whose members gathered over a morsel of veal and a salad, had, under a less pleasing form, the same defect as the singing societies; the pretensions spoiled everything. We attended one session, namely, a dinner at the most celebrated of these cabaret societies, the Joyeux in Belleville. As a meal it was quite sad, and when the triple march of songs began, the scene became only more disagreeable because of the conflict among rival personalities. There are in these societies some witty and good-humored people; they are lost and led astray there.

The Goguette des Joyeux chose Belleville's Ile d'Amour for its home, one of the most pleasant arbors in the vicinity of Paris and which has just been made into the town hall by municipal officials.[5]

Among workers, cabaret societies are abundant; they do not serve to entertain them, but only to soothe them and put them to sleep, like the songs nursemaids sing to children.

Taphanel, "Le caveau," *Le magazine pittoresque* [Paris: Bureaux d'Abonnement, 1886], 4:139–140).

[5] Like many neighborhoods just outside the Paris city limits, Belleville was home to many *guinguettes*, or drinking establishments, and *goguettes* where city taxes on wine and other goods (the *octroi*) could be avoided. The Goguette de Joyeux met at l'Ile d'Amour from its founding in 1792 until 1846 when the building was turned into the Belleville town hall. For a good contemporary account of the development and transformation of these singing societies from professional associations to the more popular *goguette,* and their eventual decline after the 1830 Revolution, see Louis Couailhac, "Les sociétés chantantes," *La grande ville: nouveau tableau de Paris* (Paris: Bureau General des Publications Nouvelles, 1843), 2:241–258: "Today we are gay because we want to appear gay. There is pretension even in pleasure.... Today egotism or self-esteem has taken the place of a convivial feast" (2:254).

The spirit of association took on such importance in public life that the simple dinner could not contain the new grandeur. Banquets were created.

They comprise all types. At their head stands the patriotic banquet; then come the military banquets, which replaced regimental dinners; philosophical society banquets; political banquets, founded to honor or defame, to praise or to blame; the philanthropic banquet, where you eat for the poor who are dying of hunger; the corporation banquets. The National Guard, both civil and military, has under both aspects multiplied banquets of all kinds.[6] The arts have their banquets; the industrial sector has its banquets; commemorations and schools have their banquets; and finally the Masonic banquets, which frighten small children.

We have not examined the moral character of these displays, their causes, their purpose, and their sincerity; it is just that the banquets now hold enough of a place in the life of our people that it is not fitting for us to neglect them: but we can

[6] The French National Guard assumed a variety of forms from its founding during the 1789 Revolution as a civilian militia to its final disbanding in 1872 after the Paris Commune. Although it was instrumental in establishing the July Monarchy of 1830, its power, numbers, and political affiliations throughout the reign of Louis-Philippe were highly volatile. In its early years "les grandes revues royales" annually celebrated the union of the throne and the militia. But it was also an independent political force and, in fact, did not support Louis-Philippe when he was overthrown in 1848. (See, e.g., Mathilde Larrère, *L'urne et le fusil: La garde nationale parisienne de 1830 à 1848* [Paris: Presses Universaires de France, 2016].)

confirm that these meals are normally no more than detestable dinners where the common dishes (cold or tepid, torn into a thousand pieces for general distribution) and the wines (unap-

preciated because of the heightened enthusiasm) form the least attractive ensemble that can be imagined. As all of us are aware, a banquet is not a pleasure, but a duty to be endured. The toasts proposed so very seriously, the long speeches, and sometimes the songs, finish off a task where the burden is borne by each of the guests. Only one kind of a banquet escapes these drawbacks, and that is the one that reunites old childhood friends. These ought to find a reprieve from our censure, particularly since, as meals, they have sometimes been tolerable.

There are, however, some banquets that are quite entertaining because of the burlesque figures of the guests and the amusing caricatures of their harangues, their fervor, and their jubilation. A famous sect gave a banquet a few years ago with the aim of regenerating mankind through pleasure, at three francs a head.

Under the Directory, the banquet of
Saint-Sulpice can be mentioned.[7] Under
the Consulate, the coachmen of Paris
held a banquet for the First Consul's
driver who had saved him from the infernal machine.[8]

The bourgeois life of Paris, regaled by
the honorary displays of the citizens' militia, has royal days, those that take place at
the Tuileries; the Parisian suburbs supply
the posts for Neuilly.[9] At the Tuileries, the
high command dines with the King; the other officers dine
with the palace's commanding officer; at Neuilly, all the exec-
utive officers, up to the rank of captain and including the heads
of the escort, take seats at the King's table; the other officers
are received by the palace adjutant. For certain provincial officers, this is quite a windfall from which they profit greatly;
their satisfaction is also a pleasing sight for the court.

In Paris, family ties are not as loose as we seem to think;
there are still private ceremonies at the domestic fireside;

---

[7] Following Napoleon's Egyptian campaign, a banquet, sponsored by the Directory,
was held November 6, 1799, at the Temple of Victory (formerly and afterward the
Church of Saint-Sulpice). Two days later Napoleon supported the coup d'état that
led to the Directory's overthrow. By all accounts, the banquet was a gloomy affair.

[8] The "plot of the rue Saint-Nicaise" on December 24, 1800, also known as the
"*machine infernale* plot," was an attempt on Napoleon's life as he was traveling to
the Opera. The bomb, a cask loaded with gunpowder, exploded as his carriage was
passing nearby, and his coachman, César, was praised for his dexterity in getting
Napoleon safely to his destination. The coachmen of Paris honored César with
a banquet, although Napoleon later attributed his coachman's sang-froid to the
fact that he was drunk at the time. (See Emmanuel, comte de las Cases, *Mémorial
de Sainte-Hélène* [Paris: Bourdin, 1842], 1:207–208, 322.)

[9] See chap. 2, n. 43.

 parties for grandparents and birth-
days, commemorations of memo-
rable dates and the first day of the
New Year are celebrated at these
family dinners, where everything
is good so long as the heart is willing to assist the stomach a bit. Paris,
under the mantel of its outward
egoism, has not rid itself of all of
its sentiment, and it owes to these
emotions pleasures that the liveliest of distractions have never
made it entirely forget. Old ways and manners resurface, like
the old crockery taken from the cupboard to adorn the table.

Sundays, for large and close-knit families, have something
that approaches these celebratory days.

Weddings and their feasts have gone away; high society
wants no more of them; the newlyweds climb into a carriage
and depart upon leaving the church. The small property owner
and the working class, and sometimes tradesmen, too, are still
naïve enough to celebrate marriage with dinner and a ball.

Men of letters, poets and writers of prose, have not all renounced this taste for pleasure and fine fare, which has been
passed down among them through the ages; today, as in former
times, they love a good dinner; but preferably at the homes of
others than at their own. Within these past few years, however,
the press has set some grand tables; but it is generally inept in
the art of receiving people well, and it does not own the secret
for fine receptions, no matter what kind of pomp it deploys.

Publication dinners were created for the use of journalists.
Following the publication of a book on Spain by the Marquis
de Custine, his bookseller gave a series of literary dinners at

the author's home for all the critical press.[10] M. Crémieux presented Mlle. Rachel at his dinners, to which he invited political figures and the writers from whom he expected publicity appropriate to the success he had promised the young tragedienne.[11] It had been very much the fashion to launch, through a press dinner, enterprises of all kinds that wished to be immediately noticed by the fashionable world.

The theater sometimes still resorts to these methods, and those for whom they are intended can scarcely repress their laughter.

The revival of *Némésis* was announced and celebrated by a dinner at Véfour. Barthélemy read, at dessert, the first song from this second appearance.[12]

Often enough, those who are commonly known as men of wit are invited to entertain the dinner company to whom their presence has been announced. These guests, who thus make up part of the menu, almost always have enough of the devil in them to say absolutely nothing; there are even some whose wit takes its vengeance to the point of speaking utter nonsense. Such entertainments belong to the banking profession; aristocrats

[10] Astolphe-Louis-Léonor, Marquis de Custine, was a writer of travelogues whose most celebrated work was *La Russie en 1839* (1843). It was preceded, however, by his less successful *L'Espagne sous Ferdinand VII*, published in 1838.

[11] Adolphe Crémieux, a Jewish lawyer and politician now remembered especially for his stands on the abolition of the death penalty and slavery in the colonies, was an early supporter and mentor of the actress Rachel (see chap. 3, n. 20), who lived in his home for a time. (See, e.g., Francis Gribble, *Rachel: Her Stage Life and Her Real Life* [New York: Scribner's, 1911], 70.)

[12] Auguste-Marseille Barthélemy published a weekly series of verse satires from March 1831 to April 1832 under the title of *La némésis*. A collection of the satires went through several editions, and a new collection of what seemed to be previously published verses, beginning with the poem "Reveil" ("Awakening"), appeared in 1845. For Véfour, see chap. 10, n. 37.

who have some taste do not allow them; they know enough not to play around with talent, a firearm that is always loaded. When several opposition speakers and writers who were standing up against him were mentioned, a statesman replied in a scornful manner, "If you wish, I will serve them up to you at dessert."

Some tables are also happy to employ, as centerpieces, foreigners of distinction and illustrious travelers; celebrated artists are also at risk of having such honors inflicted upon them.

Men of talent treated like this do not spare those who welcome them with such disrespectful hospitality. Coupigny, whose songs and angling have drawn crowds, said quite publicly, "Mlle. Mars is an ingrate; I grace her table every Wednesday, without missing a single one this year, and on New Year's Day, she gave me absolutely nothing."[13]

A man of wit, well known in Paris, was the dining companion of a banker who took pleasure in hearing him chat. The amiable guest, having naturally borrowed a sum of money from his host, just as naturally failed to pay it back. The matter, submitted to the proper authorities, had been routinely handled; there was a note, and it was pursued. The fearful debtor stopped seeing his creditor; the banker had the man who had been fleeing him apprehended physically and had him brought...to his table.

"Sir," he told him, "between you and me, things will continue in this manner until payment has been made."

---

[13] André-François de Coupigny was a songwriter, dramatist, and close friend to many in the theater world in the early 1800s. He was also well known for his wit and his "veritable mania" for fishing. (See, e.g., A.-F. de Coupigny *Dernières romances* [Paris: Delaunay, 1835], 14–24.) For the actress Mademoiselle Mars, see chap. 3, n. 10.

"As well they should," replied the other, "you owe me some vittles."[14]

And this modern Spartan, so pompously entertained by this Fontanarosa who had become a satrap, told him quite simply, after the meal of which the social climber seemed so proud, "Your dinner just saved me at least a franc and a half."[15]

Dinner has its mysteries; and so it flees from the glare and the daylight; it seeks only well-being, but it seeks it with a passion. Everything is positioned and prepared for a meal beyond reproach, where each part must have its own disposition and management, its own dishes and wines. The guests, few in number like a true elect, have arrived precisely on time; a true gourmet never makes anyone wait; dishes are eaten one by one, hot and just at the right moment. These delights, so far removed from the vulgar, hold treasures whose enjoyment is prolonged by art and infinite good taste. The shrines where these joys are protected are dinner's version of the boudoir. Paris is the city where these succulent practices, privileges of a few favored stomachs, are best preserved, their exquisite organization lending dignity to their graciousness.

Learned men have tried, on various occasions, to make the wonders of antiquity their own. The story has been told of a celebrated gourmet, Father Margon who, having received

[14] This anecdote pleased Briffault's illustrator, Bertall, so much that he borrowed it intact up to this point (unattributed) for his own book *La comédie de notre temps* (Paris: Plon, 1874), 1:399.

[15] According to Thucydides (*History of the Peloponnesian War*, Book 8), Sparta negotiated several unsatisfactory treaties with the Lydian king and satrap (Persian governor of a region), although by Briffault's time "satrap" also signified a proud and powerful man, often of voluptuous tastes. Fontanarosa is probably a reference to Dr. Fontanarose, a patent-medicine salesman in *Le philtre* by Daniel-François-Esprit Auber and Eugène Scribe, a highly successful opera, which premiered at the Paris Opera in 1831.

a substantial gift from the Duc d'Orléans, thought about consuming it all up in a supper that he beseeched the Prince to allow him to give at Saint-Cloud.[16] The priest made the arrangements for the meal; he copied Trimalchio's banquet. Petronius in hand, he executed that monstrous feast with precision.[17]

All difficulties were overcome by means of cash; the Regent was curious enough to look in on the players, and he admitted that he had never seen anything so original. This event, unimaginable when measured against the idea of the original's colossal proportions, is nevertheless confirmed in the new translation of Petronius by C.H.D.G.[18] But what has been taken for the imitation of a great painting was no doubt only a miniature.

All these parodies misfire; following antiquity step-by-step only leads to intolerable dinners. The famous Spartan black broth was also the subject of several failed experiments and trials.[19]

Under the Directory, a Roman dinner was carried out, and it was so ridiculous no one will admit to having any memory of it; long, rolling, mobile tables were put to use, like those which served the Romans who changed them with each course; three

[16] Guillaume Plantavit de la Pause, l'abbé Margon, was a religious pamphleteer employed for a time by Philippe II, Duc d'Orléans, who as Regent held power in France from Louis XIV's death in 1715 to his own death in 1723. The Château de Saint-Cloud, just outside of Paris, belonged to the Orléans family at the time of the Regency. (For more on Father Margon, see Peter Campbell, *Power and Politics in Old Regime France* [London: Routledge, 2004], 595–596.)

[17] Trimalchio, a character in Petronius' first-century verse-fiction *The Satyricon*, is famous for the lavish and exotic banquet he throws in Book 15 of the work.

[18] The anecdote regarding Father Margon was drawn almost verbatim from a footnote in the above-mentioned edition and translation of Petronius by Charles Héguin de Guerle (*Le satyricon de T. Pétrone* [Paris: Pancoucke, 1834], 1:48–49).

[19] For the "black broth," see chap. 1, n. 3.

of them were required for a dinner.[20] We have rediscovered this practice at the home of a rich Creole, who extended his extravagance up to the point of having his guests pass from one room into another: the freshness of each new setting sharpened the blunted appetites.

Several prescriptions for very simple dinners have been handed down; the Princess de Liéven dines only with a small savory pie in sauce, a mutton chop, and a glass of water.[21]

The *Journal des modes*, under the Empire, moved to adopt, for almost all the European courts, this diet, which guaranteed, they said, one hundred years of life to those who followed it.[22] *Three meals*: the first, in the morning, a glass of water without sugar; the second, at three o'clock, a meat soup, six oysters, a mutton chop, stewed fruit, a glass of Madeira; the third, on going to bed, a glass of sugared water.

Dinner has its tragedies, and here is one of the most terrible:

It was after 1830; let us bear in mind that under the active direction of M. Harel, and thanks to the talent of Mlle. Georges, the Odéon was then taking on a new life. This industrious colony—the director, the great actress, Jules Janin, and Jouslin de la Salle—lived together in a house on rue Madame.[23] Each

---

[20] The source for this is de Cussy's "L'art culinaire" in *Les classiques de la table* (1845), 1:273.

[21] Princess Dorothea von Liéven was the wife of the Russian ambassador to Great Britain, where she played an important role in the affairs of the two states from 1812 to 1834. When her husband was called back to Russia, she settled in Paris where she ran an influential salon.

[22] The *Journal des dames et des modes* was founded in 1797 as one of the first illustrated reviews of fashion. Over the years it continued under a variety of titles, including *Journal des modes*, until its final issue in 1839.

[23] Charles-Jean Harel, a journalist and playwright, was also the director of the Odéon, one of France's national theaters, from September 1829 to April 1832. Marguerite Georges was celebrated as an actress throughout Europe in the first half of the

of the place's residents cared for an animal: Janin had a goat; M. Harel owned a pig, but the friendliest pig that was ever seen; and this sweet animal was also the delight of his master from whom he never parted; he followed him to the table and then into the room where he slept; this was a pig that could have worn lace cuffs.

One day Mlle. Georges and Janin put their heads together; the two of them admired the pig: its child-like graces, its melodious grunts, its pink flesh beneath its silken white pelt, its rounded shape, plump and appetizing. It was decided that such an animal, by its very charms, was destined for a feast; Janin cited several passages from the *Odyssey* to prove that a pig was, in heroic times, food for the demi-gods:[24] to offer this pig would be to perform a praiseworthy act.

The sacrifice of the pig was settled.

M. Harel was absent; the victim was killed.

The director returned with a ferocious appetite; rehearsals had brought him to the brink of starvation. Upon arriving at

nineteenth century (and was said to have had affairs with Tsar Alexander I and both Napoleon and the Duke of Wellington). Jules-Gabriel Janin was a prolific writer, journalist, and critic up to his death in 1874. He also contributed to many of the same journals and collections as Briffault and corresponded with him. Armand-François Jouslin de la Salle was a playwright, journalist, and the director of the Comédie-Française from 1832 to 1837. Rue Madame is in the Sixth Arrondissement, near the Luxembourg Gardens, and Mademoiselle Georges was known to have lived there for a time at no. 25.

[24] Janin was probably citing from Book 14 of the *Odyssey*, where the swineherd Eumaeus slaughters and roasts a "fatted boar" as an offering to the gods and to his guest Odysseus.

the shared lodgings, he was surprised by the festive air that reigned throughout the house; the table was set with an attractive allure that proclaimed its intention to please.

All took their places; piping hot blood puddings and sausages golden from the grill accompanied the beef; M. Harel gave them a hearty welcome.

These dishes, which he abandoned only with regret, were followed by a first-course stew that he vigorously celebrated; a tongue in a spicy sauce arrived just in time to restore to his appetite a force that could have been weakening. Finally, a roast of fresh pork, wondrously colored by the flame, steaming and glistening with fat, arrived to apply a finishing touch to his bliss; the whole thing was a miracle of tenderness.

M. Harel was pleased, delighted by the excellent fare he had just had, and, in his rapture, he did not notice the somber looks Janin and Mlle. Georges were exchanging on the side. To complete his happiness, M. Harel asked, like Saint Anthony,[25] to see his darling companion.... There was some hesitation.... He had a horrible suspicion.... A table still overloaded with the remnants of that meat!... He cried out in distress.... Trembling, they admitted to him that he had just eaten his pig.... For a moment he was devastated; then, very calmly, he said:

"Really, I liked him very much; but he never gave me as much pleasure as he did today."[26]

---

[25] As the patron saint of small and domesticated animals, the fourth-century Saint Anthony of Egypt is often depicted accompanied by a pig, an animal the monastic order the Hospitallers of Saint Anthony raised to support their charities.

[26] This tale of the charming but doomed pig, named Piaf-Piaf according to Alexandre Dumas *père*, is also recounted in Chapter 125 of Dumas' *Mes mémoires* (1852–1856).

This was a scene straight out of *Gabrielle de Vergy*.[27]

Dinner, such as we have just been viewing under its various guises within Parisian life, has lost some of its appeal of earlier times. Formerly, dinner was always a pleasure; now it is often a matter of business. An Italian proverb forbids love to think; we would like dinner, freed from ideas, to consider only sensations; appetite and wit are the only two things it should be allowed to think about. Our dinners have become sumptuous, and they have sacrificed taste and delicacy to this opulence. The magnificence of our tables intrudes: gaiety is afraid of it; luxury, when it is pushed to excess, begets uniformity: from its desire to be all things from all countries, it ends up no longer being from its own. Such is the fate of today's dinner, it is no longer delectable, it is no longer joyful, it is no longer various, it is no longer, in style and spirit, French.

Two things formerly contributed to dinner's attraction; those sad squires of the carving knife garbed in black—who at the great tables, fall into the precincts of mediocrity when it puts on formal airs—were not found everywhere; this pack of rented lackeys breaks the bonds between the head of the household and his guests. Our

[27] Briffault is probably here referring to the play, published under that title in 1770, by Dormont de Belloy, based on the tale of a woman who was fed the roasted heart of her lover by her jealous husband. There were also several Italian operas on the subject by, among others, Saverio Mercadante, Michele Carafa, and Gaetano Donizetti (although the Donizetti opera was not first performed until 1869, after the composer's death).

fathers' dinners extended beyond the dining room; now upon rising from the table, we steal away; there is a general run to the exits.

A man on a romantic outing was wriggling impatiently beside his mistress:

"What's wrong with you?" she asked him. "Why are you stirring about like that?"

He replied, "I would like to be able to leave, so I can report on my happiness to everyone."

And so it is with certain persons; they have to present themselves at the Opera so they can say at the top of their voices that they have just come from the dinner at Madame Whoever's place.

This luxury, against which we are protesting, has, however, some right to our indulgence, when we think about what it has done for labor and also for all the ingenuity of its arrangements. The most poorly equipped household or a man totally isolated and without lodging will be able, in a couple of hours, to improvise a dinner, if they have the wherewithal to pay for it; a full and comfortable apartment, a table, silver- and dishware, centerpiece, vases, flowers and candelabra, wines, courses, domestic and serving staff, all will be supplied as if by pure magic. Balls and dinners can be ordered up today as easily as a funeral.

Among modern dinner innovations, two of them, to us, do not seem to be of sound taste.

Numbers of glasses placed before each guest do not have a very gracious appearance; multiplying the glassware clutters the table and embarrasses the drinker, who hesitates and worries about the choice of glass he ought to be taking. We think it would be better to return to the practice of bringing

glasses, inside those basins that were one of the most beautiful of table ornaments, with each wine served. The basins
could also be left at both table-ends, and you could then take
the glass intended for the wine you would like to drink. Also,
the head of the household himself did the honors for any
wine he wished to recommend particularly to his guests. M.
de Talleyrand did not overlook this custom; we have eliminated it.

Between two courses, there is what is called "the shot
midway"; it comes to us from Bordeaux, that town that has

a wine for every dish and a dish
for every wine. "The shot midway"
was served by a pretty and amiable
young woman, offering on a tray
Jamaican rum, absinthe, or Madeira
in crystal carafes; a tonic and often
acerbic brew. Today it is taken with
a sherry or better still with a rum
sorbet, which pairs the tonic quality with freshness.

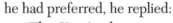

Lepeintre the younger, as an actor, had dined at both the
King's and the Royal Prince's tables; when questioned on whose

he had preferred, he replied:

"The King's, there were only
two glasses; the Duc d'Orléans had
three of them."[28]

---

[28] Emmanuel-Augustin Lepeintre was a comic
actor at the Théâtre des Variétés and
Théâtre des Vaudeville from 1818 to 1843,
known for both his obesity and slight stature.
(For a sculpted caricature of Lepeintre's

The second practice we want to criticize is the introduction of toothpicks and waterbowls onto our tables. This dual mouth cleansing, so far removed from all decent and agreeable conventions has elicited cries of disgust from our fathers and especially our mothers, and we still have not hardened ourselves

very well against these feelings. That final gargling, that general slurping and sloshing and that tepid water are a bad end to a meal where everything was done to entice and attract. This latter operation makes particular guests somewhat less seductive. Women use their bowl as a washbasin; they find it perfectly good form to cleanse their faces completely: such whimsical behavior is far from flattering.

What we do approve of without reservation is the change of setting with each course; this procedure, coming from England, is currently in general use throughout France.

The dinner is moving up to a later and later time; tables claiming to be at the height of fashion no longer dine earlier

distinctive shape, see http://parismuseescollections.paris.fr/fr/musee-carnavalet/oeuvres/portrait-charge-d-emmanuel-augustin-lepeintre-dit-lepeintre-jeune-1788-1847#infos-principales.) For information on his older brother, also an actor, see chap. 5, n. 12. The King, of course, is Louis-Philippe and the Royal Prince his eldest son, the Duc d'Orléans.

than eight; the theater and the dramatic arts complain bitterly about such lateness, which make theatrical evenings impossible. The political world, on the other hand, which does not end its deliberations until six, requires these indispensable delays. Everything could easily be reconciled; legislative sessions would begin at noon and last until four, and thus the table could be set for six o'clock.

"If this continues," said one woman of wit, "we won't be sitting down to dinner until tomorrow."

Women have been formally excluded from gourmet dinners; they must understand nothing about them. Our serious dinners, particularly the political and business ones, offer little opportunity for the deployment of their wit and charms, which always lose something next to such gravity. At a certain age, which they will never acknowledge, women are less hindered by serious conversation; but youth, that gentle adornment to our celebrations, what can youth

do in the middle of these solemn trivialities?

Post-dinner sociability has, among our recent mannerisms, yet another mortal enemy: it is the cigar, which raises a cloud of smoke between men and women.

The toothpick, the waterbowl, and the cigar! Good God! What would M. de Lauzun have said![29]

[29] Probably a reference to Armand-Louis de Gontaut, Duc de Lauzun (later Duc de Biron), who, although known primarily for his command of French forces in the American Revolution, was also celebrated for his gallantry toward women—one of

Our childlike and honest civility is no longer free from a variety of assaults,[30] about which we do not complain; social equality has won out. Formerly, a head of a household, addressing his guests, did not speak to all of them in the same language:

"My dear Duke, might I have the honor of offering you some beef?"

"My dear Countess, would you do me the honor of accepting some beef?"

"My dear Baron, would you be so kind as to take some beef?"

"My lord, allow me to offer you some beef."

"Sir, take some beef."

"Sirs, do you want beef?"

"Sirs, beef."

And finally, to the far end of the table, and showing the plate to the guests, he cries out from afar, "Beef! Beef!"[31]

Designation of places for the guests is a very delicate subject, one on which we refrain from volunteering much of an opinion.

whom was Marie Antoinette—and the dissipation of an immense fortune in his earlier years: "A Don Juan, the incarnation of the frivolous, elegant, blasé society of his time" (E. Jules Méras, "Introduction," *Memoirs of the Duc de Lauzun* [New York: Sturgis & Walton, 1912], vii).

[30] Briffault here uses the phrase "la civilité puérile et honnête," a reference to classic primers on form and etiquette going back to a 1530 treatise by Erasmus, translated from the Latin as *La civilité puerile* and the 1559 text *La civilité puérile et honnête* by Mathurin Cordier, which went through several editions. The title persisted into the nineteenth century, culminating in the popular *La civilité puérile et honnête expliquée par l'oncle Eugène* (1887) by Eugène Plon.

[31] The "head of household" in some variations of this anecdote is the statesman Talleyrand, who apparently also had a "proportional scale" for addressing guests. (See, e.g., Amédée Pichot, *Souvenirs intimes sur M. de Talleyrand* [Paris: Dentu, 1870], 234–235.)

It is necessary, as much as it is possible, to combine the men and women in their alternative places. To the right of the mistress of the house, where the high end of the table begins, the most eminent figure is seated; to the right of the head of the household is designated for the woman to whom the highest honors are due: the placement, to the right and left of the host and hostess, follows in that manner all the way down the line. To avoid confusion, the practice of writing down the names of the guests needs to be adopted; this measure, along with the benefit of positioning each individual without a problem, also identifies the guests and replaces the English fashion of presenting by name each new arrival, and naming those already there to whoever is being presented to them at the same time. What a cacophony these preliminary clarifications would avoid!

Dessert crowns dinner. To fashion a beautiful dessert, you have to be at the same time a confectioner, decorator, painter, architect, ice-cream maker, sculptor, and florist. On every table, it is the most brilliant part of the dinner. Desserts have been known to cost more than 3,000 francs. These splendors are aimed directly at the eye; the true gourmet admires them without touching anything.[32] The brilliance of dessert must not make us forget the cheese; at Neuilly, at the King's table, an officer from the suburb asked for the missing cheese; they gave him some.

[32] Observations in this paragraph were probably drawn from Alexandre-Laurent Grimod de la Reynière, "Calendrier gastronomique," *Les classiques de la table* (1845), 1:197.

We have replaced all the old aphorisms about cheese with this saying: "Cheese completes a good dinner and supplements a bad one."

One of the most eccentric of men was, without exception, Sir Francis, Count of Bridgewater, Lord Egerton, who lived in Paris for such a long time at the Hôtel de Noailles, on the site where the rue d'Algers was constructed.[33]

At a time when the health of Sir Francis allowed him to receive company, his dinner protocol presented, for us, some curious and unusual circumstances. Milord arrived in the drawing room just a moment before dinner, and hardly had he finished with his greetings when the chief steward announced that it was being served. Then Milord positioned himself near the door, and had his guests, one after the other, march past, replying with his own bow to the bowing of each. Servants, in numbers equal to that of the guests, and holding in one hand a silver pitcher and in the other a towel, had them wash up in an adjoining room. Once all were seated at the table, Milord had the dinner menu circulated. This menu was divided by the succession of courses, and included also the catalog of wines being served and the list of the hors d'oeuvres piled up on a supplementary but permanent table. Before the dessert, there was a sort of interlude, where the table was covered with nothing but cheeses and strong beer. Throughout the course of the dinner, all the dishes were brought in sequence before Milord

[33] Briffault does not exaggerate the eccentricity of Francis Egerton, Eighth Earl of Bridgewater, who was especially renowned for the dinner parties he gave his cats and dogs, all dressed in the latest fashions, down to the miniature shoes and boots on their paws (although he was also known as a serious collector of manuscripts, the bulk of which he donated to the British Museum). The Hôtel de Noailles, on the rue Saint-Honoré, was built in 1687 and purchased by the Noailles family in 1711. At the death of Bridgewater in 1829, the property was divided for sale into five separate lots and traversed by the new rue d'Algers.

who, depending on the situation, wielded knife, spoon, or spatula; after which the plate was passed to the chief steward to complete the task begun, or rather indicated, by Milord. If the host wished to honor a guest, he served him himself, before having the dish circulate around the table.[34]

Here are some details about the reception of our ambassador in China, and about the banquet that was given to our legation by the Imperial Commissioner. One of the attachés is speaking:[35]

"Ki-ing, Imperial Commissioner, Viceroy of Canton, prince and a relative of the Emperor, arrived in Macao on September 29, in the afternoon; he rested on the 30th, then came the next day, with great pomp, to make his visit to the residence of the French ambassador, where, the day before, he had been

preceded by his own life-sized portrait. His procession was led by 150 lancers on foot and ended with Manchu horsemen armed with bows and sabers but very poorly mounted. We were all in full uniform, in almost ninety-degree heat. During that first interview, professions of esteem and

<hr>

[34] This anecdote appears verbatim in the 1825 publication *Chronique indiscrète du dix-neuvieme siècle: esquisses contemporaines* by J.-J. Regnaud-Warin, Pierre Lahalle, and J.-B. Bonaventure de Roquefort (Paris: Marchand de Nouveautés. 1825), 152–153.

[35] The description is taken from a letter widely circulated in the European periodical literature of the time. (See, e.g., "Courrier de Paris," *L'illustration, journal universel* 4, no. 90 [Jan. 18, 1845]: 309–310.) The author remains anonymous, although one of the attachés of the legation was the journalist Xavier Raymond, who was also acting as a special envoy from the *Journal des debats.*

friendship were exchanged in profusion. Ki-ing and M. de Lagrené embraced several times.[36]

"Two days later (October 3), at one in the afternoon, we set out to return the visit with which the Imperial Commissioner had honored us. Ki-ing was staying in the pagoda of the village of Wanghia, a short distance from Macao. Along with the embassy staff, out in full force, M. de Lagrené had admitted into his retinue a dozen officers from the French fleet.

"We were all in sedan chairs. After the exchange of compliments, Ki-ing took M. de Lagrené by the hand, and we all entered the dining hall where, among flowers and foliage, a splendid feast served in the Chinese manner awaited us. The organizer of this banquet took care to have forks and spoons placed beside the Chinese chopsticks; but, being men with good social skills, we used the chopsticks almost exclusively. The wines of Champagne, Roussillon, Porto, and Madeira circulated about the table.

"The meal opened with the sweets, then each guest was served a cake taking the form of four Chinese words, signifying a ten-thousand-year friendship between France and China. This hope was greeted with applause. Then began a series of toasts to everyone's health, which followed in such rapid succession that the very health we were toasting was seriously endangered.

"Ki-ing had M. de Lagrené on his left; on his right, Rear Admiral Cécille. Houen, Treasurer-General of the Canton

---

[36] Ki-ing (K'i-yin or Qiying) was an accomplished statesman during the Qing dynasty who negotiated several treaties with Western powers, including the Treaty of Nanking (1842), which ended the first Opium War with Great Britain, and the Treaty of Whampoa. Marie-Melchior-Joseph-Théodore de Lagrené was a politician and diplomat who served in various positions in the foreign service throughout the Restoration and the July Monarchy. In 1843 he led a diplomatic mission to China where, on October 24, 1844, he signed the Treaty of Whampoa, which opened up trade with France and also led to the legalization of Christianity in China.

Province and a mandarin of the first class, was seated to the

left of the ambassador; three other mandarins had taken their places at the table: Ton-lin, one of the forty of Peking's academicians; Tohao, Subprefect of Canton, a large fat Manchu with the manner of a corporal of the municipal guard; Panthin-chen-tin-oua, honorary mandarin, son of an old Hong merchant of Canton who had left him an immense fortune.[37] I found myself placed between

the latter two. As for the academician, he was placed at the other end of the table, and he took it so much upon himself to encourage drinking, that toward the middle of the dinner, he was drunk enough to have to be carried out. This episode gave rise to a host of scenes even more grotesque.

---

[37] Jean-Baptiste Cécille, an admiral active in pursuing French colonial interests in Asia, accompanied Lagrené on his trip to China. "Houen" is probably Huang En-t'ung, a provincial treasurer who counseled Ki-ing during several of his trade missions; "Ton-lin" is likely Chao Tchang-ling, an academician who was a personal counselor to Ki-ing; "Panthin-chen-tin-oua" is probably P'ai Tche-tcheng (original name: Young Tinn Qua), a wealthy merchant who was frequently an intermediary between the Chinese mandarins and foreign officers; "Tohao" may be Tchang Yu-che who was a subprefect at the time and made the initial report to Ki-ing concerning the French arrival at Macao. For more on the events leading up to the Treaty of Whampoa and its participants, see Louis Wei Tsing-Sing, *La politique missionnaire de la France en Chine: 1842–1856* (Paris: Nouvelles Éditions Latines, 1957), 206–237, 245–250. For a contemporary account, see Théophile de Ferrière Le Vayer, *Une ambassade française en Chine: journal de voyage* (Paris: Librairie d'Amyot, 1854).

"Ki-ing was very vocal, he prompted M. de Lagrené to drink, then when he had emptied his glass, he reversed it to show he had drunk it all, and drained the wine into the glasses of his neighbors, who did the same in turn. Among the Chinese, it is a great act of courtesy to take a morsel from the table with the chopsticks and put it into the mouth of the person whom you intend to honor. Ki-ing did it repeatedly with M. de Lagrené and Admiral Cécille; his neighbor, the Manchu, also bestowed upon me this profession of esteem and friendship.

"During the course of the meal, birds' nests were served along with spoon worms, shark fins, sea cucumbers, wild mushrooms, etc., etc., all very good things, I assure you, well seasoned by the port and champagne our hosts served us with the most engaging enthusiasm. My neighbor, the Manchu, repeatedly showed me his full then empty glass, as a kind of provocation; also, as yellow as it had been in its natural state, his complexion took on a far more cheerful purplish color. Before we rose from the table, a Manchurian tea was served, bitter and without sugar. Then we arrived at declarations for the liveliest of friendships. 'China and France have become one!' Ki-ing cried out. Finally, after four hours downing drinks, we separated, completely enchanted with one another."

The Arabian dinner also has its singular ways. A traveler recounts one such meal, an offering of African hospitality, this way:

"After having walked a good part of the day under the blazing African sky, we found ourselves at the door of a Muslim monk, celebrated throughout the country for his holiness and his hospitality. He received us courteously, and offered us a splendid dinner, which also had, for me, some very disagreeable consequences. After the couscous and the mutton prepared in beef fat, two dishes I did not recognize were served: one was a roast that I took for a shoulder of lamb, the other a fried dish I believed to be a vegetable unknown to me. All of it was accompanied by some rolls from a sort of soft russet dough, and I found them to be quite as good as all the rest. A moment afterward, we were served the same vegetable pickled in a salad and also boiled in vinegar. With this last method, it had retained something of its original shape; having taken a complete piece of it, I examined it with care; my stomach quaked, my face turned pale, my heart jumped, and a cold sweat ran down my brow. Alas! Alas! I had just recognized, on this supposed vegetable, legs, wings, antennae, and a head equipped with strong mandibles.... It was a grasshopper. The fried dish, the salad, the boil, and everything, including the rolls, was composed of these insects grilled, boiled, fried, or dried and kneaded into cakes, according to the practice of these barbarous tribes. The monk noticed the terrible disgust these dishes inspired in me when I became aware of their true nature.

"'The Arabs, the Tartars, the Egyptians, and all the peoples of Barbary,' he said to me with some gravity, 'make a considerable business out of these insects, which they consider an excellent nutritional source. They preserve them dried or pickled, and they flood all the markets of North Africa with them. I thought offering them to you would give you some pleasure; but,' he cheerfully added, 'since you don't like grasshopper, you can go back to the shoulder of dog.'

"And with his finger, he indicated to me that excellent roast of which I had already eaten three-quarters. At these last words, the hair on my forehead bristled; unable to handle it any longer, I rose and fled into the garden where I almost died

of indigestion as I cursed the
hospitality of these grasshopper
eaters."[38]

A custom adopted by several
elite tables is to distribute among
the guests the menu, the bill-of-
fare, the program for dinner. It is
a practice followed by the clubs
and the prominent *tables d'hôte*; it

comes to us from Russia. At Russian dinners, the main dishes
are not displayed; the guests see only the dessert, the table
ornaments, and the centerpiece; the courses are served without first being shown.[39]

We will cite as a model the printed menu offered to the
Queen of England by Mr. Staples, the organizer of a banquet, a breakfast given for Her Majesty, on the occasion of
the opening of the new Stock Exchange; it was in exquisite
taste.[40]

---

[38] The source for this anecdote is likely Pierre Boitard, "Les insectes musiciens,"
Musée des familles: lectures du soir 12 (October 1844): 21.

[39] Alexander Kurakin, the Russian ambassador to the French Empire from 1808 to
1812, is generally credited with introducing *service à la russe*, where dishes were
served sequentially directly from the kitchen to the table. This method contrasted
with, and gradually superseded, the traditional *service à la française*, where large
portions of a meal were displayed for guests to admire as they arrived at the table.
Jules Gouffé in his *Le livre de cuisine* (1867) writes in praise of distributing menus
at such private affairs: "It is a result of our modern progress.... The adoption of
service à la russe, for that matter, makes it almost indispensable. Isn't it a true
advantage to be able to prepare in advance and build up reserves of appetite for
various parts of a meal?" (Cited in Barbara K. Wheaton, "Le menu dans le Paris du
XIXe siècle," *À table au XIXe siècle* [Paris: Flammarion, 2001], 97.)

[40] For the contents of the menu, see Chapter 6. The Albion Tavern, where the banquet
was held on October 28, 1844, was managed at the time by John Staples and his
brother Thomas.

On a background of white satin was a steel engraving of a view of the new Exchange, with the Duke of Wellington's statue in the foreground. The list of dishes took up the center, and garlands with the initials V.R. ["Victoria Regina"] in gold and in colors extended down each side. The menu was framed in a rich border of enameled gold, purple, and crimson; a superb fringe, made up of satin, enclosed it all.

Addison cites, in *The Spectator*, an inconceivable example of a stomach's frailties. We will let the patient himself expose the details of his health and dietary habits:[41]

"Accidentally taking into my hand that ingenious discourse written by Sanctorius,[42] I was resolved to direct myself by a scheme of rules, which I had collected from his observations. The learned world are very well acquainted with that gentleman's invention; who, for the better carrying on of his experiments, contrived a certain mathematical chair, which was so artificially hung upon springs, that it would weigh any thing as well as a pair of scales. By this means he discovered how many ounces of his food passed by perspiration, what quantity of it was turned into nourishment, and how much went away by the other channels and distributions of nature.

---

[41] This anecdote, by Joseph Addison, is drawn from issue 25 of *The Spectator* (March 29, 1711). The extract cited here is the original English version, which differs somewhat from the translation Briffault was probably using. For more on Briffault's source and Addison, see chap. 2, n. 48.

[42] Santorio Santorio was a physiologist and physician who taught at the University of Padua from 1611 to 1624. He is celebrated for his experiments in temperature, respiration, and physical weight as well as the many devices he invented, including the "weighing chair," spoken of here by Addison, in which for thirty years he weighed himself, taking account of everything he ate, drank, and excreted.

"Having provided myself with this chair, I used to study, eat, drink, and sleep in it; insomuch that I may be said, for these three last years, to have lived in a pair of scales. I compute myself, when I am in full health, to be precisely two hundred weight, falling short of it about a pound after a day's fast, and exceeding it as much after a very full meal; so that it is my continual employment, to trim the balance between these two volatile pounds in my constitution. In my ordinary meals I fetch myself up to two hundred weight and a half pound; and if after having dined I find myself fall short of it, I drink just so much small beer, or eat such a quantity of bread, as is sufficient to make my weight. In my greatest excesses I do not transgress more than the other half pound; which, for my health's sake, I do the first Monday in every month. As soon as I find myself duly poised after dinner, I walk till I have perspired five ounces and four scruples; and when I discover, by my chair, that I am so far reduced, I fall to my books, and study away three ounces more. As for the remaining parts of the pound, I keep no account of them. I do not dine and sup by the clock, but by my chair, for when that informs me my pound of food is exhausted I conclude my self to be hungry, and lay in another with all diligence. In my days of abstinence I lose a pound and an half, and on solemn fasts am two pound lighter than on other days in the year.

"I allow myself, one night with another, a quarter of a pound of sleep within a few grains more or less; and if upon my rising I find that I have not consumed my whole quantity, I take out the rest in my chair. Upon an exact calculation of what I expended and received the last year, which I always register in a book, I find the medium to be two hundred weight, so that I cannot discover that I am impaired one ounce in my health during a whole twelvemonth. And yet, Sir, notwithstanding this my great care to ballast myself equally every day, and to keep my body in its proper poise, so it is that I find myself in a sick and languishing condition. My complexion is grown very sallow, my pulse low, and my body hydropical."

A Russian dinner. It was at the home of a prince; there were forty guests; after having crossed, between two rows of richly dressed servants, several front rooms, the persons invited arrived at the picture gallery where they were received by the host; none among them was announced. At six they headed into another gallery; the table was covered with a magnificent centerpiece, overloaded with fruits and flowers. The courses did not appear. When everyone was seated, the dishes were presented every five minutes or so. A very efficient chief steward, at the buffet, skillfully carved the quarter of beef from the Ukraine, the veal from Archangel, the sturgeon from the Volga, and the turkey from Périgord. All the plates were duplicated, there were numerous servants, everything was served hot and promptly.

The courses were so many, it would have been difficult to replace for each of them the silver and silver-plated utensils. The staff, in order to move forward faster, did not wash the settings, but were content to dry them off; women were seen defending their settings from the servants, and thus escaping the danger of using their neighbors' forks.

Vintage wines were present from the beginning of the meal; a bottle, which the chief steward placed before a guest, revealed to him that he should deliver toasts with the wine contained therein, that its fine taste had been recommended.

The great Russian dinners are almost always accompanied by loud music, which stifle conversation; no discussion is possible.

Spring fruits and vegetables are very much sought-after by the Muscovite tables; entire trees appear at dessert; mention is made of a cherry tree, served in winter, loaded with fruit that was plucked off of it. This novelty cost 1,800 rubles. Almost all of these marvels have no taste. An ambassador, who had been served asparagus in the month of December, said, "My eyes confirm that I am eating asparagus, but my palate doesn't agree."[43]

On important feast days, the Malabar princes, and especially the Samorin of Calcutta, hold banquets and invite the entire country. The profusion of dishes, rather than their fine quality, makes these meals very expensive. It is not unusual to see guests overload their stomachs so much that they die from it. This occurrence is regarded only as a matter of foolishness; and in praise of the magnificence of a feast, the number of persons who died from it is tallied.[44]

Dinner cannot escape seasonal influences. It flourishes in winter; it curses the spring that sends it out into the countryside; during summer, withdrawing into the great houses, it lives off of spinach and pigeons to repair winter's breaches; in autumn it expects and welcomes the offerings of the hunt.

[43] These paragraphs, beginning with "A Russian dinner," summarize an extract from Carême's *L'Art de la cuisine française au dix-neuvième siècle* that appeared as "Un Grand Diner à Saint-Pétersbourg" in *Les classiques de la table* (1845), 2:603–606.

[44] The origin of this anecdote can be found in Jean-Henri Grose, *Voyage aux Indes orientales*, trans. Philippe Hernandez (Paris: Desaint et Saillant, 1758), 352–358, although a passage identical to that of Briffault's appears in Élie-Catherine Fréron, *L'année littéraire, année 1758* (Amsterdam: Lambert, 1758), 2: 282. "Samorin" or "Zamorin" was the hereditary title used by the Hindu rulers in power on the Malabar Coast from the twelfth to eighteenth centuries.

• V •

PEOPLE WHO DO NOT DINE

A man of wit, on a day of forced fasting, parodied some lines from Racine like this:

To the birds in the nest, he gives some feed,
His bounty stops at the authors we read.[1]

The number of individuals who get up in the morning not knowing if they will be dining in the evening is quite high in

Paris, but more considerable still is the number of those who do not dine at all.

This distress—its existence hardly suspected by people with full stomachs—strikes not only those who have been reduced to this extremity by vice, idleness, or debility; those kinds always find some sort of feed somewhere; they get it from the pity they are not

---

[1] The original is from *Athalie* (1691; Act 1, scene i): "Aux petits des oiseaux il donne la pâture,/ Et sa bonté s'étend sur toute la nature." The parody was attributed to Léon Gozlan by Maxime Du Camp in 1883 in his *Souvenirs littéraires* (Paris: Editions Complexe, 2002), 24.

ashamed to provoke, or else they know how to capture it
through force, dexterity, or fraud; if needed they will look for
it in the refuse by the side of the road and compete with the
stray dogs for it. These miseries do not belong to the swindler
and rogue who look to their impudence and appearance for
their daily bread, and who would rather carry away the restaurateur's place settings than go without dinner. The hungry who
are good and decent are also around, and their strategies are
fertile and ingenious. Addison[2] speaks of a man talented
enough to obtain three dinners a week by leaving his hosts with
the glimmer of a hope for an inheritance, and three additional
ones by getting himself invited to dinners he knew were being
prepared for some friends. The vaudeville stage, maliciously
clever at birth but then having become cruel, mocked without
pity those poor wretches who seek out their well-being without harming that of others.

Literature, the arts, everything dedicated to the worship of
thought and the imagination supplies Paris's emaciated population with an enormous contingent. Hunger, felt so often by the
talented, lays its hand also on genius. In view of the high wages
some works of art and intelligence bring, the misery of artists,
writers, and poets of times past are mocked and made light of:
these disgraces are relegated today to the realm of the abstract;
alas, they are only too real; to understand fully how much sorrow
lies within that Parisian limbo, you have to have passed through it.

Everything bumps against everything else in this city of ex-
tremes: indigestion and hunger stand next to each other. Don't
say anymore that Chatterton, Gilbert, and Malfilâtre are not to

---

[2] Briffault also cites passages from Joseph Addison, the eighteenth-century English
essayist, extensively in chapters 2 and 4.

be found among us.[3] Yesterday they were in your midst, and you let them die of hunger!

Poverty, when it attaches itself to those whom it has shaped early on in its forge, has also prepared their hearts for this condition; moreover, the poor come to the aid of the poor, just as the poet has said, "They love one another."[4]

If, within the man whom vice has driven to this extremity, all noble, sensitive, and generous instincts are extinguished, the physical suffering alone remains. If it so happens that a liberal and higher education had fertilized the seed of noble qualities; if it so happens that such a disposition had been

---

[3] The English poet Thomas Chatterton, now known primarily as the author of a series of faked medieval poems, died at the age of seventeen of starvation and self-inflicted arsenic poisoning in a Holburn garret in 1770. A popular play on his life, produced in 1835, was written by the French Romantic poet Alfred de Vigny. Having gained several pensions at the time of his death at the age of twenty-nine in 1780, the poet and satirist Nicolas-Joseph-Laurent Gilbert was for some time wrongly thought to have died in a state of poverty and madness. The poet Jacques-Charles-Louis Clinchamps de Malfilâtre died in 1767 at the age of thirty-four, reduced to poverty and hounded by creditors.

[4] The poet Pierre-Jean de Béranger was perhaps the most popular songwriter of the early nineteenth century. This particular line, "Ils s'aiment entre eux," comes from the 1812 piece "Les gueux" (The Beggars).

enlarged by study, and that talent had heated it up with its invigorating flame, and that it had been suddenly overtaken by this scourge; these precious elements, rejected by the intellectual world, are incapable of operating in the material order; they fall and are stifled by hardship's embrace and an inexorable necessity. Among the ardent young who rush to Paris from every part of France, how many lives have been thus miserably obliterated by this slow agony that exhausts the forces of body and soul and kills those who can no longer withstand these maladies.

Without doubt, a portion of these misfortunes must be attributed to wayward thinking, fatal illusions, and vain error; but isn't there then any way to snatch these foolish unfortunates from this horrible situation?

Old before their time, pale, worn down by grief, despair, and privation, they wander here and there, casting covetous glances over this city so rich in all things and so sparing of every particle of that wealth of which it is packed so full. Surely, one word would save them; there are still benevolent and kind hearts; but how could that word be spoken without awakening all that pride which nature and education have placed in their own hearts?

They suffer in silence; they fear even to arouse pity, and quite often it is under the appearance of material comfort that these torments are felt. This is a frequent circumstance in Paris among those expecting from intellectual work an existence they cannot obtain through manual labor.

The situation of unemployed workers is just as worthy of interest as that of these unfortunates.

The so very numerous gambling catastrophes drastically
increased the number of sudden accidents that removed any
chance for sustenance for the unhappy players. For these abrupt
misfortunes there was in each gambling house a charitable cash-
box called "A relief kit for the asphyxiated, drowned, or wounded."
    As for the bohemian hordes,[5] vagabond shadows without
refuge or bread, who haul, pick up, and discharge the muddy

course of debauchery, society has only
one duty to fulfill against their wicked
thoughts and criminal intentions: the
right of self-defense.
    By bizarre contrast, it is in the most
opulent places that these veterans of
Parisian misery can be seen to gather,
loafing about and on display. Chodruc-
Duclos left the galleries and garden of
the Palais-Royal only to go to the boulevard des Italiens and the Chaussée-
d'Antin. All the disciples of this Diogenes followed that
example;[6] these bands of beggars can be seen infesting the
promenades: the Palais-Royal is full of them.[7]

---

[5] Although in Briffault's time *Bohémien* or *Bohème* was coming into use to describe an
impoverished artist (largely due to Henri Murger's *Scènes de la vie de Bohème*, the
first installment of which appeared in *Le corsaire* in 1845), the term primarily
defined a vagabond outside of society, often one with criminal connections. (See
Dictionnaire de l'Académie française, sixième édition [Paris: Firmin Didot, 1835],
1:196–197.)

[6] Émile Chodruc-Duclos was a celebrated beggar who frequented the Palais-Royal
during the Restoration. Several books were written about him, as well as an
apocryphal memoir after his death in 1842 and a melodrama in 1850. He was
occasionally compared to Diogenes, the Greek philosopher who purportedly spent
his life in poverty in search of an honest man.

[7] For more on the Palais-Royal, see chap. 10, n. 21.

Another class, which we do not know quite how to charac-
terize, is made up of those young women, full of crazy ideas
and precocious perversity, who renounce work to devote
themselves to the liberties of pleasure. With them, everything
is uncertain; it is true that their heedlessness knows nothing of
planning or suffering. When the sad little girl, in her days of
solitude and abandonment, has nibbled on her last crust,
cracked her last nut, visited the depths of her jelly jar, and
eaten her last prune; when the poor little thing, this improvi-
dent grasshopper,[8] has been sought out by another, her female
neighbor, she then finds herself in tears, because she is hungry,
this child who's left her mother. So a companion comes to see
her, so they tell one another of their mutual distress; so some
others turn up, all also in search of their board; the playful
troupe dries her tears, bursts out in laughter, and thinks further only of devising a good sort of scheme that is likely to get
them a bite of dinner.

They consult one another to find out if they have all exhausted their credit in the neighborhood; those who still have
some arrows in their quiver venture to go out to order a dinner
at a nearby eating house, asking quite clearly to have the bill
brought along with the dishes. The cook's assistant, usually just
a boy, approaches with confidence; from the window and the
top of the stairs, they lie in wait for him, they catch sight of
him, they signal to him. No sooner does he reach a specified
spot than he is surrounded, each taking a dish; the one who
ordered the dinner grabs the bill, looks as if she's adding it up,

---

[8] An allusion to Jean de La Fontaine's seventeenth-century fable "La cigale et la
fourmi," usually translated as "The Grasshopper and the Ant."

and puts her hand in her pocket when one of her companions cries out: "There's no bread!"

"Excuse me, ladies," says the boy, "but I did bring some."

At this point an argument breaks out, during which the company takes flight, and when the grieving assistant asks for his dishes back, they are returned to him only in pieces broken at his feet.

The damage is paid for later, at a more fortunate time, with a price that settles all complaints.

Another time, in a house on the rue Neuve-Saint-Georges,[9] Miss Amanda, on coming downstairs, overheard the second-story maid say to the concierge:

"We're having people over for dinner. I'm going to order a vol-au-vent."[10]

This welcome news is immediately carried up into the garrets; from five to six o'clock lookouts are posted on the ground, first, and second floors. The vol-au-vent arrives, it is allowed to climb up the stairs, escaping notice from the concierge; on the staircase, it meets up with a young and pretty maid who seizes it before the attendant carrying it has had the time to recognize her, and from above someone cries out to him: "It's fine!"

---

[9] Opened in 1824, the rue Neuve-Saint-Georges was designated in 1846 as an extension of the rue Saint-Georges. In the Ninth Arrondissement near Notre Dame de Lorette, the street and its environs were known to attract the demimonde, and Balzac had already installed several of his fictional courtesans (Suzanne du Val-Noble, Esther Gobseck, et al.) in "une charmante maison de la rue Saint-Georges": "There are in Paris some houses whose function does not change, and this one had already supported the lifestyles of seven courtesans." ("Les comédiens sans le savoir," *La comédie humaine* [Paris: Plon, 1846], 10: 206.)

[10] Vol-au-vent is a rounded container of puff pastry, filled with either savory or sweet ingredients, that, depending on its size, can be served either as an hors d'oeuvre or an entrée.

The vol-au-vent, thus confiscated is devoured in an instant, leaving the dinner on the second floor in a state of anticipation that distresses the head of the household, his wife, his guests, his children, and his servants; while the confusion unfolds, those beneath the rooftops are inwardly laughing, licking their lips.

Against these uncertainties, the poor girls have some shelter. Known throughout the Parisian world, he is an old voluptuary who keeps a charitable table for gallantry reduced to desperation; a dinner, lower than mediocre and put together like those of Sir Harpagon,[11] welcomes the suffering bellies. His table is well known, it is extremely popular, and he

[11] Harpagon, the miser in Molière's *L'avare* (1668), is adept at cutting corners, including when obliged to prepare a dinner for his fiancée in Act 3.

expects to see there women once exalted by fortune; it costs him only a dinner to attract the affection and humanity of the most splendid beauties. It is a foretaste of the beatitude promised to us by heaven for the price of a glass of water given in its name. Actors and writers are subject to these bouts of scarcity. The elder Lepeintre, Martainville, and Monrose were leaving a cold bath, with only forty centimes to appease an atrocious hunger.[12] They were walking with heads down; Martainville's eyes catch sight of legs evidently belonging to a young pastry cook, those apprentices given the name of *patronet*; he straightens up, and he perceives distinctly a leg of lamb leaving the oven, carried by this charming boy on a tin-plated tray; he abruptly confronts him:

"Ah, here you are at last!" he cries out to him. "And the biscuits, where are they?

The boy stands there, dumbfounded.

"Go find them, fool!"

The kid runs in one direction, the highway robbers take off in another and seek refuge at a wine merchant's.

We'll cite some examples of heroic resignation. In order to satisfy a passion for brandy, an educated man, but one whom a state of permanent disorder had driven into the depths of misery, had resigned himself to dine only once every two days, sometimes without the certainty of being able to do even that. If, in the interim between these dinners, he was invited to one,

---

[12] All three of these actors—Charles-Emmanuel Lepeintre, Alphonse-Louis-Dieudonné Martainville, and Monrose (Claude-Louis-Séraphin Barizain)—began their careers at the turn of the nineteenth century at the Théâtre des Jeunes Artistes. Lepeintre the elder (his younger brother was also an actor) was perhaps the best known, "one of our best actors, particularly remarkable in the role of Harlequin" (Girault de Saint-Fargeau, *Les quarante-huit quartiers de Paris* [Paris: Blanchard, 1850], 264).

he boldly replied, "It's not my day. I will not eat. I will accept all the brandy you're willing to offer me." When he happened to miss his dinner on the designated day, he looked in the mirror and delivered this little monologue:

"Eyes look good; color's not bad; the hat fits; I've not dined yesterday, I will not dine today, perhaps not tomorrow... tra la la... la la," he sang, while dancing a jig before the mirror.

He sometimes said, "You can go to bed without supper, but without breakfast, that's another matter."

This was his honorary award.

A medical student lived only on bread during the course of his studies. One day, lacking a loaf, he recalled that, the previous evening, along the boulevard des Invalides, he had thrown away a morsel of bread he no longer wanted; he went to look for it, and did not find it. The thought that perhaps another person, as hungry as he was, had picked it up consoled him, and he suffered without complaint. He became one of our most distinguished professors and dean of one of the nation's medical schools.

Whatever the perspective, humorous or magnanimous, under which these events are viewed, it is nonetheless deplorable that, in the capital of a great country, there is such suffering. Men have been known to deliver themselves over to the law, admitting to thefts committed out of despair, and exchanging freedom without bread for prison with meager rations.

• VI •

BREAKFAST

If it is true that there had been four meals formerly—and that
they still can be found in some provinces—it needs to be acknowledged that our forefathers' stomachs were, like their
chests, robust, and that their diet would overwhelm our frail
bodies like their heavy armor breaks our limbs. As we have
mentioned, since the Revolution of 1789, only two of the four
meals from former times remain: breakfast[1] and dinner, and it
can still be said that dinner is the only serious one.

There was a day when breakfast had a Titan's ambition; it
wanted to depose dinner, and, a new Hecatonchire,[2] it raised
one table atop another to clamber up to the heavens; this was
under the Empire, when that shapeless and bizarre hybrid,
called the *breakfast buffet*,[3] was given birth and grew up, a
meal as barbaric as its name.

---

[1] Briffault titles this chapter "Le Déjeuner," and although its meaning was even then
shifting, it primarily signified in the author's time "the morning meal." (See, e.g.,
Dictionnaire de l'Académie française: sixth edition [Paris: Firmin Didot, 1835],
I: 500.) A more substantial "breakfast," later in the morning or in the early afternoon,
was referred to in a variety of ways, including *déjeuner-dîner, déjeuner à la fourchette*,
and *déjeuner dînatoire* (see below for the last one).

[2] In Greek mythology the Hecatonchires were three powerful giants who were generally
considered to be on the side of Zeus in the war between the upstart Olympians and
the old generation Titans in the epic battle for control of the universe.

[3] "Brunch" would also be an accurate translation for Briffault's *déjeuner dînatoire*, and
although it would have probably sounded equally "barbaric" to the author's ear, it
would also have been an anachronistic usage for 1846.

122

We have never really understood what was intended by this impudent custom, placed between two traditional habits, apparently to destroy the both of them without retaining anything from the one or the other. The breakfast buffet was no longer a breakfast; it still was not a dinner.

This meal was the delight of the chief officials of the Imperial bureaucracy, who invented it to take full and free enjoyment of their evening pleasures; some claimed that these arrangements were adopted so that the evening hours could be devoted to the theater without interruption. Whatever the case, it passed from the government offices into the world.

To begin the breakfast buffet, you usually sat down at the table around one o'clock. There was no soup, no boiled beef; the table was covered with cold entrees and cold hors-d'oeuvres; there was only one service, with everything on display.[4] The lamb chops, the blood and other sausages, immediately followed the oysters, which always began the meal. Nothing was more pitiful than this table without candles; if the guests remained calm and quiet, there was no gaiety; if they livened up, the blush of drunkenness, which under lights gives new life to a face, was hideous.

The women—and we are speaking of those who count for something in society—rarely took part in these breakfasts; the meal lasted until nightfall. For some, it was a true misfortune; it disrupted an entire day; for others it was simply tiresome. One of the most serious drawbacks of these arrangements was that the guests, upon leaving the table, were tossed back into a world that was just beginning dinner; their frustration was extreme; and for several hours, the theaters not yet being open, they wandered about aimlessly.

[4] *En ambigu.* See chap. 2, n. 60.

In general, a good deal of trouble was taken to be cheerful at these breakfast buffets, which have been disavowed completely.

We do not know how it has happened that our daily commentators have attributed almost all the dining anecdotes from the Imperial court to breakfast. We have retained only one of them, whose philosophical side has always captivated us. There was a breakfast at the home of Duroc,[5] the Grand Marshal of the Palace; artichokes were being eaten; some put sauce on them, others preferred them with oil. Napoleon, upon arrival, took a petal that he ate with neither sauce nor oil, salt nor pepper; all the others having breakfast expressed their admiration, and the most considerable among them cried out: "What a great man! You do nothing like everyone else!"

And that is what we have read, very seriously presented, in several books.[6]

From the Restoration, we know only one thing about breakfast; it is that Louis XVIII himself did the honors at the meal. Each morning a bowl of soft-boiled eggs was served at the king's table, which he offered himself to the invited guests; this was also the only meal where someone not of the royal family could sit down at the king's table.

At the Tuileries, there are no longer breakfasts; this meal is no more than a simple snack that all take at their leisure.[7]

At the homes of some ministers and some high officials, in those mansions full of aristocratic pride and opulence, and

---

[5] Géraud-Christophe-Michel Duroc was one of Napoleon's most trusted generals, and as *grand maréchal du palais* he supervised the Emperor's security as well as many of the household duties and responsibilities in his residences.

[6] This anecdote probably derives from Paul-Louis Courier's *Pamphlet des pamphlets* (1824). (See *Oeuvres de P.L. Courier* [Paris: Firmin Didot, 1861], 237–238.)

[7] The Tuileries Palace was the official Paris residence for Louis-Philippe, as it was for previous monarchs.

among the prosperous bourgeoisie, breakfast is still served, with less embellishment than formerly, but quite comfortably. These honors are reserved for people who, although desired as guests, cannot be invited to dinner. Sometimes breakfast is a business meal, an appointed meeting, a confidential encounter; the heads of the households usually see to the service themselves, but almost without laying a hand on it. All the senior political staff of the Restoration went out for the famous breakfast at the Café Desmares;[8] all of the editors of the newspaper, *Le déjeuner*, were brought into the Académie.[9]

When young men—that is to say persons who are unmarried and live without a household—take breakfast at home, they eat just a little, alone, quickly, and from off a tray. Outside, together, they eat well, a lot, with care, and take a long time.

In Paris there still exist a few fine breakfasts, but only in restaurants; we will be speaking about them in their proper place. At the theatrical matinees at the Castellane mansion, for breakfast a full and complete post-ball supper was held onstage.[10]

[8] "The Café Desmares...needs to be mentioned as a political café under the Restoration. Breakfast and dinner were served there. Chief officers of the palace guards and the division heads of the various ministries along the Seine's left bank were especially representative of its morning clientele" (Louis-Désiré Véron, *Mémoires d'un bourgeois de Paris* [Paris: Norvelle, 1856], 3:19).

[9] In his contribution "Déjeuner" for the *Dictionnaire de la conversation et de la lecture* (Paris: Belin-Mendar, 1835), 19:465–66—from which Briffault may have drawn some of his details here—the journalist and dramatist Maurice Ourry mentioned that the editors of the small satirical journal *Le déjeuner* were condemned to deportation in 1797. The preceding sentence in the article was devoted to the Société des Déjeuniers, a "literary coterie to which several members of the Académie française belonged and which opened its doors to more than one member who wished to be brought in."

[10] Initially owned by John Law, who began construction in 1718, this sumptuous mansion on rue de Faubourg Sainte-Honoré was purchased in 1829 by Comte

Breakfast is the preferred meal for the military, whose customary morning activities sharpen the appetite at an early hour; they make a wide use of it, and the leadership gladly presides over the morning table; high-ranking officers almost all have an excellent reputation in this respect. The late General Pajol gave remarkable breakfasts.[11]

The middle class invariably makes its breakfast from the remains of dinner.

The laboring classes, the workers, gladly eat in the morning; it is one of their major meals; a warm dish is necessary for them; several among them, to save on cost, buy fruit or ham and sausages, or carry cold meat with their bread, which they start to eat as they walk. There are packs of emigrants who come from the provinces to Paris just to eat the hams, the sausages, and the white bread!

Breakfast is the linkage for several kinds of business relationships; at Bercy,[12] at the vintners' warehouses, and around the central markets and exchanges, contractors and builders close no deals without breakfast.

Jules de Castellane, who held there some of the finest balls and *fêtes* throughout the July Monarchy. In 1835 a theater was built inside the mansion where both amateur and professional performances were produced. (See, especially, the chapter "Jules de Castellane" in Anne Martin-Fugier, *La vie élégante ou la formation du Tout-Paris: 1815–1848* [Paris: Fayard, 1990].)

[11] Pierre-Claude Pajol served as a cavalry commander during the Revolution and under Napoleon. Dismissed by the Bourbons, he later played an important role in the July Revolution and the overthrow of Charles X.

[12] For Bercy, see chap.1, n. 11.

The varieties of breakfast, without being of any great significance, are quite numerous.

Breakfast sets in motion the awakening of Paris, from the concierge's quarters below to the attic above: the morning visits at the grocer, the chatting around the dairy lady, and the housekeepers so busy over monsieur's coffee, and the old women shouting, and the little dogs barking; for an hour or two, it is a peculiar turmoil of movement, words, squabbles, and disputes.

Breakfast at the legal offices is also an important affair. The senior clerk goes for breakfast at the nearby café; during this time, the junior clerk, the usual supplier, visits the pork butcher and the fruit vendor, collecting the common provisions, from which he deducts his tithe: he always has a portfolio into which he slips several slices of sausage. And what a

variety of foodstuffs, from the acute triangle of Brie cheese to
the sausage grilled on the stove, to the stately slice of ham,
sparkling with aspic as if adorned with yellow, transparent
gemstones.

As for the owner of the firm, he has fulfilled his obligation
when the servant has brought the four pound loaf of bread and
the bottle of wine to the premises. These legal breakfasts have
a hierarchy; the notaries are more generous than the solicitors,
and breakfasts are better during the first trial than at the
appeal; at the bailiff's hardly any breakfast is taken; and there
is none at all at the barrister's.[13]

The mysterious secrets of breakfast have neither the charm
nor the attractions we have found in the boudoirs of the din-
ner-hour; some consist only of delights, others know only dep-
rivation; it is the champagne flûte against the student's or temporary clerk's glass of water; a breath of fresh air for some, for
others a hope for some dinner.

For artists, breakfast is the exception rather than the rule;
they love it not as a customary activity, but as a piece of good
fortune. At their homes, the pleasures of the table are always
prodigious.

---

[13] It may be useful to clarify the hierarchy of the legal professions mentioned here:
"notaries" (les notaires) were lawyers—appointed by the Ministry of Justice and
limited in number—who offered legal advice and drafted contracts, largely in
matters of property, family, and corporate law; "solicitors" (les avoués), who were
also limited in number, handled procedural matters and prepared cases for trial,
but did not appear in court; "bailiffs" (les huissiers) were extra-judicial agents who
served papers and enforced court decrees; "barristers" (les avocats) were alone
entitled to litigate a case in court but did not appear as attorneys of record. (For a
contemporary discussion of these professions, see "Account of the Various
Ministerial Offices Attached to the French Court," Law Magazine [London:
Saunders and Benning, 1830], 4: 240–251.)

Just beyond the Luxembourg Gardens, toward rue de l'Ouest,[14] was a vast sculptor's studio, fully furnished with fragments, sketches, and constructions; you climbed a narrow open stairwell to a small roost, a veritable nest of boards, which was the master's bedroom. With the exception of a private room, quite prettily furnished, everything was of a perfect simplicity. Occasionally, the studio—I was going to say the depot—was transformed into a banquet hall. At that time, like in those Flemish weddings in Teniers' paintings,[15] there was a long table loaded with courses; made up of planks positioned on trestles, this improvised table needed to be sturdy, so heavy was the mass it had to support. There, in no particular order, everything marvelous the most knowledgeable of kitchens could create was on display: cold and iced items in honor of the most illustrious chefs, admirable poultry, pâtés, veritable monuments of art and good taste, pyramids of the finest fruit, castles of ices, all the miracles of oven and pantry. A service of formidable appearance, entrées of fish, game, and venison appeared sizzling, making places for themselves. All around the studio an encircling ring of bottles of every shape and decoration dominated. Dishware and silverware, all the bright and clean table service fell into that beautiful disorder that is the merit of imaginative works; vestiges from every century were there; not a single piece resembled another one.

Twenty or so guests, each according to his fancy, gathered around this succulent arrangement; the finest names in art and

[14] In 1868 the rue de l'Ouest Briffault knew in the Sixth Arrondissement turned into a continuation of the rue d'Assas. The current rue de l'Ouest is now in the Fourteenth, near the Gare Montparnasse.
[15] David Teniers the Younger, a prolific seventeenth-century painter, was a master of several genres, including peasant scenes, one of which, *Peasant Wedding* (1650), now hangs in the Hermitage.

letters happened to be assembled there, celebrating together behind closed doors. Unexpected scenes were varied and frequent; sometimes a long procession filed past, and all returned to sit down with a treasured bottle in hand; there followed invocations to the statues observing us, the *Child with a Goat*, who, to our eyes, was laughing; a *Bacchante* and her little satyr, ever drawing her closer toward us, then a praying *Virgin*; around these works, anthems and libations were pouring forth; after that came songs and refrains and some infernal melodies; then the return to the table and the careful chatting in undertones, as if coming from the previous century. The tales, the freight of the studio, so true and so lively, the comic scenes, all the mad ideas that a frenzied gaiety can inspire, completed the entertainment. O Garraud! If you are reading these lines, my good friend, now that life is for us a little more tranquil and far from all that noise that amused us so, accept my best wishes for the fulfillment of that future we promised for you during those celebrations.[16]

We do not know if these studio breakfasts belong to the category of breakfast buffet; they lasted from noon through to the next day, to two or three o'clock, in the afternoon.

Here are some monstrosities, nameless and without a family.

---

[16] Gabriel-Joseph Garraud is best known today for his statue of René Descartes, one of the *hommes illustres*, sculpted between 1853 and 1857, for the Cour Napoléon at the Palais du Louvre. But he was also an active contemporary of Briffault, having shown work at several of the annual salons: "His debut, *Hercule délivrant Prométhée* (Hercules Freeing Prometheus), earned him a medal at the 1838 salon. He then showed *Une jeune fille jouant avec une chèvre* (A Young Girl Playing with a Goat), 1839; the *Vierge et l'Enfant* (Virgin and Child)...1840; a *Bacchante faisant l'éducation d'un jeun satyre* (Bacchante Educating a Young Satyr), 1844" (A. Perrault-Dabot, *L'art en Bourgogne* [Paris: Laurens, 1894], 247).

The *Journal des chasseurs* gave a hunt breakfast; among other things and under a considerable variety of flavors and forms, an entire deer was eaten there; at dessert, the animal was presented mounted and stuffed.[17]

Something singular is happening in regard to breakfast; while the newest English fashion took from us the breakfast buffet—what they were calling *déjeuner à la française*—our morning customs were seduced by the tea, warm breads, fresh eggs, toasts, anchovies, sandwiches, shrimp, and the wine-less breakfast of the English.

The breakfast offered for the Queen of England at the opening of the Royal Exchange was entirely French; here is the menu, provided by the Albion Tavern:[18] roast chicken, game pâtés, Westphalian hams, beef à la George IV, roast partridges, larded capons, lamb, roast pheasants, tongues, barons of beef, chicken galantines, cutlets

[17] The meal Briffault refers to here is probably the banquet given by the *Journal des chasseurs* at the restaurant Véfour in honor of St. Hubert, the patron saint of hunters. A report on the feast and an engraving of the deer mounted on the table can be found in the November 30, 1844, edition of *L'illustration, journal universel* (4, no. 92, 196–197—the drawing also appears in Aron, *Le mangeur du XIXe siècle*, plate I, between pages 128 and 129). The *Journal*, the most important hunting journal of its time, was founded by Léon Bertrand and published from 1836 to 1870.

[18] The reference here is to the meal held at the Albion Tavern on the reopening, following a disastrous fire, of the Royal Exchange by Queen Victoria on October 28, 1844. The Albion, on Aldersgate Street, was celebrated for its large banquets given by societies, corporations, and public officials. (See, e.g., Henry Leach, "The Heart of Things," *Chambers Journal: Sixth Series, 1906–1907* [Edinburgh: Chambers, 1907], 10:383.) The menu for the breakfast was published in the November 2, 1844, issue of *The London Illustrated News* (282).

with cucumber, lobster mayonnaise, chicken salads, *petits pâtés à la reine*, sweetbreads *à la romaine*, lamb ballotines, filets of sole *à la provençale*, shrimp, salads, French cakes, apricot nougats, aspics, Chantilly meringues, compotes, apple conserves, rhubarb *à la régence*, fruit jellies, almond pastries, pineapples, hothouse grapes, pears, dried fruits, ice creams.[19]

The time for breakfast extends from eight o'clock in the morning to two in the afternoon; as with the dinner hour, the more it moves up into the higher social regions, the further away it moves from morning. A disadvantage of breakfast is that it weighs down the body and thickens the mind, at a time when business affairs and transactions have need of both; it also gives to the mouth a winey breath that can compromise

[19] Not all of these dishes are readily identifiable, and terms like *à la régence* (in the fashion of the Regency), *à la romaine* (in the Roman fashion), and *à la provençale* (in the fashion of Provençe—although this preparation usually includes olive oil, garlic, and tomatoes) vary depending on the chef and main ingredients. *Petits pâtés à la reine,* however, probably refers to *bouchée à la reine,* a small pastry shell filled with minced vegetables or meat, and Chantilly meringue is usually an ice of whipped cream and egg whites. A galantine is generally deboned meat, fish, or poultry, stuffed, poached, decorated with aspic, and served cold, and a ballotine is, basically, a galantine that is braised, roasted, or poached, and often tied to preserve its shape and served warm.

the most established reputation for sobriety. There is always a degree of imprudence in a heavy breakfast.

The current state of breakfast in France has been summed up and judged by this exclamation that escaped in frustration from a celebrated expert: "Today, we don't even know how to take breakfast!"[20]

[20] The quote was probably taken from the section "Déjeuner" in *Les classiques de la table* ([1845] 2:342), probably written by Joseph Roques, a botanist and physician who was a friend of the Marquis de Cussy and Brillat-Savarin. (See, e.g., *Les classiques de la table* [1845], 2:361).

• VII •

LUNCHEON

The snack between meals is no more; but the contempt directed against breakfast is often punished during the day by a weary stomach; an irritating need resembling a lingering torment then ensues. It is at such times that fine carriages halt outside the doors of famous pastry shops, where women can be seen surrendering to those cravings for which they would be ashamed if they knew how fatal this gluttony is to their charms. We have noticed that the more thin and delicate a woman is, the more she stuffs herself with pastries, sweets, and fortified wines. Be assured also that any man who flings himself at these plates is a frail and puny being. Women who respect themselves should leave such inclinations to those who do not, and for whom they are most appropriate.

In England these transitional meals, which are taken at home, are called "luncheons"; the word is assimilating with difficulty into France, yet it is beginning to be used. One of the most cheerful of French sub-prefects, when he had the honor of being a journalist, was sent to London on the occasion of the Queen of England's coronation.[1] The entire aristocracy

---

[1] Queen Victoria's coronation took place on June 28, 1838, in Westminster Abbey following a lengthy procession from Buckingham Palace. The correspondent mentioned here by Briffault may have been François-Auguste Romieu, an acquaintance of Briffault, an occasional journalist, and an accomplished *viveur*; in

of the three realms[2] was confined within Westminster to await the hour of the ceremony; the dress was magnificent, gleaming with diamonds and precious stones; all the titled women were garlanded with their family crests. Everyone waited a considerable time for the Queen's arrival, and the coronation then lasted for several hours. Toward the middle of the day, according to the account of the French reporters, a restless movement arose among that resplendent multitude, and all the blonde miladies could be seen drawing from the pockets of their gowns of silk, of gold brocade, of silver and velvet, rosewood boxes, the kind used for pressing gloves: these small accessories held sandwiches in thin strips—containing between two slices of bread a slice of ham—that they bit into with those great white teeth seen on the other side of the channel. Following that, each lady took out an ornate flask and drank straight from it, not without a burst of laughter before, during, and after each operation; this was a bit of "sherry"; and, as our official historian[3] points out, "sherry" is a local wine a little stronger than our brandy.

During that great day of the coronation, the correspondents from the Parisian press, unaccustomed to these ways, had made

fact, by Briffault's time, he had earned the reputation of being the "homme plus gai de France" (Alfred Marquiset, *Romieu et Courchamps* [Paris: Emile Paul Frères, 1913], 36). He also served as *sous-préfet de Lauhans* before becoming Prefect of the Dordogne in 1833. Although his biographer does not mention his presence at the coronation, he does describe an 1843 trip of his to London, where he accompanied the Duc de Nemours (the second son of Louis-Philippe) as an *attaché civil et historiographe* and contributed articles to both the English and French press (Marquiset, 84).

[2] The "three realms" are England, Scotland, and Ireland, although this is a bit of an anachronism since all three were united by the 1707 and 1800 Acts of Union.

[3] "Official historian" is a translation here for *historiographe*, a term specifically applied to a person who has received an official appointment to chronicle an event, period, or institution and a position Romieu held during his London visit in 1843.

no plans; coming in great haste, they had not taken breakfast, and, around two o'clock, they began to feel a ferocious hunger. As a result of their pleas and prayers, they obtained from a gatekeeper some large biscuits, for which they paid a heavy price and which they greedily devoured; their appetites were appeased. A few moments after this meal, they felt terrible, sharp pains within their gastric regions; they asked with some dread what had been in those biscuits they had just been given. Quite calmly came the reply that they were mustard biscuits, prepared especially to give an appetite to gentlemen lacking one, and to stimulate lethargic stomachs. The correspondents from the Parisian press then understood that they would have to resign themselves to an extended torture.

The between-meals snack, the light refreshment, or the "luncheon"—whatever you want to call it—is a meal for children; and we have always thought that women of thirty or more and old dandies put on such a show of taking it in public only to make it seem that they have an adolescent stomach.

• VIII •

SUPPER

Supper:[1] if we had written this book a century ago, we would have had to yield the place of honor to supper; it was predominant then. Today, it is no more than a grandeur deposed. It was a bright and radiant star, a pillar of light beaming through the Parisian night; now it is a dull glow that stays hidden, closing the windows, the shutters, and the curtains so as not to be seen from the outside. Supper was a point of pride; at present, it is under suspicion; the police harass it and hunt it down like a thief in the night, and often even take it to be arraigned before the magistrate's court.

To write the chronicles of supper, from the heights where the gourmands and voluptuous habits of the Regency[2] had placed it to the humiliations to which the final years of the eighteenth century had forced it to submit would be both a joyous and pitiable tale. It is a tale not quite anywhere because

---

[1] The historian Lola Gonzalez-Quijano describes the "supper" of Briffault's times as follows: "Supper, which had disappeared at the beginning of the nineteenth century, was restored under the July Monarchy. Taken after the theater or a ball, between eleven at night and two in the morning, it was then emblematic of the life of the Parisian demimonde (*la vie parisienne galante*)." ("'La chère et la chair': gastronomie et prostitution dans les grands restaurants des boulevards au XIXe siècle," *Genre, sexualité & société* 10 [Fall 2013]: 7, http://gss.revues.org/2925).

[2] La Régence usually refers to the period from the death of Louis XIV (1715) to the majority of Louis XV (1723), during which time power was largely in the hands of the Regent, Philippe d'Orléans.

137

it is a little bit everywhere; these scattered memories are too much a part of the history of supper for us to want to change anything about them.

Supper, formerly the master of so many delightful dwellings, supper, which had its palaces, its villas, its apartments great and small, no longer has a single home to itself; it abides now only with the cook-caterer.

Under the Directory, supper, an aristocrat returned from exile, resided at the Luxembourg Palace;[3] it seemed even to have recovered its luxury, its finesse, and its extravagance of former times. After that, it no longer appears but in the magnificence of the gala celebrations.

We are experiencing a real embarrassment here; in our opinion, the meal that concludes a ball is not a supper; it is a nocturnal dinner and something quite different; we consent to give the name of supper only to those elegant and engaging meals that rise when everyone else is going to bed, freed from the concerns and demands of the day, delivered from obligation and business, devoted entirely to pleasure and entertainment, protected from all that is annoying, reclusive, distracted, and rowdy, mysterious and noisy, exempt from all hypocrisy, lavish and dissolute, disheveled, extravagantly perverse, but courteous, refined in wit, impertinent and mocking, delectable and debauched. That is supper as we understand it. Perhaps it is not quite as lost as we thought it to be; we'll look for it in a little while.

---

[3] The Luxembourg Palace became the seat of government for the Directory from 1795 to its overthrow in 1799, when the Senate was installed there. Briffault may be referring here to the several celebrations held at the palace in 1797 to honor Napoleon's victorious Italian campaign. (See, e.g., Ida M. Tarbell, *A Short Life of Napoleon Bonaparte* [New York: Moffat Yard, 1909], 347.)

Carême has handed down to us the recollection of two
sumptuous suppers from the Empire; his vanity, when he
speaks of his prowess, is so innocent, that his phrasing should
in no way be altered.[4]
The first of these ideal suppers took place on the occasion
of the ball the Emperor gave at the Elysée Palace. Napoleon
himself, on that occasion of the marriage of Prince Jérôme to
the Princess of Württenberg, presided over all the arrangements for this celebration.[5] Here is how the tables were laid
out: "Twenty-four savory centerpieces; fourteen pedestals
bearing six hams, six galantines, and the heads of two wild
boars; six loins of veal garnished with aspic; next, seventy-six
diverse entrées, including six of prime rib and filet of beef garnished with aspic; six of veal filet, six of calves' brains dressed
with borders of molded jelly; six of foie gras loaves, six of *poulet
à la reine* in galantine, six of aspic garnished with coxcomb and
kidney, six of red partridge *salmis chaudfroid,* six of *poulet à la
reine fricassée chaudfroid,* six of chicken mayonnaise; six of
salmon steak with Montpellier butter, six of filet of sole salad,
six of eel galantine with Montpellier butter."[6]

---

[4] Carême's account of the balls described by Briffault appears in his *Le cuisinier
parisien* (1828, on 33 and 296 in the 1844 edition; for more on Carême, see chap.
2, n. 17). But Briffault likely drew his account from Marquis de Cussy's article
"L'art culinaire" in *Les classiques de la table.* The text of Briffault's cites can be
found on 270–271 ([1845]: I), which, according to de Cussy, is from Carême's
unpublished *Memoires.*

[5] The marriage of Jérôme Bonaparte, Napoleon's youngest brother, to Catharina
Frederica of Württenberg took place on August 22, 1807.

[6] Some culinary definitions: a galantine is generally deboned meat, fish, or poultry,
stuffed, poached, decorated with aspic, and served cold. *Poulet à la reine* is a small
young chicken used generally for roasts, as opposed to *poulet commun* (used for
fricassées), *poulet demi-grain* (for marinated chicken), and *gros poulet gras* (for spit
roasting); see Alexandre Dumas, *Grande dictionnaire de cuisine* (Paris: Alphonse
Lemerre, 1873), 886. *Salmis* is a preparation involving cooked and sliced meat,

That is still only a chief steward speaking. Now listen to the poet:

"Our border garnishes were composed like this: for the salmon steaks, garnishes of pale pink butter; for the eel segments, garnishes of herbed butter; for the filet of sole salads, egg garnishes; and for the chicken mayonnaise, garnishes of the same sort; for the poultry and game *chaudfroids*, garnishes of root vegetables and truffles; all these border garnishes were adorned with jellies and aspics. The entrées were decorated only with jellies, ensuring that whatever remained from our entrées and centerpieces were enhanced and scintillating with jellies and aspics of varying hues.

"Vigorous cubes of jellies and aspics formed some of the garnished borders—a beautiful finish and a beautiful standard for our cold dishes.

"I devised our newest *suédoises* around 1804.[7] The shapes that had been given to them before me were lacking in grace and elegance. My effort, at a large adjunct of the ball given by the Marshals of France to their chief, was a huge success. The ball was magnificent; it was held in the grand hall of the Opera, adorned with hangings; it was then on rue de Richelieu. The younger Richaud managed the work for it,[8] and M. Bécar, chef

---

often game, reheated in a sauce fortified, usually, by truffles or foie gras. *Chaudfroid* is a preparation for cooked foods served cold and usually glazed over with aspic or sauces. Montpellier butter is a heavily seasoned butter served with meat and fish. Carême gives the recipes for many of these and the following dishes in his *Le cuisinier parisien*.

[7] "Before Napoleon left Paris to campaign in Germany, the newly appointed 'Imperial' generals threw a ball for him.... Talleyrand recommended Carême, who created over 30 towering *suédoises*—eye-catching layers of fruit in syrup presented in moulds with aspic and jelly" (Ian Kelly, *Cooking for Kings: The Life of Antonin Carême* [New York: Walker & Co., 2003], 68).

[8] The brothers Richaud are often mentioned with the brothers Robert, with Dartois Laguipierre (who worked for Napoleon and who died with many others on the

for the sugared desserts, had called me to support him; I made thirty-six of them for him, and for several days, from the kitchen to the Parisian salons, nothing but his *suédoises* were talked about. Such happy times! And such agreeable work!"

Will these two citations be enough to give an idea of the splendor of the ceremonial suppers under the Empire?

The Restoration had its magnificent buffets at the Tuileries; but the rich and elegant grace of the ball suppers given by the Duchesse de Berry at the Pavillon de Marsan had not been equaled by the pomp of these great staterooms.[9]

Since 1830 the palace's ball suppers have been set in the concert hall; it is difficult to imagine a sight more absolutely dazzling than this crowd covered with diamonds and precious stones, embroidered gowns, feathers and bouquets; the tiaras, the medals, and the epaulettes gleam with a glittering brilliance that intermingles with the radiance of the tableware and the sparkle of the crystal; there is a kind of enchantment in its appearance.

The dress ball given by the Duc d'Orléans at the Pavillon de Marsan was remarkable for the fine and inventive taste that controlled all the arrangements. The prince did not like excess, but he wanted everything to be well chosen, well prepared,

retreat from Moscow), and with Carême as chefs who helped revive French cuisine in the first decades of the nineteenth century. (See, e.g., Lucien Tendret, *La table au pays de Brillat-Savarin* [Belley: Louis Bailly, 1892], 28.)

[9] Marie-Caroline de Bourbon-Sicile, Duchesse de Berry, was the daughter-in-law of Charles X and the mother of the successor to the Bourbon crown after her husband, the Duc de Berry, was assassinated in 1820. Her official residence was the Pavillon de Marsan, part of the Tuileries Palace complex, and while living there, she was renowned for her expenditure on furnishings and her balls, the last of which was a famous *bal historique* in 1830, where she appeared costumed as Marie Stuart, an unfortunate presage of her own failed attempt at an insurrection in 1832. (See, e.g., M.W. Duckett, ed., *Dictionnaire de la conversation et de la lecture* [Paris: Firmin Didot, 1860], 3:72.)

and presented with charm; he wanted art, namely, a feeling for the good and the beautiful, to be apparent in the slightest detail.[10]

During the marriage celebration of the Royal Prince, there was a supper, very well managed and arranged, in St. Jean Hall at the Hôtel de Ville;[11] it was pleasurable and proceeded in an orderly fashion; small tables of two, three, four, and five settings were adopted for everyone; the use of these rounded tables is a very welcome innovation, substituting intimacy and good conversation for awkwardness; each small table, then placed under the protection of a polite and attentive steward, was served with a care and dispatch that could not be expected of waiters disconcerted and made frantic by the number and confusion of the orders and demands directed at them.

Formerly, supper was the necessary conclusion to any evening affair that valued its reputation; it was abandoned only gradually. It was costing too much; it was causing too much embarrassment and too much trouble, especially for the lesser classes, who now all wanted to have their grand evening affairs. And there is a final reason for the renunciation of supper: simply stated, it is the experience of a feeling akin to shame; supper had been banished from all celebrations where it was

[10] The Pavillon de Marsan became the principal residence of Prince Ferdinand Philippe, Duc d'Orléans and eldest son of King Louis Philippe, during the July Monarchy. Like the Duchesse de Berry, who lived there before him, he was known as a connoisseur of contemporary art and furnishings: "The Pavillon de Marsan, arranged and decorated through the care of M. le Duc de Orléans, had become like a precious and rare museum where all the contemporary fine arts were represented" (Jules Janin, *Le prince royal* [Paris: Bourdin, 1843], 240). In 1905 the Pavillon was converted into the Louvre's Musée des arts décoratifs.

[11] The marriage of Prince Ferdinand Philippe to Hélène de Mecklembourg-Schwerin was one of the major social events of the July Monarchy and was celebrated in Paris with a ball at the Hôtel de Ville on June 19, 1837.

not strictly required, because it had been sullied and disgraced by looting, gluttony, and drunkenness.

Normally, the orchestra gave the signal for supper with a fanfare. And so, a pack of hounds, hungry for entrails when the horn is sounded at the end of the hunt, stampedes with no more fury than did the ball for its supper. What more deplorable spectacle than that of the dining room—which, at first sight, was almost always so fresh, so full of elegance and splendor— being sacked and plundered and soon offering no more than a heap of filth and debris. The women, left behind, could get nothing; some owed their place at a table or a plate on their knees only to the zeal of those serving them. The dining room, packed full of turmoil and shouts, resembled a place invaded by a mob fallen into a bacchanalian frenzy; everything distinguishing good company from the bad had vanished. The younger people—and, it must be mentioned, the young women—displayed the most intense passion for this uncouth mayhem, in the middle of which erupted laughter and sometimes other outbursts to which it is difficult to give a polite name. These excesses infested all the evening affairs, and seemed even to be associated with the highest of them; not so long ago, the royal court itself was not exempt from such indignities.

One of the dancers cried out, his mouth full, "I'm eating. I've paid enough of a levy for at least that." At the last gala evening at Versailles, a supper had become impossible.

Just before supper, and when the desired moment was seen to be approaching, the dancers were heard telling each other, "I'm going to have a fine supper; I haven't dined for that very reason, so as to eat better now." During supper, there was nothing but sordid quarrels, arguing and even fighting over the dishes, with gestures, tones, and words that amused the serving staff and had them laughing up their sleeves. After supper, in the ballroom, the conversation intensified, the dancing revived, and at first the ball seemed livelier, but agitation was growing. The gentlemen, heated up by wine and the fiery atmosphere, forgot moderation; the women, disheveled, breathing heavily, their gowns ruffled and stained, with the look of a Bacchante previously unknown to us, all gave to these ballrooms—whose gracious charms were so fresh and decent a few hours before—a character from which both sight and thought turned away in sadness. It is at this stage that the mothers, alarmed, lead their young daughters away.

In the dining hall, the damage was soon repaired; table linen and dishware were promptly changed and the debris covering the floor was gathered up; the air, refreshed by opened windows and then perfumed by an aromatic fumigation, expelled the dense vapors. The savvier ones, who had allowed the devouring cyclone to pass through and were unmoved by the tempest, took their places at a restored table, and, following the deluge, savored the fine fare and the calm.

Such has been the fate of all the gala suppers.

At the Tuileries where, more than once, the deputies had forgotten the gravity of their office, the women did not always take pride in moderation. One of the Arab leaders, after having seen a supper, exclaimed, "On seeing them dance, I dreamed of paradise and the houris of the Prophet;[12] on seeing them eat, I fell back to earth."

Among the bourgeoisie, at what we will call the balls on the fourth floor, suppers made just as much noise with far less

<hr />

[12] The houris are the celestial maidens who, in Muslim belief, join the blessed in heaven.

brilliance; only the uproar was aroused by crude antics and generated by deafening songs and their refrains, or by those prodigious toasts resembling a rolling thunder of drums.

The day following a supper, in the palaces, in the great homes, and on the fourth floor the furniture was found to be greased and stained with traces of meat; from beneath the furniture the remains and leftovers satiety had tossed there were gathered up. Supper thus became a formidable scourge; but despite these disgraces, a high degree of ceremony still persists.

Buffets were tried, they fared no better; they were taken by storm, treated like conquered cities.[13]

In order to remedy these shortcomings that so dishonor our manners, refreshments replaced supper, without, however, causing it to disappear entirely. It proceeds by degrees and at an ordered pace that the most perfect taste controls. Cordials and cold drinks—*le acque* as expressed so well by the Italians—and *petit-fours* open the procession; the ice creams, the glazed fruits, the sorbets, and the bonbons come next; a little later, the punch circulates, accompanied by hard and firm pastries.

There is a break.

Other trays appear: they are loaded with English porcelain; tea, bouillon, soups thickened with small noodles or starches,[14] coffee, chocolate are offered

---

[13] Apparently, much had not changed by the time of the Second Empire: "The door to the dining room, transformed into a buffet, was opened...a shove forward, a crush...a scramble over pastries and truffled poultry, elbows digging into ribs, brutally. It was a looting and a plunder." (Émile Zola, "Chapter IV," *La Curée* [Paris: LaCroix, Verboeckhoven, 1871], 308.)

[14] For Briffault's *potages de pâtes ou de fécule*, see, e.g., Antoine Gogué, *La cuisine française* (Paris: Hachette, 1876), 181–182.

in turn; the sandwiches, which appear flanked by glasses, close the procession; the wines of Bordeaux, Champagne, and Madeira stimulate the dance without venturing to get it drunk. The liveliness of the ball profits from it, and nothing of decency and taste is lost. In the final hours of the ball, everything served during the night is brought back according to the requests made by the persons invited and, especially, the gamblers.

These precautions, so fine and so ingenious, do not always manage to guarantee order and civility. In the halls leading up to the rooms, bands of pirates cruise about and settle in. They do not dance, they do not gamble, they consume; these voracious and ill-bred vandals capture the trays and strip them bare; they let nothing pass beyond the territory they occupy. Often the head of the household or the chief servants are themselves forced to escort the trays to deliver them from this insatiable rapacity. These gluttons of the ballroom stuff themselves with everything without a thought for the women and the young girls who are suffering, devoured by thirst for the lack of a glass of sugared water they do not have the audacity to request.

One of those sound practices, which we could not come across without singing its praises, was introduced into our evening affairs: the crowd is allowed to pass through; several initiates, well informed and forewarned, do not join the progress toward the exit. When there are no more than a small number of the chosen in the rooms, the head of the household gathers them discreetly around a table hidden within some charming corner, and there, chatting over the night's events, they await daybreak; wit and appetite ordinarily recover their full independence of spirit at these privileged suppers, which have a certain flavor of forbidden fruit and of delights not given to everyone. We have never known these meals to be lacking in gaiety; often their playfulness even approaches the childlike. We will mention, as one of the most agreeable suppers of this sort, the one that ended the last reception of M. Léon Pillet, the director of the Opera.[15]

Two suppers have become famous enough for us to separate them from the pack.

One was a supper for *viveurs*.[16] Seen there was a dish without equal. Placed in the middle of the table was an object well beyond the dimensions and proportions of the finest fish. A pink veil covered it in a way designed to suggest its true form, and all of it betrayed a mysterious beauty. Around this showpiece glittered the splendors of the setting. When all were seated, the servants lifted the veil, and enchanted eyes beheld a young and wondrously attractive woman, lying within a conch shell on a bed of marine plant life; she seemed to be sleeping. Her costume was composed of coral braids blending in with her hair flowing down to her neck and coiled into

---

[15] Léon Pillet was a journalist and drama critic who served as the Director of the Paris Opera from 1840 to 1847; during his tenure he had the distinction of alienating, among others, Richard Wagner, Giuseppe Verdi, and Giacomo Meyerbeer.

[16] A *viveur*, of which Briffault himself was a prime example, was a kind of bon vivant who prized particularly food and drink above all other pleasures. See the "Introduction" for more on this species.

bracelets around her arms, into a corset around her waist, at her feet, and in long pendants from her ears. At the very moment when the carvers expected to carry her off, she sprang up to her feet, assumed the pose of a nymph as if she were going to perform the dance of the naiads,[17] and vanished, bounding over the heads of the guests, who were then presented with a salmon trout so prodigious it made them forget everything else. The chronicles of the Parisian supper boasted for some time about having had a mermaid, poached fresh in court bouillon. We offer this tale without believing in it very much; it is perhaps just a page out of *The Thousand and One Parisian Nights*.

Another supper inaugurated one of Paris's fine dwellings. The evening began with the music; the ball ran its full course, but tired no one out. At midnight, the dining room was opened. The table had altogether ten settings, all arranged exquisitely. But it was soon clear that nothing had yet been seen of the service's wonders. Ten young women, all dressed in white, with the kind of talent and beauty the public loves and admires on the stage, were arranged, playful and cheerful, around the enticing dishes that seasoned so well the tokens of admiration and praise received from all sides. This was the Decameron being served.[18] The entire company followed this design of ten-by-ten, and a sequence of feasting lasted until daybreak.

We will define the *viveur* without applying too much paint. The *viveur* has located intellectual enjoyment in the perfecting of sensual pleasures. For him, to enjoy is to act and to think; he

---

[17] Briffault's use of the term here *pas de naïades* may be a reference to *Odine ou la naïade*, a ballet that premiered in London in 1843, under the direction of Jules-Joseph Perrot, one of the most prominent choreographers of his time.

[18] *The Decameron*, written between 1348 and 1353 by Giovanni Boccaccio, was a collection of 100 stories told by ten narrators over a period of ten nights.

proclaims his independence, recognizing and following no rules, delivering himself over to his imagination, and like the economists, he wants to *be*, and to be the best possible.[19] But he is the sole judge and final arbiter of his satisfaction; he has established as a maxim these words from the wisdom of nations: *Each takes his pleasure wherever he finds it.*

Some *viveurs,* working against the tide of manners and custom, accordingly tried to revive the supper. Around the last years of the Restoration, these attempts were developed enough to arouse hopes that supper would regain possession of its former honors. It settled into all the famous restaurants, selecting, among others, the Café Anglais, whose small private  rooms, now dismantled, had so much charm.[20] Its preferred private hideaway was situated on the Place de la Bourse. This supper was esteemed at once for its spirited ways; if it could not always guard against excess, such inclinations came as surprises; it was undeserving of that accusation of "orgy" so foolishly applied to it. Like its predecessor, this supper was viewed as fine, delicate and lively, rebellious in spirit, profligate, and

[19] In his essay "Le viveur," Briffault writes that the *viveur* was "the living personification of this precept of Adam Smith: 'To be, and to be the best possible'" (*Les Français peints par eux-mêmes* [Paris: Curmer, 1840], I:371).

[20] Opened in 1802, the Café Anglais had a strong reputation throughout the nineteenth century. Many writers—from Stendhal to Proust—and their characters were patrons, and it was a favorite of Balzac, who also had characters dine there in *Père Goriot* (1835) and *Les illusions perdues* (1843). In William Makepeace Thackeray's *The Newcomes* (1853–1855), Olive Newcome writes of taking (in the 1830s) an after-theater supper there (Chapter 22). See also chap. 10, n. 30.

sometimes debauched, accepting the bad crowd, without mixing in with it, detesting impudence as much as prudery: such was the new supper, which had no reason to envy the older one other than some splendors unknown and impossible in our time. The first generation of the new *viveurs* committed a grave error; they made of supper too much of an amorous[21] meal; they spoiled it by degrading it. Those who followed them sought out and accepted feminine society for their nocturnal meals, and it was not lacking; but they never viewed it as anything other than decoration. They also retained for their supper its prized privileges, thereby preserving it from baneful control. Supper became fashionable; gallantry occupied it; and it was thus afflicted by a banality that taste should have resisted. When the gambling houses still existed, the exit from Frascati's tables filled the nearby restaurants with happy and unhappy gamblers,[22] and with women who, quite often, expected from these encounters their single meal of the day. These particular nocturnal events have no other connection with supper than the time they steal from it.

After the suppression of the gambling houses,[23] of which the true supper took no notice, these gatherings persisted, and

---

[21] Briffault uses the term *galant* here, and although it had a similar usage to the English "gallant" or "gentlemanly," it had a negative connotation in Briffault's time as well, alluding to a demimonde of prostitution and concubinage. One of the definitions the *Dictionnaire de l'Académie française: sixième édition* ([Paris: Firmin Didot, 1835], I:816) gives for *galanterie* (also used later in this paragraph) is *un commerce amoureux et illicit*.

[22] Café Frascati, founded in 1789, acted variously as a gambling house, restaurant, and ice cream salon until its closing in 1857. Along with appearances in Thackeray's *Vanity Fair* (1848), it appears several times in various guises in Balzac's fiction, as both a debauched gambling den and as a bastion of haute cuisine.

[23] On December 31, 1837, the Chamber of Deputies banned all games of chance in France, and all gambling clubs in the country closed.

this was their finest moment. The attractions of this meal had to be experienced, a meal that came after all others, and—forgetful of the night before and the day after, having no other prospect than sleep—it found its free spirit. When, in front of a few dishes as simple as they were excellent, a company of five or six—persons of taste who got along well enough intellectually with each other never to be in agreement—made up a social gathering that brought back at night all the pleasant impressions of the day; all of them cast into the bustle of Parisian life, delivered over to its emotions so lively and so various, familiar with the things and the men who cause a bit of a stir; skeptics and scoffers, far from bias, enemies of received opinions; living behind all the backdrops and in the wings backstage to the world and its events: this, the pleasure of these suppers, was a pleasure beyond compare. Such eloquence! So much wit! So many swift and sure-fire judgments! Such crazy foolishness, and still so much good sense! These nights were far more durable than the slander. Faults that they never had were attributed to them; but there was one merit that could not be denied them, that of intellect and wit: in France, that is beyond a virtue. As for their exploits each night, they seemed to belong to a legendary and heroic time; the fancies of the *viveur* carried everything to its extreme: he knew of no qualities other than those he savored with the rage and delirium of his passion.

This first generation of *viveurs* gave some statesmen to the July Revolution; some are found seated in the Chamber of Peers.[24] M. Romieu took only a single step from the supper

---

[24] The Chamber of Peers, the French equivalent of the British Houser of Lords, was created during the Bourbon Restoration in 1814, survived the July Revolution (1830), but was disbanded in 1848 after the French peerage was abolished.

table to the Prefecture of the Dordogne, the land of truffles; and now in the Department of Champagne, he is spending, as if in purgatory, trying times imposed on him by an administrative disgrace.[25]

If it were necessary to show that supper can be allied with the gravest misgivings, what more striking demonstration can be found than that of the Grandvaux supper, so renowned in the annals of contemporary politics.[26] From the second generation of *soupeurs* only a few men of wit emerged; this is not much.

When the abolition of supper was sought in the name of morality, which it did not dream of offending, it was proclaimed that it compromised public safety. However, people who, at night, were passing through the silent arcades of that cloister known as the Palais-Royal encountered only quiet there and heard only the sound of their own footsteps, never suspecting that, in all the gallery's restaurants, supper had settled into place. Police harassment pursued supper from one

---

[25] François-Auguste Romieu, a writer and high-ranking civil servant, was the Prefect of the Dordogne province from 1833 to 1843 (see also chap. 7, n. 1). According to his biographer, he had been lobbying to become the Prefect of Police in Paris, and it was unclear whether his appointment to the Prefecture of the Haute-Marne in 1843 represented "an advancement or a disgrace" (Alfred Marquiset, *Romieu et Courchamps* [Paris: Emile Paul Frères, 1913], 84). As the Prefect of Briffault's native region and a celebrated *viveur* himself—"cet autre buveur titanesque," writes Roger de Beauvoir in comparing him with Briffault (*Les soupers de mon temps* [Paris: Faure, 1868], 169)—Romieu was certainly well known to Briffault. The Prefect, incidentally, is the state's representative in a French Department, or region, and is responsible for, among other things, securing public safety and administering governmental rules.

[26] This is a reference to a minor scandal in 1835 involving the minister Adolphe Thiers who had been a participant in a hunting party at Comte Achille Vigier's Château de Grand-Vaux that supposedly degenerated into "l'orgie de Grand-Vaux" (and during which it was reputed that M. Thiers had presented his naked posterior to the assembled revelers before turning in). (See, e.g., *L'intermédiaire des chercheurs et des curieux*, no. 241 [May 25, 1878]: 318–319.)

refuge to the next, closing all doors to it; and the position of the foreigner, who found himself at night on the streets of Paris with the urge for a bite to eat, cannot be thought of without a fearful shudder: he would die of starvation, unable to obtain, even at the price of gold, a morsel of bread.

Supper haunts only the public places; it is always awkward and constrained in private residences. However, there is in the Saint-Honoré district, in those magnificent mansions, a favored pied-à-terre;[27] there it abides in all its unrivaled sensuality.

The theater world still has supper. But for the actors returning to their homes, it is only a bleak and solitary meal; for those who find places still open, these café suppers take on a certain manner: wherever they have settled in, they have adopted certain ways of being, behaving, and speaking, making it necessary, for the sake of art and good taste, never to allow our gaze to linger over these scenes.[28] The theater's brightest stars are hardly likely to have fond or sharp recollections of this sort.

Moving through the Paris night is a nomadic supper: this is the canteen lady who supplies the national guard posts and the troops in the guard houses; carried by hand on a hotplate, bouillon and coffee roam the streets. At break of day, this supper becomes breakfast.

If supper is no longer a meal for the rich, it is still one for the poor.

The Parisian worker eats three times a day: morning, at nine; afternoon, at two; and, in the evening, after six, when work is

---

[27] It is not clear which mansion Briffault has in mind, but in his time the *faubourg Saint-Honoré* was generally a district reserved for wealthy aristocratic families, government officials, and financiers.

[28] For such a "scene" (circa 1867), consult the theatrical supper vividly recounted in Chapter 4 of Emile Zola's *Nana*.

done. Women and children have also returned from the day's labor; the evening meal brings together the entire family, and it is here that the worker's life reveals its joys and sorrows. For some, order and labor provide comfort, as well as health and happiness from these meals whose aroma and appearance are a joy. For others, disorder, misconduct, idleness, and debauchery bring only misfortune, hunger, and misery; the children roll about the floor in tears to escape the cravings that torment them, while the parents deaden their suffering and stifle their remorse in drunkenness.

Misfortune and undeserved hardship, sickness and unemployment often produce these sad results. Elsewhere others are reduced to a frugality bordering on the most severe abstinence: for these later meals, some await the uncertain profits from the begging or pilfering of their younger children.

Under such destitution, families grow in size. While speaking with someone about the ease with which the poor have children, Sophie Arnould replied, "When they have nothing, it's their way of having supper."[29]

From the time that the "lansquenet" unleashed its wrath,[30] there have been suppers for gamblers who sit down at the table at four in the morning, at the same time when the bandits and vagabonds go to the market district to eat that perpetual soup from a pot, which unlike the cask of the Danaides, never runs dry.[31]

---

[29] Madeleine-Sophie Arnould was a celebrated pre-Revolution actress and singer also well known for her *bons mots*, many of which were collected by Albéric Deville in *Arnoldiana* (1813).

[30] "Lansquenet" was a term used for a particularly violent type of mercenary active in the fifteenth and sixteenth centuries, a name they also lent to a card game which was played by, among others, Dumas' three musketeers.

[31] During Briffault's time many of the cabarets in the market district ("Les Halles") were authorized to stay open all night, unlike the city's other restaurants and cafes,

The Empire did not take supper, but the Emperor did. In 1814, at Essonne, he invited for supper his generals, whose troops were dispersed in and around Paris.[32]

An early appendage to supper, which we have borrowed from the English, is the tea. Among evening pleasures, the tea has replaced the punch, which was very much in favor with Empire society.

The taking of tea was imported into Europe as a curative in 1666 by Queen Catherine, the wife of Charles II, who had picked up the habit in Portugal.[33] From England's court, where

which were obliged to close by two in the morning, although as Briffault indicates above, many of the clients in the private rooms continued to be served throughout the night (see Gonzalez-Quijano, 10–11). Thus, the market became a magnet for gamblers, prostitutes, and other nighthawks, who often dined on the *gratinée des Halles*, the celebrated French onion soup that fortified the early morning workers and those who believed it to be a preventative against hangover. The Danaides, the fifty daughters of Danaus, for having murdered their husbands, were condemned to attempt forever to fill a leaky barrel using only sieves.

[32] Before Napoleon's abdication, in spring 1814, the greater part of his available army was stationed along the river Essonne, with the general headquarters in the village of that name, and although he occasionally reviewed his army there, Napoleon remained primarily at Fontainebleau where he would meet and dine with his marshals and generals late into the night. (See, e.g., Achille de Vaulabelle, *Histoire des deux Restaurations* [Paris: Perrotin, 1855], 1:382.)

[33] Briffault may have drawn this fact from the *Bibliothèque britannique* (*Sciences et arts* [Geneva: Bibliothèque britannique, 1809], 40:272). Tea had actually been

this beverage became fashionable, the practice of taking tea spread throughout all of Europe. Among the English, it has been absorbed into the customs of all the classes: London's beggars take their tea. In Holland and in several lands where the climate is similar to that of England, it is almost a general practice; elsewhere, especially in France, it is sought out only by the leisured classes. In the morning, a breakfast tea is often accompanied by eggs, bread and butter, ham, and so many other things that a "simple cup of tea" can become a substantial meal. The evening tea also has its accessories: toasts, a heavy cake, which in former times was called a leaden cake,[34] the inevitable sandwiches, and the eminently French brioche all serve as escorts. The splash of cream is obligatory; some persons substi-

tute a dash of rum for it. Tea's affectations are infinite; it has its precious charms, along with its little pastries.[35]

For classes with a more humble or impoverished way of life, *café au lait* is their morning tea; cider and chestnuts, beer and biscuits,[36] all the varieties of mulled and sweetened wines are the teas of the small landholdings.

imported into England, through Portugal, before the Stuart Restoration in 1660 (the diarist Samuel Pepys had his first taste of it in that year), but Catherine, who was Portuguese, is still credited for having introduced it to the court.

[34] Although *gateau de plomb* is not quite the same as "pound cake," it is composed of the same ingredients: flour, butter, eggs, and sugar, all of relatively equal weight in the recipe.

[35] Briffault uses the term *mignardise* here, which can stand for a certain "preciousness" or a particular kind of *petit-four*; I have supplied the sentence with both.

[36] Briffault uses the term *échaudé* here, a kind of biscuit that is poached before it is baked.

A prefect was criticized for seducing the electors of his Department by inviting them to a table that was always splendidly set; he announced that henceforth he would restrict himself to offering them a tea. The evening before the election, he indeed invited all the electors to take tea at the prefecture. The precious infusion, with its splash of cream and its little hard and crisp pastries, was served on magnificent trays. The country electors were there in profusion that evening, and resembled rather closely the fox that was invited to the stork's supper;[37] they understood nothing of the professed taste for this insipid brew, which was for them a variation on hot water. The secretary for our prefect led them discreetly into the depths of the drawing room. The buffets were laid out there, all conveniently stocked with cold dishes capable of withstanding the heartiest of appetites. There they found pâtés, fish, galantines, and venison, with wines to match; and these good people then understood what was meant by a tea.

In France, tea is the supper of the salons.

---

[37] The tale of the fox and the stork, "Le renard et la cigogne," in which each invites the other to a dinner physically impossible for its guest to eat (the stork is meant to dine off a flat plate and the fox from a thin-necked vase), derives from Aesop, but it is also one of Jean de La Fontaine's more popular tales.

CLUBS, *CERCLES*, *TABLES D'HÔTE*, *PENSIONS BOURGEOISES*, REST HOMES

Between the dining rooms and the restaurant dining halls, there lies a middle region. It, too, has its diverse lands, but the manners and customs are not plainly drawn; they are curiously mutable and touch the national character only slightly.

The clubs, which we have taken from British tradition—and which we understand poorly and have copied clumsily—are being assimilated in France, but slowly. The Jockey Club is practically the only one that has managed to lay down roots.[1] The dinner there is that of one of the very great houses; the fare leans naturally toward English taste; the wines there are principally French. The Jockey Club's table attracts little notice; it is set luxuriously, with care and intelligence; it has a charm all of its own. Without detracting from the civility of its interactions, it leaves them in total freedom; it takes no pride in either sobriety or temperance; a noble hospitality is practiced there, directed especially toward foreigners of distinction. Discussions at the table and those after dinner in the

---

[1] The original English Jockey Club was founded in the mid-eighteenth century as a social club for aristocratic gentlemen with a passion for horses. In 1833 Lord Henry Seymour organized the Société d'Encouragement pour l'Amélioration des Races de Chevaux en France. Its name was changed to the Jockey Club de Paris in 1834, and it remains one of France's most exclusive clubs to the present day.

drawing rooms, over the billiard table, and on the balcony creatively review that part of the world's news touching on the life of pleasure and amusement. Conversation is given full rein, like at one of M. Scribe's vaudevilles.[2]

What are called "clubs" in London bear the name of *cercle* in Paris.[3] If a close review of these institutions entered into our consideration, we would easily show that the English "clubs" and the French *cercles* do not resemble each other at all. We have detached the Jockey Club from the *cercles*, because its character is distinctive and has nothing in common with other social gatherings of this kind.

Thanks to the name of the Marquis de Cussy, the suppers of the Cercle des Étrangers gained a certain reputation.[4] With the suppression of the gambling houses, the *cercle*'s rooms were closed, a matter of sharp regret for the seriously dissipated.[5]

The *cercle* occupying the house located on the boulevard in front of the Passage des Panoramas has a table with a fine reputation for its service;[6] this fame, begun at the rue de

[2] Eugène Scribe was a highly prolific and popular dramatist and librettist, active from about 1815 to 1855. During his early career, he was best known for his *comédies-vaudevilles*, and entertainments, usually with music and song, that appealed to the bourgeois public. Coincidentally, the Jockey Club was to make the Hôtel Scribe (on rue Scribe) its base of operation from 1863 to 1913.

[3] Since Briffault draws a clear distinction between the two institutions, I have retained the French term *cercle*, which is usually translated as "club."

[4] For a brief history of the Cercle des Étrangers, see Auguste Vitu, *La maison mortuaire de Molière* (Paris: Lemerre, 1880), 285. The novelist Paul de Kock also mentions it in his *Mémoires*: "'Is that a decent place?'... 'It's the best place of its kind'.... 'It's kept by an ex-chamberlain of the Emperor, the Marquis de Cussy!'" ([Paris: Dentu, 1873], 120). For more on de Cussy, see chap. 2, n. 19.

[5] Many of the early nineteenth-century *cercles* gradually transformed into gambling clubs and were forced to close when gambling houses were suppressed by law at the end of 1837. Gambling in a variety of forms, however, continued to be actively practiced in the *cercles*.

[6] This is likely a reference to the Ancien Grand Cercle, which was located under several names at the Hôtel de Mercy-Argenteau on the boulevard Montmartre until

Grammont, has grown in its new premises. All the acclaim bestowed on this *cercle*'s table is justified; it is difficult to imagine a dinner more consistently attractive and more essentially good than that from this society. Its elegance is perfection; it has borrowed from luxury all that can be taken from it to adorn without embarrassment. For the persons they invite there, the *cercle*'s members pay a price far less than the true value of the meal.

We recollect one resplendent *cercle* that one day took possession of a mansion at the end of the rue de Richelieu, near the boulevard Montmartre, and with considerable pomp settled into the palace left empty by the demise of the rooms of the Étrangers. It was called the Cercle des Deux Mondes.[7] A truly royal luxury was deployed there; the galas of the court offered nothing of greater magnificence than the standard service at that table. The dinnerware, the centerpiece, the porcelain, and the crystal had an admirable beauty; the food and all of the arrangements were of the utmost refinement. For the reception of representatives of foreign powers in Paris, a porcelain service was created with each plate bearing the emblem of the country of the diplomat being served.

1937. *Cercles* often disappeared and reappeared, consolidated, changed addresses and names, and it is sometimes difficult to identify with certainty those Briffault mentions here, although a list of *cercles* and their addresses that he supplies in an article he wrote in 1842 is helpful ("Petite physiologie des cercles," *Historiettes contemporaines*, no. 1 [Jan. 31, 1842]: 52–58).

[7] The 1838 *Bibliographie de la France* ([Paris: Pillet Aîné, 1838], 91) lists a prospectus for the Cercle des Deux Mondes with the address 104 rue de Richelieu. Coincidentally, this is also the address for the Restaurant Lointier where, according to some sources, the novelist George Sand first met her future lover, the poet and dramatist Alfred de Musset, at an 1833 dinner arranged by François Buloz, editor of the *Revue des deux mondes*, perhaps the most prestigious French literary review of the time. (See, e.g., André Maurois, *Lélia, ou la vie de George Sand* [Paris: Hachette, 1952], 182.)

The quick passing of the Cercle des Deux Mondes, which lasted only a short time, left behind a brilliant wake.

Among the *cercles* of some importance, few of them seek a reputation for fine food; but almost all chase after a false luxury and neglect true qualities; they do too much for the eye and not enough for the stomach.

Some, fortunately, escape these disadvantages. We will mention the two *cercles* currently on the rue de Grammont: the one hosting the highest political society, the diplomatic world, and the old aristocracy; the other, composed of men of leisure who love the free and easy life.[8] In the first of these *cercles*, dinner is exactly that of a fine house; it has the decorum, customs, and the amenities of one of them. In the second, we know of no other examples where the table is served with such intelligence. Portions of fish, poultry, meats from the butcher, and game, marvelously beautiful, are available at all times. The service, full of a proper simplicity, is beyond reproach, the wines are well chosen, and it is difficult to imagine a dinner being more completely conducive to well-being than this one; all the privileges so necessary for the pleasures of the table are to be enjoyed there. Sometimes this dinner takes on extraordinary proportions. Guests are summoned with the

[8] In his article in *Historiettes contemporaines* ("Petite physiologie des cercles," 54–55), Briffault identifies two *cercles* on rue de Grammont, the Cercle de l'Union (no. 28) and Cercle Grammont (no. 27). The first, founded in 1828, was one of the most elite and elegant *cercles* of the time, welcoming both the extremely wealthy and members of the foreign and French diplomatic corps. Talleyrand, Prince Metternich, and three Rothschilds were, for instance, members. (For a more comprehensive, contemporary look at *cercles*, particularly the Cercle de l'Union and the Jockey Club, see Charles Yriarte, *Les cercles de Paris, 1828–1864* [Paris: Dupray de la Mahérie, 1864].) The second is likely the Cercle de la Rue de Grammont, which had a variety of names and addresses since its founding in 1819 as one of the first of the Parisian *cercles*. Incidentally, the rue de Grammont, in the Second Arrondissement, lost one of its "m's" in 1930 to become the rue de Gramont.

sound of bugles or a fanfare of trumpets that rings out loud and clear throughout the meal; deer in their entirety have been served, along with heapings of still-life, just like those found in great Flemish paintings.

We will reprimand *cercle* dinners for their excessive haste and often a lack of order; few of these tables are exempt from these disadvantages. The excellent dinner at the boulevard *cercle* itself could not avoid them. They are not found at the two rue de Grammont *cercles*.

The *table d'hôte* is but an uncertain thing whose name no longer has any real meaning.[9] First of all, the dining rooms of several fine hotels—where the dinners, without excessive cost, offer everything that belongs to a rich and sumptuous table—must be distinguished from this mob. Paris has, over all the other cities of the world, an indisputable superiority in this respect, and these very same Parisian hotels can match their everyday service against the most famous of tables. We will mention one among all the others, that of the Hôtel des Princes, with its dazzling appearance.[10] In the midst of these splendors, reflected as well in other places, you can become acquainted with all of luxury's most alluring creations at a normal and moderate expense. This is one of the happy privileges of Paris the Fortunate. In other capitals, vast inns for travelers are to be found; only in Paris can the joys of opulence be approached in all of its conditions.

[9] As Briffault indicates, the French *table d'hôte* ("host's table," but I have retained the French term here) appeared in a variety of forms and prices, although, in general, it was a public establishment that offered single meals at a fixed price and at a set hour, often at communal tables and to a regular clientele.

[10] The Grand Hôtel des Princes et de l'Europe, which was on the rue de Richelieu and regularly hosted such dignitaries as the composer Giacomo Meyerbeer and the scientist Sir Humphrey Davy, was demolished in 1860 to make way for the Passage des Princes, the last of the *passages couverts* to be constructed in Paris.

The *tables d'hôte*, in their various modes and with their current decline, do not follow any regular pattern. For foreigners, clerks, pensioners, unmarried persons, for the population that lives alone, and all that fluctuating body of middling or busy lives, they are a humble refuge. In the school district, there are numerous dining halls inside the schools where frugality is the rule; but exceptions are frequent: it is not uncommon to see, at these tables, the prodigality of an abundant orgy following the frugality of the meal. The ordinary fare of these places is that of the large households. In the Latin Quarter, these *tables d'hôte* proliferate in all shapes and sizes. Some price with inconceivable restraint; the people who run them are generally content to get, through this speculation, the benefit of nourishing themselves. The student leads his young lady companion from her workplace to his *table d'hôte*; you chat there almost like you dance at La Chaumière.[11]

Between these two districts, another kind of *table d'hôte*, baneful and pernicious, is multiplying. All the dubious life of Paris rushes headlong toward it; the aristocracy of the bohemians swarms and prevails there; the tricks, the frauds, and the falsehoods of nomadic and suspicious lives are gathered there; death traps and ambushes, those are the two great components. These perilous tables are generally run by experienced matrons or midwives, old codgers, matchmakers and madams, kept women and Aspasias of thirty years;[12] con men and

---

[11] La Grande Chaumière was a popular Latin Quarter dance hall at the southern extremity of the boulevard de Montparnasse. Founded in 1788, it was by Briffault's time a favored haunt of students and their *grisettes*, and before its closing in 1853, the can-can was said to have been introduced there. (See, e.g., "Scandalous Dances," *The International Monthly Magazine of Literature, Art, and Sciences* 2, no. 3 [Feb. 1851]: 333.)

[12] Aspasia, the companion and consort of Pericles—the leader of Athens from roughly 461 to 429 BC—was perhaps the most prominent and influential woman in

hustlers lay their traps there, and a banal gallantry presents its case. It is here where the young libertines debut and the old rakes end up.

It is one of the most persistent of open sores in the life of Paris.

The *pensions bourgeoises* are generally clear of such stains;[13] peaceful sanctuaries open to the elderly and the convalescent, they are veritable infirmaries; they have their tempests and their storms; the petty passions, the mean-spirited harassment, and the cliques stir things up in a thousand ways; the quarrels, the back-biting and the slanders accelerate the work of discord; but these are only wayward quirks and not vices.

Physically, rest homes and convalescent homes maintain both pharmacies and restaurants; the odors from the cooking and the medications mingle together; a detestable fare is generally prepared there. Morally, rest homes and convalescent homes are similar to the noxious kind of *table d'hôte* and *pension bourgeoise;* the perversity of the first is often found to be joined with the nonsense of the second.

We know of only a few exceptions to these rules perhaps a bit too general.

Classical Greece. In her earlier life, however, it was rumored that she had been both a prostitute and the owner of a brothel.

[13] The *pension bourgeoise* is a kind of *table d'hôte*, although one contemporary dictionary makes the following distinction: "[the *table d'hôte*] is usually located at the place of a restaurateur or *hôtelier* who makes a business of buying food to sell it, and offers meals to all comers, while the *pension bourgeoise* is usually installed in a private dwelling that brings together several persons to live at joint expense; furthermore, these terms are quite commonly confused" (*Dictionnaire de la conversation et de la lecture* [Paris: Belin-Mazdat, 1838], 43:45). In the first chapter ("Une pension bourgeoise") of Balzac's *Père Goriot* (1835), the "respectable établissement" of Madame Vauquer is described as catering almost exclusively to the elderly, until the arrival of the young Eugène de Rastignac.

The *tables d'hôte*, even those meriting distinction, fare poorly for all men curious about living well; everything is done in haste; these are places where taste pays a visit only in passing, and where certain habits should not be acquired. Its strict regimen, where the hours are inflexible, is not compatible with an independence that ought never be surrendered. The inflexible order of the service impedes the imagination incessantly; and the wonders that may have seduced the guest at first become a succession of embarrassments and mishaps. Conversation is not possible for any man of sense or wit at a *table d'hôte*, short of chatting with a friend in a low voice.

The *pension bourgeoise* is infested by a pair of harpies: pretension and boredom.

In several of these places, cleanliness and proper form are offended incessantly and treated like something superfluous.

The majority of the *cercles*, the *tables d'hôte*, and the rest homes have only one goal, one that they pursue relentlessly; this goal is gambling, which has prostitution as its partner. At the tables that are set here, it is always a danger to sit down where pleasure is a trap and every brew has its provocative drug.[14]

---

[14] Although there are no specific borrowings, Briffault's opinions echo many of the sentiments in an earlier article titled "Les tables d'hôte parisiennes" by Louis Desnoyers (writing under the pseudonymn L. D. Derville), a journalist colleague of his, including their association with gambling and dangerous characters (*Paris, ou le livre des cent-et-un* [Paris: Ladvocat, 1832], 6:289–317). This piece, too, ends with a warning: "Be wary, gourmets; be wary, merry guests, of the *tables d'hôte* of Paris, whether it is a cheap eating-house [*gargote*], a *cuisine bourgeoise*, a *pension bourgeoise*, a *table d'hôte*.... For whoever wants to dine well, dine cheerfully, only one thing in the world is worse than dining at a *table d'hôte*: that is not to dine at all" (317).

• X •

THE RESTAURANTS OF PARIS

A century ago Paris did not have restaurateurs; only cook-caterers[1] and grill masters were known: some ran those *tables d'hôte* where the hosts never sat down; the others delivered around town or served on their premises the dishes, dinners, or meals that were ordered. In 1751, a little less than a hundred years ago, the "Hermit of the Chausée-d'Antin" dined at one of the houses located on the rue des Boucheries under the signage "A la Croix de Malte." Here, in his article of February 13, 1813, is how he spoke about his memories of sixty-two years before:[2]

---

[1] I have here borrowed Rebecca L. Spang's translation of "traiteur" (from *The Invention of the Restaurant: Paris and Modern Gastronomic Culture* [Cambridge, MA: Harvard University Press, 2000]), which nowadays is translated as "caterer." But the "traiteur" of Briffault's time and before played a wider and more various role (often regulated and restricted), occasionally running establishments similar to inns or *tables d'hôte*.

[2] This lengthy citation is from "Les restaurateurs," number 66 of the articles appearing in the multi-volume set *L'hermite de la Chausée-d'Antin* (1812–1814) by Victor-Joseph Étienne de Jouy, a journalist, critic, dramatist, and librettist who was elected as one of the forty members of the Académie française in 1815. He was probably best known as the author of a series of satirical essays published in the *Gazette de France* and brought together in the above collection. The observations on the "Maltese Cross" and other establishments in the citation are those of the "Hermit," a fictional narrator who gives his birth date as 1741 (Jouy was born in 1764) and would therefore be in his prime in the years preceding the Revolution; it is unclear, however, from where Briffault derives the date "1751," since it does not appear in "Les restaurateurs" (*L'hermite de la Chausée-d'Antin, ou observations sur les*

"The Croix de Malte," he says, "was not noted for the magnificence of its dining rooms, for the profusion of silver dishware, for the grace and elegance of the lady at the counter; but wholesome and abundant fare could be had there for a good price. Three tables of walnut wood, covered by a *toile d'Alençon* tablecloth, formed a half-circle in a vast hall where a ribbed vault supported, instead of Thomire or Ravrio chandeliers, two enormous brass lamps, each of the three spouts enlightening, in a manner of speaking, those who came to sup in that house.[3] From noon to three, the dining hall never emptied, and pretty good company could ordinarily be found there. The old Boindin came there to quarrel, 'in his shrill falsetto,' with Marmontel, and from there he left to go preach atheism in a corner of the Café Procope.[4] Piron and Crébillon *fils* arranged to meet there every Saturday, outdoing one another with their jokes and epigrams;[5] Saint-Foix took part when, by chance, he

moeurs et les usages français au commencement du XIXe siècle [Paris: Pillet, 1817], 3:85–104). The rue des Boucheries, incidentally, was one of the streets absorbed by the boulevard Saint-Germain in Georges-Eugène Haussmann's renovation of Paris during the Second Empire.

[3] *Toile d'Alençon* was a kind of canvas woven from hemp, an important part of the textile industry in the Norman town of Alençon during the eighteenth century. Pierre-Philippe Thomire and André-Antoine Ravrio were sculptors noted particularly for their bronze furnishings and mountings during the First Empire.

[4] Nicolas Boindin, a dramatist active in the first half of the eighteenth century, was portrayed as having a "fausset aigre" in Voltaire's satire *Le temple du goût*, a characterization he would carry with him, along with his professed atheism, into posterity. Jean-François Marmontel, an essayist, historian, and contributor to Denis Diderot's *Encyclopédie*, was elected to the Académie française in 1763. The Café Procope, opened in 1686 and still in existence today, was a gathering spot for the intellectual and theatrical elite of the eighteenth century. For an interesting portrait of Boindin at the Café Procope, see Emile Colombey, "Les cabales littéraires aux XVIIIe siècle," *Revue contemporaine* (Paris: Bureau de la Revue Contemporaine, 1861) 24:149–168.

[5] Alexis Piron, a dramatist active during the reign of Louis XV, was known primarily for his epigrams. Claude-Prosper Jolyot de Crébillon (known also as Crébillon *fils* to

had not received some swipe of a sword during the week;[6] finally, Patu and Portel developed a very tight friendship, and formed, three times a week, the core of the frequent theatergoers of the Comédie-Française, a gathering quite different at that period than that of today.[7] A good dinner, at a time when the science of gastronomy was still in its infancy, meant barely more than some good wines and congenial guests; both one and the other were found at the Croix de Malte. You were served there—I have not forgotten her—by a beautiful Burgundian girl named Catherine. In all my life, I have not seen such an extraordinary example of energy, memory, and presence of mind: she found a way of serving and pleasing at the same time thirty persons of differing desires, tastes, and moods. Even M. Mercier, who had his lucid moments, said some years afterward that he had known in France only two heads so well organized: the serving girl at the rue des Boucheries and M. Turgot."[8]

distinguish him from his father, a famous tragedian) was a novelist and playwright who, in 1729, helped found the literary and singing society Le Caveau, to which Piron and the composer Jean-Philippe Rameau also belonged.

[6] Germain-François Poullain de Saint-Foix was a musketeer in the service of Louis XV until the age of thirty-six when he quit to devote himself, with some success, to literature, the theater, and the duels he often provoked.

[7] Claude-Pierre Patu, a friend of both Voltaire and Casanova, was a dramatist and translator who helped introduce Shakespeare to the French public. His most successful comedy was *Les adieux du goût* (1754), which he wrote in collaboration with Michel Portelance, a lesser known dramatist and probably the "Portel" (lengthened to "Portellaure" in later editions of *L'hermite de la Chausée-d'Antin*) mentioned by Jouy.

[8] Author of some sixty plays, Louis-Sébastien Mercier was also a journalist, essayist, novelist, and critic—one of France's most prolific men-of-letters both before and after the Revolution and until his death in 1814. Anne-Robert-Jacques Turgot, Baron de l'Aulne, was a statesman and political economist who served under both Louis XV and Louis XVI in a variety of posts, retiring from government service in 1776.

M. de Jouy, today one of the forty of the Académie française—and in whose hands we leave all responsibility for his
historical erudition, his grammatical knowledge, and his
opinions—continues:
    "Perfection of any kind is reached only through trial, error,
and experimentation. Around the year 1772, at various cooks-
caterers, the standard *tables d'hôte*, with their meals at fixed
hours, gave way to tables with settings of a dozen and a half-
dozen that were replenished as many times as a sufficient
number of guests were found. This practice was kept up in the
Latin Quarter; it was in place a few years ago in a house of this
type run by three elderly women whom the students called
'the three sisters.' The Hôtel d'York, rue Jacob, where you
paid one hundred sous a head, was the meeting-place for the
wealthiest of persons. Then came the Hôtel Bourbon, rue
Croix-des-Petits-Champs; the merchants and traders preferred to gather there, and the price was one-half less than
that of the Hôtel d'York. You dined at the same price at the
Hôtel du Nom de Jésus, in the cloister of Saint-Jacques de
l'Hôpital. This hotel, famed particularly for its fish, was inade-
quate to hold the crowds of customers descending upon it
during meatless days and the entire period of Lent.[9]
    "It was at the end of the year 1774 that the first restaura-
teurs were established. I am annoyed that I cannot restore to
the memory of modern gastronomy the name of the founder
of the 'dinners from a menu.' I recall nevertheless that the

---

[9] Of the three *hôtels* mentioned here, the most notable is the Hôtel d'York, for reasons
other than gastronomic, since it was on these premises—where David Hartley, the
representative from England was residing—that, on September 3, 1783, Benjamin
Franklin, John Adams, and John Jay signed the Treaty of Paris, which recognized the
independence of the United States. For a more comprehensive description of the
hôtel garni in the late eighteenth century, including the three mentioned by Jouy,
see Albert Babeau, *Paris en 1789* (Paris: Firmin-Didot, 1889), 153–159.

foundation for this great institution was laid in the rue des
Prêcheurs, and that this inscription, in dog Latin, could be
read on the signage for this father of the restaurant:

> *O vos qui stomacho laboratis, accurite,*
> *Et ego vos restaurabo.*
> Oh you whose stomach cries out, come running
> And I, I will restore you."[10]

The first restaurateur in Paris was a man named Lamy.[11]
He opened his dining rooms in one of the dark and narrow
passageways that then surrounded the Palais-Royal. Joining
forces against him were the cook-caterers, but they could not
drive him off. Originally, the restaurateur did not have the
right to put linen on his tables; they were covered with a green
or mottled oilcloth.

Beauvilliers was the one who first attracted a large part of
the world.[12] He never left a mark as a chef, but he had a quality

---

[10] The name Jouy is seeking is "Boulanger," one that frequently surfaces in histories of
gastronomy as the founder of the restaurant trade: "Up to 1774, only *tables d'hôte*,
serving at fixed hours, were known; a cook-caterer, in the rue des Prêcheurs,
named Boulanger, had the idea of offering to his guests bouillons, eggs, chicken,
and other restoratives. He placed above his door this verse from the Bible: Venite
ad me omnes qui stomacho laboritis, et ego restaurabo vos. Such is the origin of
the restaurateurs" (Charles Harmand, *Manuel de l'étranger dans Paris pour 1824*
[Paris: Hesse, 1824], 232).

[11] Perhaps the most thorough discussion of the genesis of the Parisian restaurant can
be found in Rebecca L. Spang's *The Invention of the Restaurant: Paris and Modern
Gastronomic Culture* (Cambridge, MA: Harvard University Press, 2000). Her
choice for the first true "restaurateur" is Mathurin Roze de Chantoiseau, who
founded his "restaurant" in 1766. Briffault's candidate, "Lamy," is not mentioned
in Spang, but this fact, and much of the observations in this and the following
paragraph seem to be drawn from Marquis de Cussy's "L'art culinaire," reprinted
in *Les classiques de la table* (1845) I:287–288.

[12] Antoine Beauvilliers opened his first restaurant in the mid 1780s and then
established La Grande Taverne de Londres in the Palais-Royal (1787?), perhaps

that in our time is no more than a dead tradition: he paid full attention to the persons who came to dine at his place and roamed his halls incessantly to make sure his diners were satisfied. At the slightest doubt, he would have one dish replaced by another, descend into his kitchens, and roar loudly at the negligent worker. With the return of the Bourbons,[13] Beauvilliers became an object of ridicule, since he made the rounds of his tables in a pre-Revolutionary jacket and knee britches, a sword by his side.

Our ancestors ate at the cabaret, our fathers went to the cook-caterer, we dine with the restaurateur.[14]

Brillat-Savarin tried to define the restaurateur.[15]

According to him, "a restaurateur is one whose business consists in offering the public a banquet always at-hand and whose dishes are itemized in portions at a fixed price, at the behest of the consumer." An obscure and ponderous definition!

He goes on: "The establishment is known as the 'restaurant'—in the south of France they say a 'restaurat.' The one who runs the establishment is the 'restaurateur.' The nominal roll of the dishes, with price information, is called the 'menu.' and the 'menu to pay' for the note with the quantity of dishes supplied and their price." Today that's known as the "bill."

Finally, according to the master: "Among those who crowd into restaurants, few of them imagine that it's impossible for

the first true luxury restaurant in Paris. He is best known as the author of *L'art du cuisinier* (1814).

[13] First in 1814, and then after Napoleon's "Hundred Days," in 1815.

[14] Étienne de Jouy makes a similar observation in "Les restaurateurs" mentioned above (*L'hermite de la Chaussée-d'Antin*, 3:88–89).

[15] Briffault cites here the opening of "Méditation 28" from Jean-Anthelme Brillat-Savarin's *Physiologie du goût* (1825).

the one who invented the restaurant not to have been a man of genius and profound observation."

The establishment of the restaurateurs was a social act. Under the regime that they replaced, fine dining was the privilege of the affluent; the restaurateurs put it within the reach of everyone. The man who can, perhaps once in his life, spend twenty or twenty-five francs on his dinner—if he knows how to choose his dishes and if he sits at the table of a first-class restaurant—is treated better than if he dined at the home of a prince:[16] he is served with as much splendor as inside a palace; he orders at his pleasure; neither his taste nor his will meet any obstacles; released from all concerns, he obeys only the whims of his fancy and the delicacy of his palate.[17] The restaurateurs have thus taken a large step toward social equality, which is far better founded on the community of pleasure than on theories that will never succeed in placing the poor on the same level as the rich.

Europe asked us for our restaurateurs, like civilization's missionaries.

Under the Empire, the reputation of Parisian restaurants was raised so high, that in Europe they did for our cuisine what the

---

[16] At a time when a first-class prix-fixe dinner could cost two francs (and a full-course dinner at a luxury restaurant could cost twenty-five), the average worker was earning about two francs daily, while a skilled worker could earn as much as four francs a day. (Cited in John McCormick, *Popular Theaters of Nineteenth-Century France* [London: Routledge, 1993], 78.) See also "Introduction," n. 53.

[17] These observations are similar to views expressed by Brillat-Savarin in *Physiologie du goût* ("Méditation 28," No. 138).

seventeenth and eighteenth centuries had done for our literature; they made it universal. This splendor of the Empire's restaurants, with all due respect to the luxury of our current
public tables, has not been equaled. We are not talking here
about the vain brilliance owed to the decoration; we are talking about the actual merits of the entire service.

The restaurateurs, in their wanderings, have followed the
stages of Parisian migrations. The boulevard du Temple, which
was formerly the place where high society granted all of its
favors, had famous restaurants: the Cadran Bleu, the Galiote,
and other houses experienced triumphs that Deffieux or the
Méridien and the Capucin never achieved.[18] It is true that the
halls of these famous establishments were more often occupied by great dinners rather than by individuals; the private
rooms were especially in demand. At the same time, the fame
of the Rocher du Cancale[19]—whose perfection had been carried so far and whose fine dining and wines had qualities that
the most opulent tables could not always reach—was on the
rise. The boulevard du Temple had the privilege for a long
time—and it has not yet entirely lost it—to what were generally called "wild parties": you rarely dined there alone. The
Rocher de Cancale was, then, the homeland and classic sanctuary for the finest dinners, for those valuing genuine and

[18] Of these, the Cadran Bleu was the most renowned. Founded in the eighteenth
   century by Jean-Baptiste Henneveu, it was known in the next century for hosting
   wedding receptions and its private dinners. Balzac's Vautrin (*Le Père Goriot*) was
   familiar with it and Madame Cibot (*Le Cousin Pons*) shucked oysters there.
[19] Founded in 1804 by Alexis Balaine, Rocher de Cancale was celebrated for its
   seafood, as well as its singing-society dinners and wine-cellar banquets. A good
   deal of the *Human Comedy*'s population, as well as Balzac and other celebrated
   authors dined there. (See especially Anka Muhlstein, *Balzac's Omelette* [New
   York: Other Press, 2010], 44–57.)

complete superiority. The concert dinners, the cellar breakfasts, and all the wit expended there were viewed only as an

outstanding standard. To appear
alone in these places was rather
ill-advised: the solitary guest, relegated to the desert of the common
hall, was neglected; he received
neither the care nor the consideration of the waiters he watched
passing right in front of him; he
ate his food cold, and with insup-

portable delays. Persons of some experience did not venture
into this sort of brig.

Foreigners, new arrivals from the provinces and the terri-
tories, and officers passing through or on their return invariably
gathered at Legaque's and at Véry's.[20] These two restaurants
dwelt in long pavilions on the Terasse des Feuillants near the
first entry grill of the rue de Rivoli. They flocked into their
narrow rooms; the breakfasts and dinners there were packed
constantly. This vogue was deserved; at one of them it continued on with brilliance.

At the Chausée-d'Antin, the
breakfasts at Café Anglais; Hardy's
celebrated shellfish and Riche's
kidneys à la brochette attracted
the young and elegant world. It

---

[20] Chez Véry, which moved to the Palais-Royal in 1801, was famous during the Empire
for its elegance and expense. Rubempré, in Balzac's *Illusions perdues*, lost a good
deal of his illusions (and francs) there. Legaque, its neighbor, lasted only until
1817. (See Muhlstein, 41-44, and Robert Courtine, *La vie parisienne: cafés et
restaurants des boulevards* [Paris: Perrin, 1984], 15.)

was cheerfully said that "you had to be very rich to dine at Hardy's and very hardy to dine at Riche's." The Palais-Royal was then the center for all those whose lives were spent in pleasure;[21] gathered there were the restaurateurs who made the most noise, headed by Véry and those "trois frères provençaux," whose memory will not perish. Grouped around the Palais-Royal were distinguished houses: Beauvilliers, Robert, and that other trilogy made into a play on words by gastronomy: Rô, Méot, and Julliette. The Veau qui Tette, that land of Cockaigne for the Parisian bourgeois, was also worth a mention.[22]

At that time, each house had a well-known specialty. Robert excelled in all preparations for beef and commissioned dinners; the Veau qui Tette owed its prosperity to lamb trotters; there were some who praised the grilled tripe; the Trois Frères Provençaux made their fortune with cod and garlic—the illustrious brandade—and their cellar beyond reproach; at the Rocher de Cancale, Balaine prospered from the high quality of his wines and his excellent fish; the Cadran Bleu and its gallant mysteries made a success of Henneveu.[23] Some gourmands, more extravagant than refined, enjoyed visiting the

[21] Built by Cardinal Richelieu in the 1630s, the Palais-Cardinal became, after his death, the Palais-Royal and a royal residence. By the Revolution, it had become a huge complex of buildings and courts, its vast galleries filled with boutiques, restaurants, cafés, brothels, and gambling houses, transforming it into the entertainment capital of Paris. (See, e.g., Philip Mansel, *Paris between Empires: 1814–1852* [London: John Murray, 2001], 41–44.) For a contemporary portrait, see Briffault's own article "Le Palais-Royal" in *Les rues de Paris: ancien et moderne* (Louis Larine, ed. [Paris: Kugelman, 1844], I:185–204) where he chronicles its rise to glory and its decline: "It was a libertine who led a joyous life, but you have converted it, given it back its health, and now it dies of boredom" (I:240).

[22] Listed here and in the preceding paragraph are the names of most of those restaurants that transformed Napoleon's Paris into the restaurant capital of the world.

[23] According to Brillat-Savarin, Cadran Bleu owed its prosperity to "the mysterious fourth-floor boudoirs" (*Physiologie du goût*, "Meditation 28," No. 143).

wonders and masterpieces of each kitchen all in the same day; others amused themselves by dining backward, beginning with the dessert and finishing with the soup: a madness of delirious bellies, indifferent to all flavors.

Orbiting around these glittering stars were quite commendable satellites and secondary planets, which had also gained a deserved popularity within the middle regions.

The special character of the Empire's restaurateurs was the care and scrupulous attention applied to every detail of the service; almost all of them had been trained in their profession by experience, both early and long. At their places, the public was handled, served with a conscientious integrity; they proved to be polite and obliging, ready to fix anything that could frustrate satisfaction or well-being. The luxury of these establishments was far from what it is today, but everything there was correct and elegant.

Evenings, the presence of these Parisian restaurants, their bright lights suddenly on display, made every movement shine, generating an abundant liveliness; everything was enhanced under this favorable influence, and the public, happy with these new benefits, took ecstatic delight in them.

The years 1814 and 1815, saddened by the two invasions, were for the Palais-Royal days of great joy and jubilation.[24] The Palais-Royal and its rotunda were a universal meeting

---

[24] This is a reference to the Allied occupations—after, respectively, Napoleon's abdication in 1814 and his defeat at Waterloo in 1815—when multitudes of European officers and their troops got their first taste of what Paris had to offer.

place. The story is told of two officers, old school friends, running into each other during a cavalry charge made by their two regiments: this was at Jena;[25] the trumpets sounded, and the two classmates had only enough time to exchange swiftly these exclamations:

"In Paris!"

"After the campaign!"

"At the Palais-Royal!"

"Before the rotunda!"

"Five o'clock!"

"Day we're back!"

They were both promptly on time for the rendezvous, and the dangers they had gone through added to the pleasure of seeing each other again.

When the whole of Europe rushed in arms against France, all the leaders of that multitude had only one battle cry: "Paris! Paris!" Such was the cry proclaimed from the edge of the Rhine to the banks of the Seine. Once in Paris, what did they ask for first of all? The Palais-Royal! A young Russian officer entered there on horseback. And at the Palais-Royal, what was their first wish? To sit at the tables of those restaurateurs whose names, which had come down to them in all their glory, they were citing.

We require no further testimony of what the restaurants of Paris were like under the Empire.

From 1815 to 1830 that grandeur did not appear to diminish; but perhaps, because of expansion, it was less genuine, less solid, and less enduring than in the previous age. Thus, the

[25] This anecdote refers to an earlier incident, since the battle of Jena, between French and Prussian-Saxon forces, took place in 1806.

number of restaurants increased; these establishments, with admirable intelligence, appealed to every need and every amusement; they were placed at all levels of society, and spread new amenities, the signs and traces of which were found nowhere else, into the life of each individual and the general public. This was the first and truest merit of the Parisian restaurants during these fifteen years. Have these advantages, which were all done for the community, lessened the delights of the privileged? For the answer to that question, we will let the facts speak for themselves.

Old reputations antagonized young ambitions. Not being able to challenge them over the qualities that recommended the venerable houses to public favor, the new houses competed against them in two ways, through the luxury of surroundings and tableware, and by a drop in price. The veterans did not collapse under these blows, but distaste sapped their energy and their zeal; some fell, but several retreated by degrees and retired with a wealth of spoils. It so happened that almost all the restaurateurs—in this frenzy of growth that multiplied the new establishments—descended from the heights; mediocre houses were created everywhere and the superior houses disappeared one by one.[26]

So, for this fifteen-year period, Paris was blanketed with quite decent places, but it saw the elite kitchens extinguish their oven fires. Some brilliant comets flashed across our

[26] "The hundred or so restaurants found in Paris in the late eighteenth century increased by a factor of six during the first decade and a half of the new century. By the 1820s the city counted over three thousand restaurants of various types that ranged across the social as well as the culinary spectrum" (Priscilla Parkhurst Ferguson, *Accounting for Taste: The Triumph of French Cuisine* [Chicago: University of Chicago Press, 2004], 87).

space. Where are those emerging lights? And what stars have spun out of sight?

On the boulevard du Temple, weddings and banquets reduced everything to petty proportions. On the Chausée-d'Antin, for how long did they shine, those pompous dining rooms, today deserted and neglected, and those sumptuous corridors, so often visited by disaster? If we had to speak of everything we no longer have and everything believed to have been replaced by gilding both within and without, we would see how much genuine quality has been lost beneath these splendid appearances and these glittering vanities.

When a restaurateur has set his tables in magnificent surroundings; when his service has driven to excess the pomp of his tableware, his glassware, his linens; when he has assembled all the elements of an irreproachable novelty, he thinks he has been released from all other obligations; the very promises of his buffet are only a decoy. And is it surprising that the public is not taken in by these deceptions, and that it does not agree to pay the price for this superb magnificence that has done nothing for its true happiness! Today we are no longer misled or attracted by this arrogant deceit; we wait sensibly for time to pass over all of that. The noise and quackery no longer fool us. We know the traps and devices hidden beneath those draperies; we see all the tribulations prepared for us in those private rooms so stylishly furnished and so discreetly arranged; we enter only with suspicion: we have learned all too well that all the wonders on the walls will end up on the bill. That right there is the secret behind the ruin,

so swift, of those gilded boxes and cages that we have seen collapse. We could cite one formidable example of that decline that followed in the wake of luxury. A café, heir to a well-established reputation, received considerable company in the private rooms on the ground floor and the mezzanine: this was Socrates' place, always grand enough when it was full of true friends. He had an attack of vanity: after renting the first floor, he constructed, gilded, and richly furnished some large dining rooms; they remained empty and were visited by bankruptcy: he had to clear out. Another came to set up shop there; but the site is cursed. No one goes there any more.

These catastrophes did not afflict only the high flyers. Entirely abandoned districts attest to the fickle cruelty of fash-

ion. The boulevard de l'Hôpital, just beyond the Jardin des Plantes erected temples to dining: the Arc-en-ciel, the Feu Éternal, and the Panier Fleuri had some fine days: the popular tide had carried the fashionable world to them. We had just dropped by, they were already gone; the disgrace of the boulevard du Temple had rolled them into the abyss.[27] And what has become of the Veau qui Tette, that witness to so many joyous parties, that theater for so many banquets?[28]

[27] The "disgrace" is likely a reference to the attempted assassination of Louis-Philippe, which led to the deaths of eighteen people. It took place on July 25, 1835, as he was passing by in a procession on the boulevard du Temple.

[28] Unlike the other restaurants in this paragraph, the Veau qui Tette had a long history, tracing its origins back to a sixteenth-century butcher shop in the place du Châtelet, where it remained until the redevelopment of the place between 1855

We will divide the restaurants of Paris into three classes: outside of that, no more than a hodgepodge; lower than that, darkness; lower still, chaos and hideous sewers.

The first-class restaurants have a feature that identifies them right away; high prices are, for them, a matter of pride. Within almost the entire commercial hierarchy, this singular aristocracy is one where a fee is paid for grandeur and loftiness. Among the restaurateurs, this trait is more prominent than in the other professions.[29]

These houses, almost all run with a great deal of ostentation, are never entirely defective; but they do not always rise to their reputations. In recent times, the most celebrated restaurants seemed to have faltered, only two or three still upholding their ancient honor. A pitiful spectacle was that slow and painful agony of the first of these establishments, the Rocher de Cancale, fallen from so high. The retreat of the Trois Frères Provençaux either just followed or preceded this fatal event; the Café Anglais was no more; the Café de Paris appeared only in the shadows; the Maison Dorée never made a serious effort.[30] Paris, cluttered with so many emerging restaurants over

and 1858. Poiret the younger, from Balzac's "Les employés" in *Scènes de la vie parisienne*, dined there regularly.

[29] An early twentieth-century critic, Stoddard Dewey, quotes a late proprietor of the Maison Dorée on this matter—" 'I make you pay dear so that you may not have a rabble around you!' "—afterward offering the following comment: "A similar policy was common to all the restaurants of Paris renown until the advent of democracy" ("The Passing of the Maison Dorée," *Macmillan's Magazine* [London: Macmillan's, 1903], 87:417–418).

[30] Rocher de Cancale closed in 1846 but opened at another location, where a restaurant of that name still exists. Trois Frères Provençaux, established in 1786, was sold in 1836 and lost much of its character (the publisher, Jacques Arnoux, had a very disappointing meal when he dined there in the early 1840s in Gustave Flaubert's *L'éducation sentimentale* [Part 1, chapter 5]); it regained its reputation in the Second Empire, under Adolphe Dugléré, but closed in 1869. The fame of Café

every point of its surface, found itself lacking almost any good tables. For a time, their hope for salvation rested on those two illustrious twins, separated only by a simple partition in the transverse gallery of the Palais-Royal. Alone, they bore the burden of a fame difficult to uphold; near them, the inheritors of the Trois Frères Provençaux and, at the other end, the Café Corazza (of succulent origins), came to their aid, and prosperous times seem finally to have returned.[31] We do not hesitate to repeat that, in our opinion, you are less well treated by the restaurateurs than you were formerly. Preparations and seasonings assume a depressing uniformity. Two sauces reappear constantly: one is brown, it represents the gravies and the reductions; the other is white and yellowish, used for all the fricassées. All that is brown is not yellow, and all that is yellow is not brown: it is impossible to depart from these limitations.[32] The

Anglais, founded in 1802, may have diminished when it was sold by the Delaunay family in 1836, but it recovered in 1866 when Dugléré took over its kitchen. (The banquet Babette cooks for the Danish sisters in the movie *Babette's Feast* is reminiscent of a meal she prepared as head chef at the Café Anglais.) The first Café de Paris opened in 1822, became the height of fashion around 1840, then faded in the following decades, closing in 1856. The Maison Dorée opened around 1840 on the boulevard des Italiens near the Café Anglais and Tortoni's. (In Chapter 7 of *La dame aux camélias* [1848], Armand Duval stations himself at the Maison Dorée [or Maison D'or] to watch his future mistress, Marguerite Gautier, on one of the Café Anglais' balconies, picking the petals from "les camélias de son bouquet.") Despite Briffault's disparagement, Maison Dorée quickly gained a reputation and would become one of the Second Empire's more elegant restaurants, not closing until 1902. (Many contemporary recollections of these restaurants can be found in Courtine, *passim*.)

[31] The "twins" is likely a reference to Véfour (not the Grand Véfour, opened later in the century), situated between numbers 79 and 82 at the Galerie Beaujolais, and Véry, in the same Galerie at 83 to 86. Frequented by Jacobins during the Revolution and later by the young Napoleon, Café Corazza was primarily a café and ice-cream shop until it was turned into a restaurant by Eugène Douix, a former chef of Charles X.

[32] This is not as much of an exaggeration as it might first appear. In his chapter on "les grandes sauces" in *L'art de la cuisine française du dix-neuvieme siècle*, Carême

names of these two inevitable sauces vary and are transformed with an ease and agility that answers all needs. Unfortunate outcomes from dubious dishes derived from highly susceptible foods—like eggs, fish, and game—have become more frequent. The quality of the wine has suffered from harsh assaults: driven from the kitchen, integrity has not found refuge in the cellar. Without doubt, there are honorable exceptions; but the general condition has been altered and is deteriorating more and more.

First-class restaurants have made notable progress in another area; the special dinners they formerly held were affairs of cardboard and artificial flowers, the burden of which they have shaken off, and their meals, now enhanced by everything that can enliven them, have boldly headed down the path to which the elegant and comfortable life is accustomed. Apart from the indelible differences, we do not hesitate to place the special dinners of our top restaurateurs above the best of the city's tables.

One example, which we borrow from a book authoritative in gastronomic matters, sheds light on this truth.[33]

This was at the Rocher de Cancale. It began with six small Marennes oysters and enough spoonfuls of soup to neutralize the sensation of cold from the oysters; several soups were sampled, followed by the glass of Madeira. The opening service was worthy from the start. The narrator expresses his admira-

proposed four master sauces—*l'espagnole, le velouté, l'allemande, la béchamel*—from which all others were derived (Paris: Renouard, 1847), 3:1. Depending on the proportion of ingredients, all four can take on either a brown, yellow, or white coloration.

[33] Briffault cites here passages from *Encyclopédie des gens du monde* ([Paris, 1837], 8:233–234), describing a dinner at the Rocher de Cancale given by a "Lord W.," and written by Frédéric Fayot. The piece was also reprinted in *Les classiques de la table* ([1845], 1:299–403), the "authoritative" book referred to above and from which Briffault often cites and borrows.

tion as follows: "It wasn't that there was a great number of plates; but they were so well modulated, and the style, the aspect, the freshness, the force, and the flavor were so excellent that everyone had to admire them." The historian complains here that for "the shot midway" a punch *à la romaine* was used rather than a rum sorbet.[34]

He adds: "We were served with warmed silverware, of English plate, in perfect taste and in brilliant candlelight." He then names some exquisite dishes, and next exclaims, "The rest of the small and magnificent dinner was perfect. If you want to get an idea of it," he says, "imagine M. de Talleyrand or Lorenzo de Medici giving a dinner for nine of his gourmet friends." We will take enthusiasm's role into consideration in such praise, but it could still have been given without being charged with exaggeration.

The chronicles of the old Rocher de Cancale are replete with exploits of this kind.

That dinner, given by Lord W . . . and shared by nine guests, cost 100 francs a head. We will match it with a truly original dinner M. Romieu gave some years ago. He wrote Borrel in the morning to have ready for him at two o'clock, for six persons, cabbage soup, beef, bacon and sausage, pork and beans, a mutton stew with potatoes, a goose stuffed with chestnuts, a lamb's lettuce salad, and an apple tart, coarse country bread, spare linen, pewter place settings, earthenware and common glasses. For wines, the most expensive of all that was there.[35]

---

[34] "Punch à la romaine" is more like an alcoholic frozen lemonade than a punch. It has the distinction of being the last "punch" served the night the Titanic sank. See chapter 4 for "the shot midway."

[35] For Auguste Romieu, see chap. 8, n. 25. Pierre-Frédéric Borrel succeeded Balaine as the proprietor of Rocher de Cancale.

M. Romieu had adopted for his meals, even at restaurants, a practice originated by M. Jules Didot,[36] who in summer dined in white jackets and in winter, all the guests included, in nightgowns.

One day a military orderly from the ministry, having seen M. Romieu and his companions in that outfit, reported that he had found him dining among Turks.

Another time, three gamblers went to find Borrel and told him: "After having won a lot, we lost almost everything; for all of our profit, we've got nothing left but this 1,000 franc note. We want to eat it up all in one meal." The honest restaurateur pointed out to them that their wish was no easier to fulfill than that of the grenadier who asked for coffee at six francs a cup. They insisted. It did no good to demonstrate to them that the thing was not possible, that at the very least the number of guests would have to be increased; all objections were useless. They began to think about what there was that was most expensive. One of them came up with a singular idea. It was the month of December during a cold wave that had frozen all the waterways. He proposed eating a plate of frogs, going to fish for them after breaking through the ice. For this expedition they brought together fifty workers, who asked for five hundred francs for a hundred frogs, which were made into a soup that no one touched.

At Trois Frères Provençaux, a dinner for wine lovers was established in the justly celebrated cellars of that restaurant.

The special dinners at the first-class cook-caterers play today a large role in contemporary manners; no longer do just the banquets, birthdays, and professional corporations take over

[36] This is probably the Jules Didot who was a member of a well-known family of publishers, printers, and typographers.

the beautiful dining halls built for that function, but there are private dinners as well; what was known for a long time only at the Rocher de Cancale can now be experienced everywhere.

Second-class restaurants are numerous; they can be found in almost all the popular districts. They favor the wider streets, the boulevards; many of them are at the Palais-Royal, next to the three or four chosen ones always in demand by the dining aristocracy. Sometimes these restaurants deploy greater luxury than those above them; but they do not have the secret for excellent dishes, offering only things that are scrupulously good. The wines especially, at these places, never depart from this honorable mediocrity.

At the third rank, we will place a still larger number of houses that are commendable but cannot incur the necessary expense to raise their level and serve with distinction; they huddle together in a lower range and have no more than a single ambition, to do small things well. There is generally some honesty within these middle regions; less of a show is found there than at the top, and less deception than at the bottom.

These second- and third-class restaurants are those the average diner haunts; their public is composed of that common

crowd that lives placidly between opulence and poverty: it is the temperate zone of the social sphere.

In the first-class dining rooms, even those on the ground floor, figures from all the high social stations are found; the nobility, dignitaries, and those of intellectual distinction converge there. Foreign families come there to take their meals; the manners and tone of these colonies of visitors indicate the rank they occupy in their own country. It is in the first-class restaurants where those opulent fortunes of a day are seen, enjoying a few prosperous hours as if they owned an eternity of wealth. Also there, strutting across the tiles, are the vanity of the snob and the vainglory of the fool.

By tacit agreement, for which the grounds would be difficult to explain, the three classes of restaurants are devoted to this or that meal. Breakfasts at the Rocher de Cancale went out-of-fashion; breakfast was taken at the Véry's in the Tuileries: and no more at the Véry's in the Palais-Royal; at the Trois Frères Provençaux, breakfast was almost unknown; breakfasts at Tortoni's and Corazza's had always been popular and were done well; the prize for regular and special breakfasts belongs to Tortoni; from the Café de Chartres, Véfour inherited all the breakfasts of the wood- and glass-paneled galleries. At the Palais-Royal, supper was taken at all hours; if nights at the Café Anglais are excepted, supper was taken on the Chaussée d'Antin only intermittently.[37]

[37] Café Tortoni, which like Carozza began as an ice-cream shop, was celebrated throughout the nineteenth century for the writers and artists who were its patrons. It appears not only in Balzac, but also in the fictions of Stendhal, Maupassant, and Proust. Café de Chartres was purchased by Jean Véfour in 1820, and the name "Café de Chartres" still appears in its frontage at the Palais-Royal, where the restaurant continues in operation as Le Grand Véfour.

In recent years, the Rocher de Cancale wanted to resume its "singing breakfasts." No one understood what that meant; it was an anachronism.

For a number of persons, a life spent dining in restaurants is an absolute necessity; the uncertainty of their hours and the need to control expenses turns, in certain situations, this habit into a law. We do not hesitate to say that for these people, whatever may be the delights they gather around themselves, this life generates only satiety and disgust. It works only for some blasé stomachs that have gotten used to it, pretty much like Mithridates got used to poison.[38]

These particular drawbacks are amply redeemed by the advantages the restaurateur's presence offers to the greater number. The choice of a particular time is itself a valuable quality for both business and pleasure; travelers and the wandering public find at every turn a hospitality always ready to welcome them and for a price that can be easily determined.

For the purpose of observation and for people who do it for simple amusement, dining out is a resource whose range, in some ways, is almost impossible to measure. The whole of society comes to pass under the gaze of the diner, who contemplates and studies it at its most expansive. It is hardly worth even trying to give an idea of this picture so constantly in motion. It is not the smart society of the drawing rooms, the busy world of the streets, the poses and pretensions of the boulevard promenade, the concerns of the theater and concert hall; it is a multitude struggling with sensations that have carried it away despite itself. To follow the gradations of conversation

---

[38] Mithridates, an Eastern monarch during the time of the Roman Republic, was said to have acquired an immunity to poison by taking small doses of toxins throughout his life.

at neighboring tables is a study full of interest. Usually the early stages are reserved and restrained. Rather than speaking, people observe themselves and others; but soon uninhibited emotion emerges, rises up, and is revealed: it is a general confession and one of the most entertaining. It is said that in dreams each one of us speaks about what interests us the most; the same is true about the outpourings over a meal. (All prudent and discreet intrigues, by the way, whether matters of interest or of gallantry, sentiment or opinion, ought to dine in private rooms.) That the series of characters is unending and constantly renewed increases still more the charm of this spectacle: there are groups of burlesques, there are isolated caricatures of all ages, of all features, and of every nuance; the characters on the stage have nothing to compare with this variety. At every moment, the panels of this magic lantern change and the images are renewed. At the restaurants, a freedom of style and manners also reigns, which, for those burdened by the yoke of relations and conventions, is even more of a triumph and a joy. The silence of some, the chatting of others; embarrassment, timidity, clumsiness, audacity and self-confidence, impudence even, cries of impatience, transports of satisfaction, all those characters so diverse and shaken by so many passions; the tastes, the obsessions, the surprises, the disappointments, the raptures, the anger of these here and the bliss of those there, all form a succession of sudden contrasts, full of attraction.

To really enjoy this feature, you must not halt at the threshold, that is to say, in the front dining rooms; you have to penetrate as far as possible into the sanctuary.

All those who frequent the first-class dining rooms do not run up an enormous expense; there are those young lions who disrupt an entire house to be served a cutlet, a compote, or a carafe of ice water. You are not ever isolated in a restaurant, without even mentioning that ebb and flow of eaters who leave not a single seat vacant; you meet, you gather together, you bond, like in a coach. At Véry's and at the Café de Paris, we have seen societies of diners seated as if in a refectory, where each eats his share; they were quite cheerful there, and more than one witty fellow gained his dinner at the point of his barbs.

Certain delicate natures have difficulty getting used to the shock of the smells and fumes emanating from these dishes, these substances, these foodstuffs so numerous and so intermingled. There are also harsh contrasts: a diner beginning and a diner ending a meal are ill served by proximity; the bowl of soup and the fingerbowl take a dim view of each other.

These infirmities are those of life in public.

Below the third class, no other places are to be found except those where dinner is an activity devoid of all sensuality; headed there are the good people who eat to please an appetite and satisfy a need. The houses serving that function are numberless and colorless; however, truth leads us to recognize that in these places there is less distance between price and value than in the superior class; the benefit diminishes with the quality; but we also think there is more integrity within the small markets than in the large. The fourth-class restaurateurs come very close to those for whom it is no longer possible to assign a rank.

Along this extreme frontier, the *cuisine bourgoise*,[39] a kind of Maritornes of the dirty apron,[40] can be found, and here the

[39] According to Louis Desnoyers' "Les tables d'hôte parisiennes," the *cuisine bourgeoise* was a kind of *table d'hôte* that, at 25 sous, was less expensive than a *pension bourgeoise* but provided a few more amenities (such as napkins) than the cheapest of eating houses (*Paris, ou le livre des cent-et-un* [Paris: Ladvocat, 1832], 6:297–298).

[40] Maritornes is an innkeeper's misshapen servant in Cervantes' *Don Quixote*, who one night winds up in the knight's bed: "Neither touch, nor smell, nor anything else

uniformity of the table suits only those mechanical bellies that, like the mortar harried by the pestle, grind and digest without sensing a thing.

Beyond the *cuisine bourgoise* lie the cheapest eating-houses.[41] At certain hours of the day, these houses, populated at breakfast and dinner by workers, present a spectacle, swarming like that of a mass of insects. If the table is not bare, it is covered with a shockingly stained cloth. Mornings, the bowls are filled and a course of ragout is served; at three o'clock boiled beef and vegetables are eaten; wine is paid for separately, and bread is brought.

In some of these places, the low nature of these dishes can only be matched by the voracity with which they are swallowed.

about the good lass that would have made any but a carrier vomit, were enough to undeceive him" (Part 1, chapter 26).

[41] The term "gargote" that Briffault uses here and elsewhere refers generally to a small, cheap restaurant or cabaret, but it is often used disparagingly: "She lowered herself to the 'harlequins' in the shady 'gargots,' where, for a sou, she got a pile of fishbones mixed with scraps of spoiled roasted meats" (Émile Zola, "Chapter 12," *L'assommoir* [1877]).

Elsewhere, in this respect, progress is evident, the quality of the foods is fair.

There are two kinds of these eating-houses, quite distinct. In one, there is a pretense toward luxury and refinement; favored dishes are served: flourishing there are rabbit, venison and game stews, hashes, ragouts, and the "harlequin," that *olla podrida* of the Parisian bohemian.[42] Slipping into these perfidious preparations are also the pseudo-rabbits,[43] game from the Montfaucon charnel houses,[44] fish fresh from the gutters, and desserts snatched from the dumps, and for some time now, goats in sheep's clothing. The second kind of "ordinary"[45] are meals soundly composed of roasted and boiled meats, everyday vegetables, and common fish; in these, everything is healthy

---

[42] There was an active trade up to the end of the century in the remainders of meals from wealthy tables, eventually to be sold at market stalls and in the cheapest restaurants. There were a variety of names for these tradesmen and their products, one of which was *arlequin* (in Balzac's story "Gambara" [1837] a *regrattier* trades in "the debris of the most sumptuous meals"): "Amongst the curiosities of Paris life decidedly are the small carts which from five to six every morning call at the back gates of embassies, palaces, *ministères*, restaurants, hotels…to purchase the remains of the entremets, desserts, and dinners…sold every morning by their cooks to the emissaries of a race of costermongers called 'arlequins.'…By twelve o'clock those scraps off rich men's plates are eagerly bought up." (Cited from the "French correspondent of the *London Star*" in "Foreign Notes [Oct. 24, 1868]," *Every Saturday: A Journal of Choice Reading* [Cambridge: Fields, Osgood, 1868], 6:543.) The term *olla podrida,* a Spanish stew composed of a variety of meats and vegetables, is also used metaphorically in both French and English to denote a "hodgepodge" or a "mixed bag" of things.

[43] For the 1838 scandal involving the "massacre" of cats and the confusion between *gibelotte de lapin* and "cat stew," see Rebecca L. Spang, "Ingestion/Pulling a Rabbit out of a Cat," *Cabinet*, no. 35 (Fall 2009), http://www.cabinetmagazine.org/issue/35/Spang.php.

[44] Montfaucon, Paris's great charnel house, was where much of its horse population was laid to rest.

[45] Although in England at the time an "ordinary" could refer both to a tavern or eating house serving a standard meal, usually at a fixed price, and the meal itself, the French term *ordinaire* is used more generally to denote a meal usually taken regularly.

and sound. Our epicures scorn these places and prefer what they call the good stews.

Generally, working and service people are well fed in Paris; only the lazy and the debauched are exposed to the rubbish. But it needs to be added that if there is one fraud in the popular diet against which nothing can shield the small consumer, it is the wine; it flows through streams, like water in the rivers, for everyone. The rich do not always escape these tricks, but the poor are delivered over to them without mercy.[46] The worker's meal is infected with adulterated wine just as the porter's breakfast is afflicted with tampered milk.

Thirty years ago one dining hall where coachmen took their meals was like this. You came in preceded or followed by a girl armed with an enormous tin-plated copper ladle filled with a greasy water called bouillon. The hall was an enclosure contained within four walls blackened from top to bottom; the table was long and narrow; the cups and beakers were tin-plate, the silverware iron; the meals there were frugal, but not bad. These customs have undergone some superficial modifications, but the substance is the same.

[46] For more on fraudulent practices in the wine industry, see chap. 1, n. 9.

The backrooms, the mezzanines, and sometimes the first floors of wine merchants host lively feasts; but almost always the sausage and cold meats bear the brunt of the costs for these often quite appetizing meals, which share none of the revolting habits of the cheap eating-houses.

As for those places where the soup was served from a hollow carved into the table and where the bouillon was distributed from the piston of a horse syringe, these are memories as historic as those of Mother Camus.[47]

In the lower depths, the sleazy dives and the greasy dumps are found.[48] We do not venture into these dens, and we will make them known by a single feature. M. Gisquet,[49] being chief of police, during heat waves ordered an assessment of the meat offered for sale by the pork butchers and sausage makers, too often left hanging out for excessively long times; those corrupted meats were thrown away as garbage into a mass grave: the next day, not a trace of them still remained; all of it had been carried off during the night. And so it is with the spoiled fish and all the leftovers that had been thrown into the outlying dumps; it is this mixed salad that takes the spirited name of "harlequin." Those cheaper eating-houses with good taste buy the debris sold by the servants from off of the great tables.

---

[47] Jacques Arago (*Comme on dîne à Paris* [Paris: Berquet et Pétion, 1842], 71–72) tells of a restaurant on rue de la Mortellerie where bouillon is served (and removed from those who cannot pay) "à l'aide d'une seringue." *La Mère Camus* (1803) was a vaudeville comedy written by M-N. Balisson Rougemont.

[48] Briffault uses here, respectively, *tapis franc* and *bouge*. Both are always pejorative, the first used for an establishment whose character is suspect or criminal, the second for a "hovel" or "dump."

[49] Henri Gisquet, Prefect of Police for Paris from 1831 to 1836, was known for his excessive zeal, particularly during the 1832 cholera epidemic when he was responsible for public health.

In the dives, the popular character, in all its aspects, naïve
or perverse, with its good or bad instincts, with its tendencies
and inclinations, has an honest vi-
tality of singular energy, the vigorous expression of which is heated
up and developed by drunkenness.
Parisian restaurants have their
own prescribed districts. Rue Mon-
torgueil and its oyster breakfasts
and seafood;[50] Bercy and its eel-and-fish stews; the neighbor-
hoods around the central market with their cuts of butcher's
meat and their always fresh fish; the Champs-Élysées and its
country menus, all form so many separate countries, all with
their native customs.

There is another family of restaurants, the offspring of
which are surprisingly numerous; we would like to talk about
the prix-fixe restaurants.

The first-class ones are at two francs: that is the first of
the seductions to which foreigners and provincials succumb.
A choice of four dishes, complemented by soup and dessert, a
half-bottle of wine, and all the negotiated exchanges that can
be carried out attract and dazzle them like fool's gold. New
clerks, worn-out dandies, doctors without patients and lawyers
without briefs, the young writer whose first article was posted
that morning, the provincial actors waiting for work on the
chairs of the Palais-Royal, and noncommissioned officers on-
the-town decorate the two-franc tables. Sundays, the hosier is
found there partying with his lady, his young man, and his
girls. From this price, passing down through all the levels and

---

[50] The site of Rocher de Cancale.

from one reduction to the next, it falls to eighty centimes, with two or three dishes, soup, dessert and a small carafe of wine.

Within the abyss of the prix-fixe are absorbed all of the offal and refuse of the butcher and all the suspect supplies. A few years ago the notices for these restaurants specified day-by-day the delicacies and the small plates promised by the menu for the entire week. The public, for these smaller prix-fixe dinners, consists especially of those individuals going by the name of "poor wretches," whom everyone knows and no one talks about. The regulars at these tables always eat a lot of bread, which they get on request; they are so unsure about the next day that, for them, stuffing their stomach is like filling their pockets. An emerging literature has taken note of these races of raptors and rodents.[51] The prix-fixes proliferate especially in the Latin Quarter and the neighborhoods around the Palais-Royal. Have we said that those of the lowest rank compete at Montfaucon to supply their pantries?

In the Latin Quarter, next to the prix-fixe but above it, stand the dirt-cheap restaurants: the maximum is thirty centimes a dish, at the disposal of the gentlemen-scholars. That solemn moment of the day, which kitchen and restaurant staffs call the "dinner rush," runs its course with an unparalleled

[51] The "emerging literature" is very likely a reference to Eugène Sue's immensely popular *Les mystères de Paris*, a serial novel published in 90 parts from June 1842 to October 1843. Its first chapter—in which the author promises to introduce the reader to "hideous, frightening types, swarming in these polluted sewers like reptiles in the swamps"—is entitled "Le tapis-franc" or "The Sleazy Dive." This "tapis-franc" is the "Lapin-Blanc" ("White Rabbit"), where "harlequin" is on the menu and beds can be had for three sous a night.

violence; young appetites pounce furiously upon the substantial dishes. A general cry of distress rings out when the chef proclaims in a resounding voice this terrible sentence: "There's no more beef!" Two or three restaurants on the rue de la Harpe and rue Saint-Jacques, at the head of which we place Rousseau and Flicoteaux—the immortal Flicoteaux whose dynasty founded its fiefdom near the Place de la Sorbonne—are distinguished among all the others.[52] On the tables, the carafes are gigantic; the wine within is what could only be expected.

Priggish pedants, a species not yet extinct, fill the gaps left by the students.

Near the Palais-Royal something similar to the Latin Quarter restaurant has been created for the artistic world.[53] There also, at the dinner hour, clouds of voracious locusts, taking off from the tavern and the studio, can be seen flocking into Rouget's and its like, swooping down on all the combinations of roasted or boiled beef, of veal and of lamb of every type in their simplest varieties. In these parts, wine is known, but only in small doses, in little carafes or quarter bottles.

The restaurant waiter forms a class separate from all the other categories of the service; there are waiters who age along with the house, and from whom the secrets, the clientele, and all the wiles of the seraglio can keep nothing hidden; for a major establishment, these old servers are priceless; they know

---

[52] Restaurant Rousseau ("where so few bottles and so many water carafes were emptied under the proprietorship of Rousseau the Aquatic") appears in Hugo's *Les misérables* (Chapter 2, "Marius Poor"). An extended description of its rival, Flicoteaux ("this temple of hunger and misery"), can be found in Balzac's *Illusions perdues* ("Part 2: A Distinguished Provincial in Paris").

[53] On the rue de Valois, to be precise, "where earlier literature in distress found pasture. I really believe that you always eat at Rouget, but do you dine there?" Auguste Villemot, *La vie à Paris* (Leipzig: Hetzel, 1858), 2:68.

so much they are not easily fooled. When a waiter is intelligent, allow him to take the lead, and profit and satisfaction will follow; if he has had proof of your generosity, and if you have been congenial and polite with him, he will serve you with zeal and good taste: do not annoy him and rely on his knowledge. When the stinginess or bad humor of those he is serving irritate a waiter, there is no end to the tribulations he invents to antagonize his victim: he proves to be both ingenious and barbarous in inflicting torment. General rule: to be happy with the waiter, make sure the waiter is happy with you.

In the private and reserved rooms, the waiter's service is more intimate; it requires greater mutual trust. The mysteries of the restaurants are not the least interesting chapter among the mysteries of Paris; the waiters get to the bottom of all of them; but they are discreet. Occasions for laughter are often available to them, when in the ingénue of the day they recognize the coquette of the evening whom they will perhaps see with a new admirer the next day. The memoirs of a private-room waiter would contain spicy revelations; he would be a Gil Blas in an apron.[54]

There are ideal waiters for whom a single glance says everything and makes everything clear and understood. Chéron, at Véry's, served in private all the men of substance, who treated him with a kindly familiarity; the young women all smiled when passing before him; and, for the profligate, he was an informal banker who discounted the menu. Chéron was like the slaves of Lucullus;[55] the private room where the

[54] The eponymous hero of the picaresque novel *Histoire de Gil Blas de Santillane* (1715–1735) by Alain-René Lesage.

[55] Lucius Licinius Lucullus, one of the late Republic's wealthiest generals and politicians, was known for his extravagance, and Plutarch, in his *Lives* ("The Life of Lucullus"),

table needed to be set was indicated to him, and that was enough, everything was said. Chéron died without leaving a successor.

The restaurant waiter should be nimble, alert, quick to respond, clean, charming, a little bit of the picaresque and of Frontinus;[56] he needs to have a certain refinement in his language and bearing; he is youthful; formerly in a powdered wig, today his hair is curled quite naturally with a hot iron. If the white cravat becomes lost, it will be found again around the neck of a restaurant waiter. He should never be embarrassed; it does not matter if he comes or does not come when called; what is essential is that he is never at fault. He has two replies always at hand for requests that prove embarrassing to him: "Sir, it's not yet ready!" or better still: "Sir, there's no more!" And also the famous "Voilà!" which is an answer to everything.

In 1837 for the supper at City Hall during the ball held for the newly married Duc d'Orléans,[57] the prefect for the Seine had the table served by a brigade of restaurant waiters under the command of Chéron; the service was admirably swift. This approach is followed in the Tuileries and in several great houses.

The waiter is especially admirable during the dinner rush; he is everywhere, serving twenty tables at once; he carries stacks of dishes with the skill of the most accomplished tightrope walker, without breaking a thing; he forgets nothing,

describes how his mere mention of a particular dining room was sufficient for the servants to determine the nature and expense of an upcoming banquet.

[56] Sextus Julius Frontinus was a first-century (AD) aristocrat best known for his technical expertise and tenure as Commissioner of Waterworks.

[57] See chap. 8, n. 11. The wedding itself was at Fontainebleau.

knows how to fix and manage everything. In these moments he lets his voice ring out like a mule proudly ringing his bell.[58]

Especially on Sundays, when everything bends and bows under the invasion of the bourgeoisie, the waiter appears in all his glory. In those solemn moments when a waiter calls out to you, "Right away, sir!" you've been condemned to a very long wait.

The customary offering to the waiter is worked out like this: five percent of the bill's total in the dining rooms; ten percent in the private rooms. There are numerous exceptions to this rule, to which each is his own judge.

The provinces still do not understand the tip, this tax that has leached into every detail of Parisian life.

The ladies and misses of the counter, the entire feminine side of the service, are enthroned there or flirting about, and the dishes they write down they season with shy glances and

---

[58] This would seem to be a reference to La Fontaine's "Two Mules," although the mule that proudly "made his bells ring out" does come to a bad end.

smiles; the further down you go, the bolder this game becomes. The small prix-fixes are served by women known as "the girl."

Two scourges afflict restaurants: theft and credit; waiters rarely fail to detect petty theft and thieves; they have an exquisite flair for just that; they know all of Cartouche's tricks,[59] which the multiplicity of mirrors almost always expose. As for credit, that is more difficult, especially when it hides beneath a decent, elegant, and polished surface. The story is told about Véry who, having been duped over a bill of thirty francs by one of these penniless gastronomes, reproached him first for having dined so well and then for having chosen him as his host:

"Listen," he told him, "I'll forgive you, but on one condition; that you go and do exactly the same for my neighbor Véfour."

"Alas," replied the diner, "he's the one who sent me here to pay for the bill I left there."

These unfortunate events do not prevent a good number of restaurateurs, especially at the summits, from making quick and considerable fortunes. It is true that at the secondary and lower sectors the list of disasters is long.

There are improvisational restaurateurs: wine merchants who have risen to that position; in Paris there exist many illustrious examples of such advancement.

In the first-class dining rooms, guests of modest appearance are often seen; but far more often, at the humblest of restaurants, pompous displays of grooming are to be found. The saying of our fathers is thus still true: "Velvet on the back, bran in the belly."

---

[59] Louis-Dominique Garthausen, or "Cartouche," was the iconic highwayman of his day. He was captured and executed in1721.

For humankind dinner seems to empty the heart in filling the belly. A poor beggar, seated on the first step of the stairs to the Trois Frères Provençaux for the last thirty years, always received alms from those going up, never from those coming down.[60]
The Parisian restaurateurs are charitable. Every morning they distribute to the poor the leftovers from the bread and the meals of the previous night.

The Chinese are now our neighbors. And so it is completely appropriate to speak of the Chinese restaurateurs. Here is how one traveler reported on a supper in Java:[61]

"The show [a Chinese theatrical spectacle] finished, the crowd headed *en masse* into the restaurateurs' small shops lining the square; all sorts of foodstuffs were spread out along the storefronts: lobsters, small shrimps, sea cucumbers, birds' nests; all the fine fruits of Java offered at every opportunity to the Chinese gourmet. We followed the surge that swept us into the Véfour of the place. The owner, quite proud to see French officers in his shop, seemed to duplicate himself in an effort to serve us all that he had of the best.

"Onto a small table, immaculately clean and furnished with eating utensils, namely microscopically small plates in magnificent porcelain and pairs of small ivory chopsticks, a whitish jelly on which lay several slices of fish was first brought to us: this was kind of a birds'-nest purée, spiced to scorch the palette; we concluded from this that the favored dishes of the Chinese

---

[60] Although the phrasing is his own, Briffault likely took this anecdote from Étienne de Jouy's "Les restaurateurs" cited earlier in this chapter (*L'hermite de la Chaussée-d'Antin*, 3:92–93).

[61] This extract is drawn from the account of the explorer Jules-Sébastien-César Dumont d'Urville of his three-year exploration (1837–1840) of the South Pacific and the South Pole (*Voyage au Pole Sud et dans l'Océanie* [Paris: Gide, 1844], 7:31–32).

needed to be enlivened, and so not to have disappointed him, we swallowed with great care. Our host observed our efforts with happiness; his small eyes sparkled with pleasure. After that we watched as an array of small plates arrived. Whoever you may be, if you ever dine in a Chinese restaurant, I recommend to you the lobster and shrimp salad in soy sauce. It is an excellent sauce, made, I believe, with a meat broth into which go many aromatic seasonings.

"We were finding all of this to be excellent, when we were brought, with great ceremony, some very thin slices of a whitish meat over a jelly spun out like macaroni. Our host showed us the dish with a look of pride, the look of someone saying to us: 'Eat. This is my crowning glory.' We then made use of the small chopsticks, and each of us swallowed it down. It was good, but this meat had a very singular taste, and before moving on to a second bite, we wanted to know what we were dealing with. Our man understood us perfectly, and lowering his hand within a foot of the floor, he let out two very distinct barks; there was no mistake about it, this was dog; without doubt some poor and inoffensive poodle the wretch had brained in the street. Our first thought was to toss the dish into the Chinaman's face; but we reconsidered, and continued to eat with great satisfaction.

"At one table, next to us, were seated two large Chinese elders with double chins; the satisfaction of the gourmet was imprinted across their wide faces. They savored with great delight the fine birds' nest, two gallant gentlemen rejoicing; but, alas! All is fleeting here below; and when the time to pay came, it was a pleasure to see the sour looks and great sighs that accompanied every rupee emerging from their purse. As for us, we had ours for ten rupees, twenty-two francs in our currency."

· XI ·

ECCENTRICITIES

Paris sets its tables beyond the enclosure of its walls; at Belleville, La Courtille holds gigantic feasts that climb the hill and form hedgerows on both sides of the country road.[1] There, in a revel whose fervor is never extinguished, everything takes on Cyclopean proportions, the wine flows like water, the ovens blaze like furnaces, and entire veal and sheep and sides of beef turn on spits, while more sheep, more veal, and more sides of beef hang from the wall. The cookware seems designed to prepare meals for giants, so wide, large, and deep are its dimensions. In some places, the roast above the flame appears to have found the secret of perpetual motion; it does not stop and the orchestra keeps it company; supper and the ball are always

---

[1] La Courtille, like its neighbor Belleville, was just outside the walls within which municipal excise taxes needed to be paid and like Belleville it, too, became a center for dance halls, taverns, restaurants, *guingettes*, and other establishments where food and drink could be sold at lower prices. It was especially known for *les bacchanales* held there on Mardi Gras and *la descente de la Courtille* when the revelers returned to the streets of Paris in a disorderly procession on Ash Wednesday morning. (For a contemporary account, see Léon Gozlan, "L'hiver à Paris," *Nouveau tableau de Paris au XIXe siècle* [Paris: Charles-Béchet, 1835], 5:369–371; and for Belleville—"where joyous pilgrims on Sunday can be seen streaming past in waves toward the rendez-vous of pleasure that rarely stays within the bounds of temperance"—see Georges Touchard-Lafosse, *Histoire de Paris: ses révolutions, ses gouvernements et ses événements* [Paris: Dion et Lambert, 1853], 5:581–583.) Life in Belleville and its environs calmed down somewhat with its annexation into Paris in 1860.

ready; it is there that the profits from a life gone wrong, the proceeds from vice and those from crime are expected and spent.

The entire city is surrounded by a ring of cabarets and restaurants; some, like Le Père Lathuille of Batignolles, and on the lawn of l'Étoile, and under the chestnut trees of Bercy, have a fashionable popularity in the summer that grows and declines according to the good graces of the crowd.[2] The suburbs, in the sections adjacent to the Paris walls, are places of refuge for the *tables d'hôte* and *pensions bourgeoises* that want to escape the excise tax. Everything there is cheap. We have dined at La Chapelle-Saint-Denis[3] with the entire choir of the Opera; after dinner they gave us a choral concert, and they sang with an enthusiasm that could never be bought; they performed the soldiers' chorus from *Les Huguenots*,[4] and some of the most amusing of bawdy cantatas. A considerable amount of champagne was drunk, and when the time to pay came, the share for each was twenty francs; the fact is, we had dined at

[2] During the mid-nineteenth century, Le Père Lathuille and its neighboring cafés were the haunt of many Montmartre writers and artists (see, e.g., E. and J. Crépet, *Charles Baudelaire: étude biographique* [Paris: Vanier, 1908], 49), and it was, in fact, the site for one of Edouard Manet's last paintings, *Chez le père Lathuille* (1879). There were many cabarets and cafés on the lawn near the L'Étoile barrier, particularly after the opening of the first Hippodrome there in 1845 (see, e.g., A. L'Esprit, "Les Hippodromes," *Bulletin de la Société Historique d'Auteuil et de Passy* 8, no. 7 [1915]: 246); and although there was a restaurant Aux Marronniers in Bercy during Briffault's time, he is probably referring here to several "under the chestnut trees" for which, along with its wine depots, Bercy was well known. (See Aron, *Le mangeur du XIXe siècle*, 68; in fact, in 1872 one of the more venerable of the trees was toppled in a storm, "crushing more than 30 barrels of wine" [P. Mouillefert, *Traité des arbres et arbrisseaux* (Paris: Kliencksieck, 1892–1898), 711].)

[3] La Chapelle-Saint-Denis, also known as la Chapelle, was another nearby town incorporated, to a large degree, into Paris by Georges-Eugène Haussmann's annexations of 1860.

[4] *Les Huguenots*, with a score by Giacomo Meyerbeer and a libretto by Eugène Scribe, premiered in Paris in 1836 and quickly became one of the most popular and frequently performed operas of the century.

one franc, twenty-five centimes a person. Such is the old story of this kind of thrift.

The public institutions contained within the great city—the hospitals, the prisons, and the schools—do a colossal amount of cooking every day. Isn't the stewpot of the Invalides one of the seven wonders of the Parisian world?[5]

Paris has a global hospitality; it is not enough that it summons to it products from all its provinces and that it offers those coming from different countries whatever can remind them of their native land. The cuisine of Parisian restaurants is cosmopolitan. All nations have here their representatives and their national dishes. Spain, Italy, Russia herself, and Germany have their restaurateurs in Paris; the English especially have conveyed here all the details of their particular habits, at every level, from the most modest tavern to the splendors of the Hôtel Meurice.[6] English life has found a home in Paris. Within the entire neighborhood of the Chausée-d'Antin haunches of beef

---

[5] Founded by Louis XIV in 1670, the Hôtel des Invalides eventually housed five to six thousand wounded and retired veterans in its large complex of buildings. It was gradually converted, to a large part, into a military museum, but tourists continued to converge on the site throughout the nineteenth century to visit (after 1840) Napoleon's tomb and what was reputed to be one of the largest cooking pots ("la grande marmite") in the world: "There are three things I want to see first [in Paris]; they are La République, the Pont-Neuf, and the cooking pots of Les Invalides!" (Valory [Jean-Joseph-Charles Mourier] and Saint-Gervaise [Philadelphe-Maurice Alhoy], *L'amitié d'une jeune fille: mélodrame en trois actes*, II, vii [Paris: Marchant, 1833], 17).

[6] The Parisian branch of the Hôtel Meurice opened in 1815 on the rue Saint-Honoré and moved to the rue de Rivoli in 1835, where it continues today to overlook the Tuileries Garden and welcome an elite clientele. From its founding as a Calais coach inn in 1771, it catered particularly to the English traveler: "If you cannot speak a syllable of French and love English comfort…[if] you will have your English companions, your porter…and your brandy-and-water…with your best English accent shout out boldly, 'Meurice!' and straightaway a man will step forward to conduct you to the Rue de Rivoli" [1840] (William Makepeace Thackeray, *The Paris Sketch Book* [London: Smith and Elder, 1870], 16–17).

can be seen that the Saint-Antoine district could not view without some surprise.[7] Only recently have colonies from Normandy, Marseille, the Auvergne, and Brittany planted their tents, adapted their games, their bagpipes, their dances, their songs, their tastes, and their foods to the Parisian turf; all of Europe and the rest of the world need to be invited to this banquet.

It is a voyage taken around the world, fork in hand and without ever leaving the table.

Around the barracks, Paris, which yields so easily to all its fancies, becomes a garrison town; like a fortified city, it has its officers' lodgings and military messes; each regiment finds the customary ways of Lille and Strasbourg established here as if they were part of the military gear.[8]

To be fully at ease in the restaurants of Paris, the language of the waiters needs to be understood; their kitchen French often sounds sarcastic and insulting. They'll reply to you that you're on the grill, roasting on the spit, or in the pan; they'll bring to you, at the top of their voice, "your head of veal" and "your pig's feet"; they'll propose a beef for you, a veal, a mutton,

[7] Rue de la Chaussée-d'Antin, on the right bank, was largely a commercial strip with retail stores on the ground floor and, often, bankers' offices above: "Today, the opulent street begins with a pork butcher and ends with a wine merchant; grocery stores are interspersed everywhere" (Louis-Amédée Achard, "Rue de la Chaussée-d'Antin," *Les rues de Paris: ancien et moderne*, Louis Larine, ed. [Paris: Kugelman, 1844], 1:39–40). The faubourg Saint-Antoine, a suburb west of the Bastille, was a crowded working-class district, with a considerable amount of small industry, poverty, and political volatility. There is also an article titled "Rue et faubourg Saint-Antoine" (by Georges Touchard-Lafosse) in *Les rues de Paris* (1:115–150), and Briffault himself contributed two articles to the collection, one titled "Place de l'Hôtel de Ville" (1:22–38) and the other titled "Le Palais-Royal" (1:85–204).

[8] Situated at the borders of Louis XIV's expanding kingdom, both Lille (annexed in 1668) and Strasbourg (annexed in 1680) remained *villes de garnison* (garrison towns) into the nineteenth century.

a sardine,[9] a lark, a pea, and an asparagus. They'll offer you a "beef plain" and a *tête-tortue*.[10] From a distance and with loud cries, they exchange with the kitchen, the wine cellar, and the back office questions and answers that ring out during the busiest of hours like commands from a battlefield. To baptize new dishes, noble godparents are no longer sought out as before; ignoble names are of interest. We encountered one restaurateur who, to draw regular customers to his menu, dreamed up the idea of giving his dishes the names of actresses or the characters of fashionable novels, all of it seasoned with slang. This ridiculous effort failed miserably.

A venture for Omnibus-restaurants was also undertaken;[11] the sound of a small bell was needed to alert the residents to the passing of the vehicle that would bring to each household its dinner piping hot. The establishment of small delivery services between the market and kitchens was also attempted. All these fine projects, dead in the street, are still alive in some imaginations.

There is in Paris, in the outlying neighborhoods, in the districts of Saint-Jacques, Saint-Marcel, Saint-Denis, and Saint-

---

[9] Actually *goujon*, or gudgeon, a small European freshwater fish still on many menus in France but more often used as bait than seen on menus in England.

[10] Probably *tête de veau en tortue*, a fairly complicated dish that Carême prepared, consisting of all the components of a calf's head boiled, diced, and then stewed in, usually, a tomato-Madeira sauce and served with a variety of garnishes.

[11] Following the construction in 1836 of a huge building containing fifteen kitchens, the Vicomte de Botherol launched La Société des Omnibus-Restaurants, and by 1837 some fifty vehicles were delivering, variously, hot and cold dinners and wines throughout Paris. Requiring huge infusions of cash, however, the company lasted only about six months before failing and becoming an object of derision in many circles. (See, e.g., Hubert Bourgin, *Fourier: contribution à l'étude du socialisme français* [Paris: Société Nouvelle de Librairie et d'Édition, 1905], 130–131; also the website: https://bothorrel.wordpress.com/2015/06/25/la-societe-des-omnibus-restaurants.)

Martin small hotels and inns; life is lived there like in the middle of the countryside.[12] Near the Palais-Royal, we have seen a real innkeeper.

At the market there are public soup kettles, like in military canteens, permanently present from five in the morning to midnight.

The prix-fixe restaurants of Lyon have adopted a measure that we recommend to the Parisian ones. They have made a common currency out of the cards they distribute, with which customers can receive discounts by the meal in their own neighborhoods without having to go any farther.

One of the liveliest inclinations of the Paris population is for dinner on the grass; these pastoral meals have lost none of their primitive attractions; the parks and the forests, which the railroads have made into Parisian gardens are, on summer Sundays, strewn with those nomadic groups seated around a pâté. These idylls have the advantage of a certain thrift that the high cost of the village restaurants has made necessary.

Cardinal de Retz did not want the regular mealtimes of Parisians to be disturbed.[13] Still, there exist rebellious spirits who do not recognize the sundial's yoke, and who arrogantly rebel against the names given to meals; these persons neither take breakfast nor dine, and deny both the snack and the

[12] The *quartiers* mentioned here are all located near or just outside a gate in the city walls.

[13] Briffault here uses the verb *désheurer*, clearly referring to a popular maxim from the *Mémoires* (1717) of Jean-François-Paul de Gondi, Cardinal de Retz—and from 1644 to 1662 Archbishop of Paris (although he was often in residence elsewhere, including in the prison at Vincennes)—describing his ease at dispersing a mob just before dinnertime: "À Paris, dans les émotions populaires, les plus échauffées ne veulent pas ce qu'ils appellent se désheurer" ("In Paris, regarding public sentiment, even the most aroused do not want disturbed what they consider their regular hours").

supper; they eat every time their stomach cries out for them to eat; these are philosophers whose doctrines have made few proselytes, but among whom are some good but misguided spirits who have dreamt for a long time, and perhaps still dream of a revolution in the ordering and timing of meals. The initial effect of a reform like this would be to make all relationships uncertain, since it is so true that within the harmonies of social existence, there is nothing irrelevant and isolated.

Bric-a-brac, which has overwhelmed everything, has not spared the table; along with some fine and pretty fancies of dish- and glassware with which we have been favored, along with some small porcelain gifts coming from Japan and some charming debris from Saxony and old Sèvres,[14] how much ridiculous stuff has it inflicted on us? The young lions, always searching backward for an experience that they do not have the courage to carry forward into the future, have everything confused. At the home of one, a yatagan[15] is used to carve a pheasant; with an Albanian dagger another cuts slices off a venison's haunch; one peels a pear with a double-edged Venetian stiletto; another cracks nuts with a fine blade from Toledo. At a banker's home, the glasses have no stems, so that, unable to be balanced on the table when full, they are drained in a single draft; an author of plays had goblets of human skulls mounted on silver stems and adorned with funereal ornaments marvelously crafted.[16]

---

[14] Both Sèvres, a town just to the southeast of Paris, and Meissen, a town to the north of Dresden in Saxony, were well known since the eighteenth century for the manufacture of fine porcelain.

[15] A sabre, with a curved blade, used by the Ottoman Turks.

[16] The dramatist referred to here remains unknown, although in an homage to an earlier toast from a human skull by Lord Byron, the poet, novelist, and occasional playwright Théophile Gautier, along with a group of his bohemian friends known

Savages eat as much with their fingernails as with their
teeth; with them, the first sign of a refinement in their manners is revealed by the use of fingers to seize the food they are
taking without first tearing it to pieces. Other people, more
advanced, serve themselves with chopsticks and pointed rods:
that's progress; the fork with two prongs is in use in northern
Europe; in England, a steel trident with an ivory handle, the
fork of three prongs, is the weapon of choice; in France we have
the fork with four prongs: it is the very height of civilization.

as both the Petit Cénacle and Les Jeunes-France, drank wine from a human skull,
brought to them by Gérard de Nerval, who had first attached a drawer handle to
it. The incident occurred in the early 1830s, although it first appeared in print in
Gautier's memoirs, written just before his death in 1872 (Théophile Gautier,
Histoire du Romantisme [Paris: Charpentier, 1874], 50–51).